DEADLY ESCAPE

J.R. Kendall

For my Mother – you have given me the world.

I will forever be grateful.

1

"We've got a floater." Randy, the investigator for the State Attorney's Office, was anxious to get out to the latest crime scene and didn't care that he was interrupting his boss's telephone conversation with another attorney.

Jesse ignored the interruption and kept talking on the phone, "No, I'm dead serious. I oppose you continuing this case. You didn't take any depositions this term, so why should I agree to a continuance?" The defense attorney on the other end of the line pleaded with her, dreading the idea of asking for an opposed continuance in front of the Judge, especially knowing that he hadn't done a thing on his client's case since the last pre-trial conference.

"Jesse, seriously, come on, we've got something." Since the investigator had left the Sheriff's Office seven years ago, his opportunities to go out in the field had dwindled and he wanted to go to the crime scene before the clean-up began.

Jesse glanced up at Randy this time and said into the phone, "Mark, I've got to go," she paused, listening to the begging for a moment more. "Fine, you get one more continuance, but I better receive a 'Notice of Taking Depositions' with every witness's name on it before we get to pre-trial on Wednesday. If not, I'm laying it all out for the Judge. I've got to go. Bye." She brusquely hung up the phone and turned to Randy. "What?"

"A body was found at the north end of the county. Let's ride."

"What do we know about it? When was it found?" She didn't wait for him to answer before firing more questions. "Never mind. More importantly, what is the scene like? Can I get away with changing into sneakers or do I need to change clothes completely?" Jesse always kept a change of clothes at the office for occasions like this even though dead bodies were few and far between in their small, rural town.

"The body is back in the woods in a pond and it's already hot as Hell out there, so you probably want to change. Not to mention the whole property is around five hundred acres and I don't know how much of the property we'll have to walk through."

"Let me change and I'll meet you up front. Do we need a warrant?" Jesse's prosecutorial mind was already racing.

"We're already working on it. We may not need it, but we're drafting one anyway. I've got the driving directions to the property and one of the detectives is going to e-mail me photos of the front of the property to attach to the warrant. He has the probable cause together also."

"Good deal. I'll meet you up front in a couple of minutes."

As Jesse walked to the front of the office, she could already sense that the office personnel were buzzing with gossip. It wasn't everyday that a body was found in a pond in the middle of the woods in their rural county. Since it was such a small office, word always spread quickly when anything big happened. Actually, word spread quickly whenever anything happened; new haircuts, new dates, new anything was fair game for the gossip mill.

"Darby, send my calls to voicemail. I'm going to be out for a while." Jesse said as she passed the receptionist.

"All right," she answered back, "call us and let us know what is going on."

"Sure thing." In actuality, Jesse had no intention of calling, but it was easier to placate the receptionist than to explain why she couldn't give out the details of an ongoing investigation. The office had recently had a problem with leaks. Actually, no one knew if the leak was coming from the Sheriff's Office, the State Attorney's Office or the Clerk's Office. Jesse certainly wasn't going to take any chances that it was within her own office.

Jesse and Randy did not talk while riding down in the elevator. It was too easy to be overheard that way. However, once they were outside anyone's earshot, the floodgates opened.

"Okay, so what do we know?" Jesse asked, keeping in line with her all-business personality.

"Right now, we don't know who the decedent is, but I'm fairly confident we can rule out suicide."

"Why is that?"

"Have you ever seen a person who committed suicide be able to wrap themselves up in a tarp, tape the tarp up and throw themselves in the water?"

3

She smiled at his smart aleck comment. "Point taken. What else do we know? Who found it and how long do we think the body has been in the water?"

"Some guy from out west was out here hunting on the land and walked up on it. Doug thinks the body has been there for about a week based on the bloating but the body is about to burst; oil is coming out of the part of the tarp that isn't sealed. We'll be able to narrow down the time of death once we know who the victim is. I say he because they can see part of the face; the hair and portion of the face that they can see appears to be male." He paused and then went on after consulting a new text message that just came in on his phone. "Okay, the warrant is drafted. They just need to get it reviewed and signed by a judge."

Jesse heard Randy's response but was distracted by the mention of Doug's name. Doug Wescott was a detective at the Sheriff's Office. He was also the man Jesse thought she was going to spend the rest of her life with – until two weeks ago when she found out he had been cheating on her for the past eight months. Since that time, she had neither seen nor spoken to Doug. She put her emotions aside and forced herself to stay on track. "Other than land, what is there to search?"

"This place is basically a hunting camp. There's a 1,000 square foot hunting lodge and numerous deer stands on the property. I looked it up on the property appraiser's website, Dean Witherington owns it."

"Dean Witherington?" Jesse paused to think. "Isn't he the guy that lives in that enormous gated estate off of 47?"

"That would be the guy," Randy said as he unlocked the car and got in.

"Has anyone made contact with him yet?" Jesse joined him in the scorching car.

"The Sheriff's Office sent someone out there, but I haven't heard anything yet. As you can imagine, they are stretched pretty thin right now."

"Did anyone send you the photos yet?"

Randy glanced at his iPhone. "Not yet, but I'll just have them sent directly to LeAnne. She's the one you will want to review the warrant before it goes to a judge, right?" LeAnne was an experienced prosecutor at the State Attorney's Office.

"Yeah, that's fine. She's on-call this week anyway. I'll call her as soon as you finish telling me what we know so far to give her an overview of everything we have."

"Okay. The vic was found by a guy named Lance Finnigan. He's from Montana and is here on a hunting trip. Evidently he and Witherington are friends. Anyway, he was out there hunting and stumbled across the body. He got away from the body as quick as possible and called 911."

"Why would he be hunting here? The deer are so much bigger out west."

"I think Doug said that the guy is here to hunt turkey. He is some big shot and is on a trip to shoot every type of wild turkey that exists. Something like that, anyway."

"Um, okay. I didn't know there were different types of wild

turkey." She paused for a moment, reflecting back to her days as a misdemeanor prosecutor, recalling different hunting seasons, bag limits and illegal baiting. "Is it even turkey season right now?"

"I have no idea. You know I don't hunt."

She smiled at him. "But you are just such a wealth of useless knowledge, I thought you might know." She also thought about Doug. He hunted on occasion, so he would certainly know the answer. She wouldn't be asking him.

"Well I don't know the different hunting seasons." Randy's phone rang before he could say another smartass comment. "Hello?" He listened for a moment. "Okay, who all is out there?" The caller was brief in their response. "Give me a minute and let me run it by Jesse."

Jesse looked imploringly at Randy as he sped out of town with only his left hand on the wheel so he could hold the phone with his right hand.

"All right. Here is what we have. Todd just went out to the landowner's estate and he isn't there. He spoke to the maid and she said that Witherington has been gone for at least seven or eight days. He let all of the support staff have two days off the weekend before last. They returned on Monday, a week ago, and he wasn't there. But the maid says it isn't unusual for him to up and leave like that."

"Ask him if the maid said she saw anything suspicious at the house."

Randy put the phone back to his ear. "Did you hear Jesse just now?" he paused and listened. "No. Did the maid see anything suspicious at the house?" Randy made a face as he held the phone out in front of his face and yelled into the phone. "Hold on, let me just put you on speaker." He pressed the right button on the call screen to turn on the speakerphone. "Go ahead."

"Can you hear me?" Todd asked over the phone.

"Yes." Jesse and Randy said in unison.

"Ten-four. No, I don't think she's seen anything to raise her suspicions. She's been at the house for a week now. She returned last Monday and stayed through this past weekend. I haven't asked her specifically, but she didn't say anything was out of order when she returned."

Jesse asked, "Who else has been at the house since the last time Mr. Witherington was seen?"

"Probably just the housekeeper and the yard man. She said that the yard man comes on Mondays and Wednesdays. He's here now; just finished mowing the back yard."

Jesse said, "Get the lawn guy's name and contact information, if you will. Also, until we know where Mr. Witherington is, it would be best to secure his estate also. Find out from the housekeeper if anyone else is there, has been there or if anyone else is expected to show up. Also, find out all of the contact information the maid has for Witherington. Until we know who the victim is, I want to preserve every possible location of the murder site, assuming this pond is just the dump site. It's possible that Witherington is connected to all of this since the body was found on his land and he is nowhere to be found." Jesse's mind was stepping out of her normal role as prosecutor and assuming a part of the investigation. In her mind, that was one of the perks of the job though she couldn't overstep too far.

"Will do." Todd paused for a moment. "Are you thinking Witherington did this or that Witherington is our floater?"

Jesse answered the young deputy, "It's too soon to tell. There's no reason to speculate until we have more facts. All we know right now is that the owner of the land where the body was found is not at his house and has been gone at least a week. But, according to the maid, that is not unusual. We need to find out more about Witherington. What exactly does he do for a living? That might help us narrow down a way to find him if he doesn't just pick up his cell phone when we get his number and call. It could be nothing. It could be that someone knew Witherington's hunting land had a secluded pond and capitalized on it. Witherington may have nothing to do with this at all; it's too soon to tell."

Todd responded, "All right, I'll gather all of the information I can and try to secure the residence. I get the impression the maid pretty much lives here, but I think she has family she can go stay with in town."

"Okay, just let us know the contact information and find out who else has been at the house."

"Ten-four." Randy laid the phone down freeing up his hand to put on the wheel again.

"Is that it? Nothing else to go on?" Jesse asked.

"Nothing else at the moment. FDLE should be arriving at any minute. We just need to get the warrant signed and the sheriff's office is going to let FDLE do all of the searching."

8

"Works for me. I'll call LeAnne now." Jesse quietly cursed as she realized her phone wasn't in her purse. She finally caved in and upgraded to a smart phone and was less than pleased at how quickly the battery lost power. "Here, let me use your phone, I don't have my state phone with me; I left it charging in my office."

Randy handed her his phone and Jesse quickly entered the number.

"State Attorney's Office." Darby, the ever cheerful receptionist answered.

"Darby, it's Jesse, may I speak to LeAnne?"

"One moment."

After a brief pause, LeAnne came on the line. "This is LeAnne, may I help you?"

"Hey, it's Jesse. I don't know if you've heard yet or not, but we've got a body. Looks like it is a homicide. A draft of a warrant is headed your way and I just wanted to give you a heads up."

"Yes, I heard about it just a minute ago and I'm pissed at you for not telling me about it. I would've liked to have gone to the scene." LeAnne was able to take many liberties with her supervisor since they were also friends.

"You can come out to the scene, but I need you to review the warrant first. Let Barry review it with you. He hasn't done one yet." Barry was the newest felony prosecutor. "The probable cause is pretty straight forward; a man was out on the property hunting turkey and he walked up on a body floating in a pond. The body has a tarp wrapped around it and tape wrapped around the tarp. The guy that found the body is a friend of the landowner, Dean Witherington."

"Dean Witherington?" LeAnne sounded puzzled.

"Yes, why do you ask like that?"

"I don't know. I know his name for some reason. I'm thinking that I may have a case with him as a witness, or something. I'm not sure. Hold on a second and let me look in STAC." LeAnne quickly typed in Dean Witherington's name into the office's case tracking information system. "I remember now," she said as she opened up the relationship screen to see all of the names involved in the case. "I had a female defendant arrested in this guy's car. You might recognize her name – Kerri Hall. She is a frequent flyer; mostly small time drug cases but nothing has really ever stuck. Anyway, he claimed the car was stolen after the cops contacted him about finding it, but he didn't want to pursue charges. Nor had he reported it stolen before the cops stopped Kerri Hall in it. Claims that he didn't even notice his $80,000.00 car was missing. The officers chalked it up to being a crack rental and he just didn't want to get outed."

Jesse knew the slang term meant Witherington was supposed to have "rented" his car to Kerri in exchange for cocaine or some other type of drug or even sex. "Well, if the investigation points to Witherington, that could possibly be something to pursue. At this point, we don't even know where he is. The last the housekeeper saw him was on a Friday, ten days ago, when he let the support staff go for the weekend. We'll get Doug to send you the draft of the warrant."

Jesse turned to Randy, "Is Doug going to be the affiant?"

"No, Marty is," he answered.

Jesse's mind started spinning. If Doug wasn't going to be the

10

affiant, then he might still be out at the crime scene and she may have to face him. She tried to put the thought aside and turned back to the phone. "Sorry, Marty is going to be the affiant, so just clean the warrant up if it needs it, print it and make copies so it is ready to be signed by Marty and the judge when Marty gets there. I don't know if Marty will have Doug's camera or how they are ultimately going to get the pictures to you to attach to the warrant."

LeAnne asked, "Do you want Barry to ride out there with me once we're done with the warrant?"

"That would be great. I hate for his first body to be a stinker, but that's how it works out sometimes. Be sure to wear flats, we're going to be in the woods."

"Okay, will do. See you in a little bit. Bye-bye."

"Bye." Jesse turned to Randy, "Are we almost there?"

"Yeah, it's somewhere right up here around this corner. There may still be a bunch of patrol cars parked along the road. But they could all be gone now."

"Please tell me that we didn't have a bunch of deputies walking right up to the pond, where they could have contaminated the scene."

"No, no. They just heard it on the radio and those that weren't on a call ended up coming out. It's a good ways into the woods and only a few people have been to the body itself. They're keeping a crime scene log, so we won't run in to problems like we did on the Kingsland case."

"Don't remind me of that nightmare. At least the Sheriff's Office learned their lesson from that one." The Kingsland case involved a stabbing at a bar, which resulted in serious bodily injury to the victim. Unfortunately, the integrity of the scene was not maintained during the initial hours, so the defense was able to make reasonable allegations about tampering or at the very least improper handling of some of the evidence, which in turn made the State prove each and every link in the chain of custody. Normally, the State didn't have to prove each part of the chain of custody to move evidence in at trial unless the defense could show a reasonable probability of unreliability. That almost never happened, but it did in the Kingsland case, which almost cost the State an acquittal due to some of the key evidence being kept out.

"Here we are." Randy did a U-turn in the middle of the road and pulled onto the shoulder, behind one of the remaining detective's cars. There were still about ten different cars parked along the road. A driveway with a gate was also visible. Someone had put a yellow strip of crime scene tape up, blocking entry to the property.

The Florida Department of Law Enforcement, crime scene truck was the only vehicle inside the gate. Jesse and Randy walked around the gate since there was not a fence connected to it. They had to walk about fifty yards before joining the detectives and the crime scene investigators from FDLE in a small clearing.

"Hi everyone," Jesse gave a small wave to the crowd. "How's it going?"

"We're sweating our balls off out here waiting for the warrant to come back." Elmer, one of the homicide investigators, was always crude, no matter who he was talking to.

12

"How long ago did Marty leave here?" Jesse knew that since Marty was the affiant, the time it would take for the warrant to get back was dependent on him. She hoped that Doug was with Marty since he was nowhere to be seen, at least so far. She was extremely uneasy about seeing Doug. Their history together was complicated and she wasn't looking forward to being forced into a case with him so soon, especially since her feelings were still so raw.

"About twenty minutes ago," Mary Shiver piped up after consulting her crime scene log. "I'm putting you two down on the log. Are you going to go on back and check the body out?"

"Absolutely." Jesse responded and then turned to two similarly clad people. "Brad, Amy, how are you two doing? It's a shame we always run into each other like this." Brad and Amy were the FDLE crime scene technicians. Brad was actually an analyst but he often came to the scene to collect the evidence too. When a case did not look too complicated, the local crime scene investigator from the Sheriff's Office would handle the case, but if it looked complicated or messy, FDLE was usually called in. FDLE had the honors this time because the scene was messy and somebody was going to have to get wet.

"Great," Brad sent Jesse one of his beaming smiles. Even wearing his standard BDU's and polo shirt, Brad was always a head turner. He was the epitome of tall, dark and handsome. "You want me to take you back to the pond?" he asked Jesse.

"Yes, that would be great," she responded.

"Hey, wait up!" Doug yelled out as he jogged up to the group.

13

Jesse's stomach immediately turned into a giant knot. She couldn't let her emotions show in front of all of these people. She knew that, but merely seeing Doug again almost brought tears to her eyes.

Brad turned and greeted their new addition, "Hey man, long time, no see. How's it going?" He reached out and shook Doug's outstretched hand.

"You know how it is, working hard." He paused and added, "Just taking it day by day." He looked pointedly at Jesse as he said the last comment.

"Knowing you, you're hardly working rather than working hard." Brad joked.

"Yeah, don't you know it?" Doug joked back. The truth of the matter was that Doug was the hardest working detective in the entire agency. He didn't have any aspirations of ever running for Sheriff, but everyone knew that he was the smartest person at the Sheriff's Office.

"You got here just in time. We're about to go back to the body. You coming?" Brad asked.

"Yeah, I was already out there, but I want to see it again, before you take it out of the water."

Brad, Randy, Jesse and Doug were the only ones that went back into the woods this time. The other detectives had already had their fill from the smell of the decomposing body. In fact, Wes, one of the younger detectives had already lost his breakfast over the stench. That would become the butt of many jokes in the next coming weeks.

Jesse normally enjoyed being outdoors. She would've enjoyed the

14

current walk in the woods if she didn't have to face Doug. Her job didn't allow for too much time outside of the office setting, so even though somebody had died, it was always a welcomed change of atmosphere. Plus, as a prosecutor, it was absolutely invaluable to go to a crime scene, as photographs only capture so much. When you are actually there, you can take in the entire scene and later relay that to the jury. You can make the jury feel as though they were actually at the scene by being able to describe the minutia first hand, from your own experience.

They walked single file down a small, worn path with Brad and Randy leading the way and Doug pulling up the rear. Jesse spotted a deer stand off to the left, but the ladder going up to it was so overgrown with vines, that she doubted anyone had used it in quite some time. The underbrush was also thick on both sides of the path. Though not afraid of snakes, the thought of how many must be in these woods did cross Jesse's mind.

While turning her attention back to the path, away from the deer stand, Jesse stumbled on a root and started to fall. Doug quickly grabbed her from behind. The mere touch of Doug's hands flooded Jesse's head with memories of the first time they ever walked in the woods together.

When Jesse was first transferred to the Columbia County State Attorney's Office over two years ago, she wanted to integrate herself with the law enforcement officers, so she spent many Friday and Saturday nights doing ride-a-longs. Her philosophy was that she could build a better relationship between the State Attorney's Office and the

Sheriff's Office if she was actually friends with the officers too.

As a matter of course, she ended up riding with Doug on multiple occasions. Even though he was a detective, he still conducted patrols quite often. It wasn't until much later that Jesse found out the reason he did the extra patrols was as an excuse to get to know her. They had an immediate connection. The first time Jesse rode with Doug, they talked as though they had been friends their whole lives. Jesse was a pretty reserved person, so it was not very common for her to meet someone like Doug and immediately hit it off.

When Jesse first started doing the ride-a-longs, Doug actively patrolled the county. However, as time progressed, he would find a shadowed area to pull the car over to "watch traffic." It was really an excuse to have quiet time with Jesse. Both of them knew that they were developing feelings for the other, though neither of them would say it out loud.

Late one Saturday afternoon, Doug called Jesse and asked her what she was doing. She was actually a hot mess, as she had just finished a six hour Schutzhund training session with her German Shepherd, Xander; yet, she told him she was completely free. Doug asked Jesse if she wanted to do a ride-a-long; that he wanted to show her something. Jesse readily agreed and joined Doug within the hour. Normally he drove a car, but this time he was in a 4 x 4 truck.

Doug took Jesse to a huge fenced property. The front gate was open, so he just drove straight in. Jesse asked him, "Should we be driving back here? It looks like private property."

"It's fine. I have permission."

Jesse silently assented. "So what is it you want to show me?"

Doug cut a glance her way. "You're just going to have to wait to find out."

Doug spent the next half hour showing Jesse the variety of terrain that Florida has to offer. During the tour, Jesse learned that the property was over 1,300 acres. They first drove through a field spotted with two hundred year old Live Oak trees. The grass swaying in the breeze would eventually be bailed for hay. From there, they drove past several areas of planted pines. The straw on the ground would likewise be bailed and sold. That was just one way large properties such as this one could get an agricultural exemption, thus lower the property taxes.

After passing a stocked fishing pond, the well-worn drive turned into nothing more than a path that entered the dense woods. Now the 4 x 4 made sense. The woods were magnificent. This was Florida in its natural state – as it had been prior to the taint of man. They drove deeper and deeper, the path almost unidentifiable. They eventually went down a steep embankment, only to hit a sharp curve that brought them back up again. Doug parked the vehicle and turned it off.

"We're stopping?" Jesse asked the obvious question.

"Yes, follow me."

Jesse grew up in Florida and had always enjoyed walking in the woods. She figured they were just going to go for a little walk. It would have seemed perfectly natural for Doug to grab Jesse's hand to lead her down to the sinkhole he wanted to show her, but they weren't to that point yet. Not quite.

Jesse jumped down from the large 4 x 4 and walked alongside Doug. She knew she seemed tiny compared to his large frame. Jesse was attractive by all accounts. She had deep blue eyes and long brunette hair that glistened in the sun. She was thin, but she also had tremendous curves. In her younger years, she was extremely self-conscious about how large her rear-end was, but in time, came to learn that it was one of her biggest *ass*ets. Literally.

Standing at just under 5'2", she only came to Doug's chest, as he was nearly 6'3". Doug was definitely a man's man. He had broad shoulders that received regular work outs. While approaching 40, he was still in excellent shape, tipping the scales at 200 pounds. Unlike many other men his age, Doug still had a full head of hair that was so dark brown in color that it appeared black. His dark brown eyes caught Jesse's attention. "This way."

Doug led Jesse down a fairly steep path. Algae-covered limestone rocks jetted out of the ground. Jesse couldn't help but admire the natural beauty. "Is this what I think it is?"

Doug chuckled, "It depends on what you think it is."

"Are you taking me into a sinkhole?"

Doug held up his hands in surrender, "You got me."

Jesse paused. "Is it safe?" Florida was littered with sinkholes. It was not unusual to turn on the news to see a house swallowed whole by a newly emerged sinkhole.

"Yes, it is. You know I would never put you in harm's way."

While still slightly concerned, Jesse continued on behind him. After descending another twenty feet, Jesse could distinctly hear the trickle of water. "What's that?"

Doug ignored the question. "We're almost there."

The path Doug created was blocked by a fallen tree, about fifty inches in diameter. Since it had fallen from lower than where they were, it created a bridge against the incline. Doug simply jumped up on the tree and turned to help Jesse. She ignored his outstretched hand, opting to climb up onto the tree using nearby rocks as steps. Doug jumped down, which put his head at the level of Jesse's knees.

Jesse looked around and realized she was too high up to safely jump down. Doug reached for her. She didn't really have a choice, did she? Jesse reached down to Doug's shoulders as he placed his large hands around her small waist. He lifted her down with ease. Jesse had been anticipating a moment such as this one. Was he finally going to kiss her?

Doug held Jesse's eye as he helped her down from the tree. He wanted to kiss her so badly but he just couldn't tell if she was receptive to it. He almost said to Hell with it and kissed her in that moment, while he still had his hands on her, but he held back. The extra seconds of him holding onto her did not go unnoticed.

Jesse felt awkward. "Thanks."

"No problem." Doug let her go and pointed. "It's right this way."

What awaited them was absolutely breathtaking. Thousands of years ago, this area had been an underwater cave. Florida had been experiencing a drought for quite some time, so water wasn't covering the normally submerged mouth of the cave. After the sinkhole opened up, it exposed the cave.

19

"This is beautiful."

"I thought you would like it."

"How on earth did you find this place?"

"I stumbled across it while hunting."

"I didn't know you were a hunter."

"I get out from time to time. It's really just a way to escape from reality."

Jesse let that pass, knowing that he was going through a bitter divorce. While Doug hadn't shared a lot about it with her, he had told her some, including that he was terrified about what would happen to his unborn son. She looked at him. "Thank you for sharing this with me."

Doug looked directly in her eyes. There was so much he wanted to tell her - that she was the most amazing person he had ever met - that he wanted to hold onto her and never let her go - that she would never know how much talking to her had been helping him get through the worst time in his life. Instead, he said nothing.

Doug and Jesse sat on a rock in silence for a long time, soaking in their surroundings. With some people, silence is extremely uncomfortable. Not so with Doug and Jesse. It felt like they could've sat there forever, but the waning sun prevented that. "We should go. It's going to be dark soon."

Jesse's private thoughts interrupted. "Yes, of course. Lead the way."

Doug stood and reached his hand down to help Jesse up. She took his hand. Before she realized what was happening, Doug leaned down and kissed her. Deeply. Self-assuredly. It was like nothing she had ever experienced . . .

"Are you okay?" Doug's words and look of concern on his face brought Jesse back from her ruminations

She hesitated. "Yes. I – uh – I'm fine. I just." She wanted to tell him so badly how much she missed him. "Sorry. I just tripped on a root or something."

Doug just looked at her. "Okay. It's not much farther."

After about a hundred yards, they came to a curve in the path. No announcement was needed to say that they were almost to the body. Jesse had been smelling it for about forty yards, but didn't want to comment on it, lest she appear weak.

After walking in silence a while longer, Brad said, "Okay, here we are."

Jesse choked out, "Thanks for stating the obvious."

Brad ignored her and walked right up to the murky water's edge. The pond did not appear to be large, but Jesse could not see the whole thing because it was a kidney bean shape. There was a tree lined path that went all the way around the pond. The other investigators had already walked around it and did not find anything of evidentiary value; at least nothing in plain sight.

The body was only about eight feet from the water's edge. The entire tarp was not yet visible, as only the torso was sticking up out of the water. There were round pools of burnt orange colored oil gathering around the body on top of the dark water, an indication that the body was organically breaking down. The upper most part of the

21

tarp had been torn off by buzzards, that were capitalizing on the small window of opportunity before the body popped, let the gases escape, and sank back down into its final resting spot at the bottom of the pond.

But, because of the assistance from the buzzards, a portion of the face and neck was visible. Fortunately, the birds had only had enough time to rip the tarp open. It appeared that the damage to the face was minimal; at least one closed eye and the swollen lips were still intact, though they appeared to be shedding the outer layers of skin.

Jesse could feel the bile rising in her throat, but used every bit of will power she had to not think about throwing up. She had found in the past that if she thought about the act of throwing up when she had such strong smells around as a stimulus, then she would. If she concentrated on the task at hand, then she would probably be okay. Probably.

"What is that up by his throat?" Jesse pointed. She wondered if it was some sort of a strangulation device.

"Looks like it is a hat - the back part where you snap it closed." Randy answered.

"Oh, right, I can see it now." Jesse thought it strange that someone would take the time to throw the hat in with the body and wrap all of it in the tarp rather than just leave the hat wherever the victim was killed. That may indicate that the perpetrator did not want to leave a trace of the victim having ever been wherever the murder site was. Then again, maybe the killer was someone close to the victim and threw the hat in because it was the victim's favorite hat. Who knew? It was definitely too early to be able to tell anything.

"The smell isn't that bad when the wind is blowing away from us." Randy commented.

That was true enough, but Jesse preferred to not even think about the odor at all – whether it was a strong or slight odor. "What about the guy that found him, what did you say his name is?" She looked at Randy.

"Lance Finnigan."

"Do you know if he has been interviewed yet? If he knows the victim, then I bet he could make an ID off of the portion of the face that is visible."

"They asked him if he recognized the person but he didn't know. After he came around the last curve there and got a good whiff and realized it was a human body, he threw up and took off. He called law enforcement immediately. They let him go on into town so he could give a formal statement at the criminal division."

"Maybe he can look at a photo of the face when you interview him. It is a shot in the dark, but he may know the person." She turned to Brad and asked, "Do you think the M.E. will be able to get any prints off of this guy?"

"I think there is a good chance. He's pretty far gone, but I've seen worse that still had prints left. I bet his hands are going to be real swollen but it is certainly worth trying. We just have to be real careful in handling him; that skin is going to practically fall off."

Jesse said, "Let's get back to the rest of the guys and see if the warrant is here. The sooner we get him out of the water and the scene processed, the sooner we'll know who he is."

2

By the time Jesse, Randy, Brad and Doug made it back to the clearing, Marty had arrived and read the warrant to the vacant hunting lodge. The officers always felt silly reading a warrant to an unoccupied building or a car, but it is one of those quirks of the law – do it, or your evidence may get suppressed. Not that reading a long warrant to an individual sitting before you in handcuffs is much better, but at least you are talking to a live person.

After the arrival and reading of the warrant, Brad and Amy got to work. They loaded two pairs of boots, some waders, a garden prong, multiple boxes of gloves, evidence markers, cameras, paper evidence bags, a body bag and an array of other items onto a gurney similar to what you would see in an ambulance.

"So, who is going in the water to get Mr. Doe out?" Brad scanned the crowd, hoping someone would volunteer to help him.

"I ain't getting in the water, but I'll help you get him out." Randy had worked for the Sheriff's Office before becoming the investigator for the State Attorney's Office and had no problem dealing with rotting corpses. Jesse admired him for that and his go get 'em attitude when it came to things like this.

Seth, a veteran road deputy piped up, "All right Wes, you're the lead on this, so you get to help too. Look good 'cause here comes the Sheriff." Wes was not the lead on this case, but everyone knew Wes wouldn't get his dress shoes and slacks dirty trying to remove the body. But Seth had to get his ribbing in because of Wes' earlier display of weakness.

The Sheriff walked up and Jesse could sense a change in the officers around her. It was always stressful at the Sheriff's Office when it was an election year. She already knew that several of the officers around her were secretly supporting the current Sheriff's opposition in the election. The problem was that the Sheriff did not know it yet. If he had known, then the officers would have been shifted around to have horrible hours, or possibly even fired.

"Madam Prosecutor, Gentlemen, Mary." The Sheriff, dressed in his long-sleeved dress uniform, greeted everyone with beads of sweat glistening on his forehead. It was only a matter of time before the newspaper would be out at the scene. The Sheriff loved to have his photo in the paper, especially during an election year. The photographer wouldn't be able to go beyond the gate to join where everyone was now standing, but with a zoom lens, he would be able to get pictures of the clearing, the cabin and the people standing there. Jesse knew that the Sheriff always put himself in pristine position for photographs, so it was time for her to move away from him.

"Sheriff, it's good to see you again," Brad shook the Sheriff's hand. "We're about to go pull him out if you want to join us."

"That's quite all right. I just wanted to come out and see that everything is in order. It looks like you have us in capable hands."

"Yes, sir. Well, if you change your mind, follow your nose." Even though they were well away from the body, when the breeze blew just right, you could still smell the body. Brad turned to Jesse, "Are you coming?"

"Sure, I wouldn't miss it for the world." Not to mention it gave her an excuse to get away from Doug since he would have to stay to update the Sheriff.

Brad turned to Wes, "How much longer until fire rescue gets here? We need the rescue board to scoop under the body to get it out of the water."

"Last I heard on the radio, they left their station about fifteen minutes ago, so they should be just about here."

"All right, well, we're going to take our gear down, take the initial photos and mark any evidence out there for individual photos and collection. When they get here, just send them our way."

"Will do." Wes was visibly relieved he didn't have to go back to the body.

****

It didn't take long for Brad and Amy to take the initial photographs, both from a distance and up close. Next, they put down numbered markers next to anything and everything that could possibly

27

be evidence. For this particular crime scene, that consisted of six cigarettes that looked fresh, a Mountain Dew can and a small piece of duct tape thrown in the bushes. Amy took close-up photographs of each item of evidence individually and then stepped back and took several photos of all of the markers and evidence collectively.

Jesse and Randy were standing back out of the way while Brad and Amy worked. Within minutes the firefighter EMT's showed up with the rescue board.

Brad noticed the new arrivals and called out to the lead EMT. "Hey man, you might want to take your straps off of the rescue board. We won't need them and they'll get ruined if you don't."

"Sure thing." Henry, the EMT walked to the edge of the water, surveying the body. "I don't think we'll be wanting this back at all. This guy is a real stinker. Whew." He exhaled and walked away from the water's edge.

"All right, then what we can do is get the rescue board behind this guy and try to scoop him up. The holes on the side should allow the water to strain out." Brad said as he pointed to the far side of the body.

Randy said, "Yeah, I don't see how we're going to actually get the body in it though."

"That's why I brought this prong." Brad held up a normal four prong gardening tool. We'll use it to hook a bit of the tarp and pull the body a little closer to us. Then we'll get the rescue board next to the body and roll the body right onto the rescue board."

Jesse just stood back and watched the spectacle. It didn't go quite

28

as smooth as everyone had hoped, but it was not long before the body was out of the water. Part of the problem in getting the body out was that the leg area still had what appeared to be clothesline wrapped around the tarp-covered legs. But the clothesline was not just holding the tarp closed; it was also tied to weights at the bottom of the pond. The men were able to get two of the fifteen pound weights out of the water along with the body, but they knew that there were still more weights left in the water.

"What do you think - send divers in or drain the pond?" After removing his gloves, Randy walked over to Jesse , who had moved pretty far back in an effort to get upwind from the stench. It did not really help her because as soon as they started moving the body, the odor got ten times worse.

Jesse responded, "I want it drained. That water is so dark, there's no telling what the divers would miss. Oh, and Randy, will you try to see who manufactured those weights?"

"Sure, but Amy is already taking photos of them and the body."

"I know, but I just want to know for when they search the cabin. Not that I expect to find a weight machine with matching weights in a hunting cabin." She paused and reflected, "Actually, I don't know what to expect in a hunting cabin. I've never been in one. I'd expect a bunch of mounted deer heads and guns, I guess."

"You are probably right. But, we'll see in a little bit."

Randy and Jesse's involvement with the body was over. Brad was going to put it into the body bag, in the same condition as it was in when he removed it from the water. The funeral home on rotation had already been called, so the body would be transported to the M.E.'s office in Jacksonville within hours. Tomorrow, the forensic scientist at the M.E.'s office would have the joy of opening the body bag, and taking the tarp off. Then the medical examiner would have his turn. That was definitely not an enviable job, especially with a body as far gone as this one was. Not to mention the smell would be even worse tomorrow after the body had been stored in the body bag over night.

While standing there, no one knew it would be a mere eighteen hours later when they would learn the identity of the victim was none other than Dean Witherington. With one shot to the chest and one to the head, somebody had meant business.

3

Not surprisingly, the search of the hunting cabin did not yield anything of evidentiary value. As suspected, the officers found mounted animal heads, fish and even a few mounted ducks on the walls. There were also several gun safes, but each was locked and appeared to be undisturbed. Regardless, Brad and Amy dusted the cabinets for prints, and then opened the cabinets to inspect each gun to see if it had been fired recently. None of them had, but each make and model was cataloged anyway.

Since the search of the cabin the day before had not been fruitful, with day two of the investigation underway, the best lead Doug Wescott and Marty Newsome had to go on was that the victim was shot with a .45 caliber handgun. The M.E. had a light load and performed the autopsy first. That, or he wanted to get the stinking body out of his morgue. It was likely the latter.

Fortunately, one of the shots to the chest was not a through and through. The bullet was lodged just beneath the T7 vertebrae. If the gunshots had not killed Witherington, then he definitely would have been paralyzed. But, it is not often that you see someone survive an execution shot to the head. If a weapon was ever located, then ballistics would be able to test fire it with the same type of ammunition actually used in the killing and compare the test bullet to the surviving bullet found in the victim's body to confirm that it was the same weapon used in the murder.

More evidence was yet to be discovered; or so they hoped. All they could do at this point was go and interview the last people known to have seen Dean Witherington alive. The detectives started with the maid, Maria Hernandez, who was now staying with her mother in a small, run-down trailer just inside the city limits of the small, rural North Florida community.

A shriveled old woman promptly answered to the sounds of the clacker she had meticulously installed on the front door many years before. It was not often that she had guests. "¿Puedo ayudarle?" She peeked out the crack in the door, with the security chain still fastened.

Doug did not remember much Spanish from high school, but he could still introduce himself and say enough to get by. He said slowly, "Mi nombre es Doug. Yo trabajo con el sheriff oficina." He hoped he had introduced himself and told her that he worked for the sheriff's office. With the woman not responding, he went on, "¿Puedo hablar a Maria?"

"Ahhh, Maria, yes, sí." Finally she understood something he wanted. The old woman turned and yelled, "Maria, hay dos caballeros altos aquí para verle. Dicen que son de la oficina del sheriff." Why she yelled was not obvious, as the trailer was a small single-wide. You could sneeze on one end and hear it on the other end as though the person were standing right next to you.

Maria quickly came to the door, peering out the crack just as her mother had. She closed the door and the two detectives heard the security chain slide as Maria unlatched it. Maria opened the door, turned to her mother and nearly yelled, "Gracias servir ma má. Estaré detra's pronto." Now the two visitors realized that the older woman could barely hear. Maria turned to them, "Excuse me, we are not prepared for company, may I join you outside? She spoke with perfect English, yet seemed quite unsure of her words.

"Yes, of course," Doug backed down a step of the rusted front steps and gestured with his right hand to the small, yet colorful front yard. Maria yelled something else to her mother, which neither detective understood, and then joined them outside.

"Is this about Señor Witherington?" She had a genuine look of concern on her face.

"Yes, ma'am, I'm afraid it is." So far, Marty had not said a word, as was his usual posturing with people. "I'm sorry to tell you that Mr. Witherington is dead." Doug started to go on, but the tears welling up in the eyes of the petite woman stopped him. She seemed as though she really cared about her boss.

"I prayed to Santo Maria that this was not the case. But I knew something was wrong. Ohhh something was oh so very wrong." She wrung her hands in despair. "I prayed to Eleggua, for safe passage, for, I had a very bad feeling for Señor Witherington."

"I'm sorry, Eleggua?" Doug pronounced it, "El-egg-uah."

"It is Santeria, my religion," she responded. Marty already thought as much, having noticed the black fist hanging from her necklace.

33

Doug got back on track, "Why did you have a bad feeling about Mr. Witherington?"

The first tear spilled over, yet she maintained her calm. She just let the tear fall, not bothering to wipe the trail it left down her face. "He let me go tend to mi ma má for the weekend. That was not unusual, for he knew she was ill. It was not even unusual that he did not come back during the week, but it was very unlike him to not have fresh flowers delivered Wednesday at precisely 3:00 in the afternoon. It was like clockwork. He would always call the flower shop at a particular time; make a very specific order, asking for a different arrangement each week. When he did not call the flower shop, they called the house to see if he was unhappy with them. It did not matter whether he was at the house or not, he always ordered the flowers. I knew then that something was wrong."

"Did you make any calls to check on him?" Doug asked.

"Oh, no sir. There was no one to call. The only person I could call was Señor Witherington himself, which I did. I called his mobile telephone over and over and over again. At first it would ring, but eventually the recording would pick up right away."

The fact that the calls went straight to voicemail probably indicated the phone was turned off or the battery was dead. The phone had not been found yet, so it would be worth it to try to see if they could use the GPS feature on it to find its location. They also needed to subpoena the phone records to see who all Witherington had talked to and when. That would help narrow down who the last person was that talked to him while he was still alive.

"Why didn't you call any of his business associates?"

"Señor Witherington was very private about his business. He never did business around me. Only behind closed doors." This raised a flag with the detectives. Perhaps Witherington had something to hide. "The only thing he did say about his business is that he was global. I think he meant he could go anywhere to do business because he was always going somewhere."

"Did he usually tell you where he was going before he went?"

"No, but sometimes he would talk to me about where he had gone, once he got back."

"Do you know anybody that he works with?"

"No, no Señor Detective. Not at all. Like I told you, he never did business around me. I always kept busy elsewhere in the house."

"Did he have many friends or people that would visit?" Marty finally asked his first question.

She paused, looked away from them and made the slightest involuntary sound. She glanced up at them, said, "no" quickly and looked away again.

Marty took a step closer to her, sensing that his actions would intimidate her. "Maria, look at me." She was resistant. He put his hand around her upper arm, trying to direct her tear filled gaze back toward his face. "Maria, listen to me now. This is very important." He stooped his head closer to hers. "Somebody did something very bad to Mr. Witherington. It is obvious you care about him very much. It sounds like he was very good to you. This is your chance to help repay him. Help us find who did this to him. Anything you know

35

could help. We are not going to go air the dirty laundry; we just need to know where to go from here. You hold that key."

She slowly looked up at Marty and looked him straight in the eye, her bottom lip trembling, "I am not supposed to know. He would always try to clean up after the visits so that I would not know, but a woman knows these things."

"A woman knows what things, Maria?"

"A woman knows when another woman has been in her house." She stammered, "Not my house. I was not romantic with Señor Witherington, but I am very protective over him. I look after him in every way. I could tell that he had been having a woman over. His whole personality changed in the last couple of months."

"How do you mean?" Marty pushed her to tell more.

"At first, when I noticed someone had been there, I also noticed that Señor Witherington seemed very happy. I believed it was because he was being a man and having his way with a woman. I found, uh, um." She stammered and blushed deeply.

"It's okay, you can say it," Doug soothed her.

She looked at the ground as she said, "I found condoms wrapped up in the trash can in his bathroom." That was a little weird that she would look through the trash, but the detectives kept listening. "And then about two weeks ago, he started acting strangely."

"How so?" Doug asked gently.

"Well, he did not sleep good like he usually did. He would stay up all night and then stay up all day. But he was full of energy. He would buzz around the house, making phone calls with that ear piece

36

in his ear and then dart back in his study, where he would work hours on end, without a break, not even to eat. I would get concerned for him and try to make him eat but he always said that he was not hungry. He would not even eat his favorite foods. Then, after several days of acting like that, he went to bed and just did not get back up."

Both Doug and Marty were thinking the same thing, but neither said their suspicions aloud. "Did you notice anything else unusual in the trash?" Marty wanted to confirm his suspicions.

Maria thought for a moment before answering. "You know, now that you mention it, there was something that I thought was very unusual a couple of weeks ago. He had an empty box of aluminum foil in his bedroom. He never did anything in the kitchen, so I had no idea what he had been doing with the aluminum foil; it made absolutely no sense to me."

The detectives knew, but did not let on their suspicions to Maria. "Do you have any idea who the woman was?"

"I am not supposed to know."

"But do you know?" Marty stared straight into her eyes; which, by this time, had stopped spilling tears down her cheeks.

"Sí. Two weeks ago, I got back from the grocery store and there was a car without a top to it, with the horse on the side. What is that kind of car called?"

"A Mustang convertible?" Doug asked her.

"Sí, sí. It was very loud yellow, like a banana. It was parked in the middle of the drive, right between the fountain and the front door." The detectives knew from a previous drive by that the driveway

37

immediately in front of the front door was circular, with a fountain in the center.

"This was very unusual for someone to leave their car there. I went around back and parked where I always park. I could hear music coming from upstairs. I did not dare go up to see who was there, but every now and then I could hear laughing and loud talking. After about thirty minutes, Señor Witherington came downstairs to the refrigerator. He did not know that I was there, for he was not wearing any clothes. But instead of covering himself when he saw me, he simply greeted me in the strangest way. His words were all jumbled together and he was not walking normally. I believed he had been drinking, but when he came and hugged my neck, I could not smell any alcohol." She wrung her hands together and continued, "He has never hugged me before," she paused, then sobbed, "and never will again."

Everything she said was confirming the detectives growing suspicions that Dean Witherington had gotten tied up in drugs; specifically, methamphetamine.

"Then a girl came stumbling into the room. She bumped right into the door frame and just laughed. I was terribly embarrassed because she was naked as well. She just came into the room, grabbed Señor Witherington's hand and dragged him back towards the back stairs. She even gave me a wink as she told him to come back to bed."

"Do you remember what this girl looked like?" Doug was ready to bet all odds that she had shoulder length blonde hair with a single black streak in it

"She was very thin. She also had very large, well, um…" She looked away, embarrassed to talk about such things with two men.

"It is okay, go on, we understand what you mean. What color was her hair?" Doug wanted confirmation

"It was almost like her car. I think you call it blonde – is this the right word?" She didn't wait for a response before continuing, "But it was very strange. It had a section just off of the middle that was as black as midnight."

Now they both knew who the next person to interview was: Kerri Hall, one of the most spoiled rich girls in town. She was known to party hard and hang around some of the local meth heads. With her unique car and unique hair, there was no question that Kerri Hall was the one visiting with Dean Witherington. From the sounds of it, she also got him hooked on methamphetamine, one of the most addictive drugs that existed. They say that the first hit is a hundred times better than the best orgasm you will ever have. The addiction kicks in because you chase that high, but are never able to feel a high as good as the first one, so you up the dose with every hit you take. When that doesn't cut it, you up it again. Over and over again.

"That was two weeks ago?" Doug started to do the math.

"Yes! Sí, two weeks ago. I know it was a Monday because that is when I go to buy groceries. I go every Monday."

"Are we talking about the same week that he let you go home for the weekend?

She thought back for a moment. "Sí, now that you say that, yes, sí, it was the same week.

"Did you see the girl again?"

"No, not even when she left. I made sure to make myself scarce. There are some things that just are not my business."

Marty decided to change tracks for a moment. "Did Mr. Witherington work out?"

"No, he worked in the house. He had a study, or sometimes he would take his little portable computer to his room to work." She meant laptop.

"No, I mean, did he exercise at the house? Did he have a home gym at his home?" Marty thought better of his wording and added, "did he have any machines that he would use to exercise with?"

"Ohhh, I see. Yes, he had several machines. There is a bike that stands still, a machine that he walks and jogs on, a bench that has a bar that he puts round weights on and lays back to push it up and down, let's see, there's also…"

Marty interjected, "what do the weights look like? The ones that he puts on the bar?"

"They are silver-ish gray, with letters sticking up."

Both detectives thought they may be on to something. "How many of these weights did he have?" Marty was starting to get excited, but hid it from Maria.

"There were many of them, in all sizes and weights." She stopped to think about it. "You know, I have just realized something. He keeps the different weights on a rack that separates the weights by sizes. I go into his exercise room to dust everything on Tuesday's. Last Tuesday I noticed, some of the weights were missing."

Bingo. "What do you mean, missing?" Marty knew this would seal the deal for the search warrant.

"They were not there; they were just gone. There were some very big and some very small weights. The small weights were there, but the big ones were gone. I thought it was strange, but I had forgotten about it until you mentioned it."

Doug still had photos of the crime scene on his digital camera. He had taken photos of the weights used to weigh the victim down. If Maria could identify them as the same kind her boss had at home, they would have no problem getting a search warrant. They already could have gone to the home, but the State Attorney's office always preferred that they get a warrant. The detectives had been told that a search of a bedroom in an old case got thrown out once because an overnight guest was found to have standing to challenge the search of the home and the officers should have gotten a warrant before doing the search. They certainly didn't want anything to screw up the future prosecution of the perpetrator who committed this murder.

It sounded like Mr. Witherington didn't have anyone actually staying at the house other than Maria, but there was no telling what had gone down during the weekend Maria was gone. One thing was for sure - Dean Witherington was dead and someone very likely used his own weights to sink him to the bottom of the pond. "Señora, would you excuse me for one moment, I want to go get my camera to show you something."

"Sí, no problem."

As Doug walked back up to Marty and Maria, he turned on his

41

camera and set it to view the photos off of the memory card. He took particular care to not let Maria see the screen while he scrolled passed photos of the body. He found the picture he had been looking for, a close up of one of the fifteen pound weights. He held the camera out so she could see the LCD screen, "Maria, look at this photograph and see if you recognize it at all."

She looked at it and said, "No sir, I have never seen that picture before."

Doug was slightly flustered, "No, I don't mean have you ever see this particular photo before, but have you seen what is in it before? Look closely."

Maria instantly understood what he meant and without even looking again said, "Yes, sí. That looks just like the weights Señor Witherington has at his house."

"Are you absolutely sure?"

"Sí. I am sure."

"Can you think of anything else that struck you as unusual or out of place?" They now had enough for the warrant, but Doug wanted to make sure there wasn't anything else they had missed.

"You know, I just remembered when I was talking about getting groceries. I also go to a warehouse store to stock up cleaning supplies. Well, I thought I had plenty of bleach, so I did not buy any last Monday. I could have sworn I had a box that had four fresh gallons, plus a used one. When I went to clean last week, all I found was a single jug with just a little in the bottom. I like to disinfect the garbage can every week with the bleach, so I did not even realize I was low

42

until I tried to clean it. So, I just bought a new case on Monday before the young officer came to the house. I just don't know what could have happened to all of it."

Doug and Marty had a strong feeling as to what may have happened to it. Doug asked her, "Is there anything else?"

"No, no, Señor. Not that I can think of right now."

Doug pulled a business card from his wallet and handed it to her. "If you think of anything else, give me a call, day or night."

"Sí, Señor," she paused as she looked at the card, "Señor Wescott."

"Oh, and one more thing, we'll need to get Mr. Witheringron's cell phone number from you."

"I have his mobile telephone number in the house. Un momento."

Maria returned with a small piece of paper with a very neatly written phone number. Doug and Marty both thanked Maria for her time and left. They were very happy with the progress they were making. Maria actually ended up being a fountain of information even though she didn't think she knew a thing that could help the investigation. With phone number and probable cause in hand, they went to the gated entry of Dean Witheringron's estate to take a photograph. With that done, they drove straight to the State Attorney's Office. After all, they had a subpoena that needed to be issued for phone records. Not to mention a search warrant for the house.

4

"Hi Darby, is Jesse available?" Doug asked the State Attorney's Office's receptionist. It was a question Doug had asked a hundred times before, but never with butterflies in his stomach. This case was the first one that had come along after he and Jesse had problems. Everything was fine for almost two years while they secretly dated. But that happiness was doomed to end due to his own stupidity.

The phone rang yet again before she could answer the two detectives. "Give me just one moment and I'll check. The phone has been ringing off the hook." It took the receptionist a moment to transfer all of the phone calls to the right people but she soon had Jesse on the phone. "Jesse, there are two detectives here to see you." She briefly listened to her boss and then asked the two detectives their names. With so many officers it was difficult to keep them all straight. Not to mention the detectives were in dress clothes, not uniforms with name badges.

Doug leaned in to the glass opening. "Just tell her Doug and Marty are here and need a warrant for the murder."

Jesse overheard the key words which got her up and moving to greet the detectives at the locked entrance to the office. She was glad the case was progressing, but instantly became nervous about seeing Doug. So, she did want she did any time she was nervous – she put her game face on. She opened the door and greeted them, "Gentlemen, welcome. I'm dying to know what we have." Her little giggle was as much stress relief as laughing at her own pun.

Doug started explaining to her what they had as the three of them walked down the deserted hallway to Jesse's office. "We need two things. First, we need a subpoena for the victim's phone records. We just got his personal cell phone number from his cleaning lady. Second, we need a search warrant for the victim's house."

"What is your probable cause to say he was killed there?" Jesse sat down behind her executive desk. She loved the fact that it was deep mahogany, her favorite color of wood.

"Our best P.C. is that the gym weights used to weigh the vic down are the same as Witherington owned and had in his home gym. The maid recognized them and said that all of the heavier weights are missing. Probably just as good is the fact that four gallons of bleach went missing from the house too. The maid seems pretty meticulous about things. She has a shopping schedule and a cleaning schedule. When she went to use the bleach last week, she noticed four gallons were gone. Sounds to me like someone had a mess to clean up."

"That doesn't necessarily mean the murder actually took place there, but it is enough to get us into the house. Give me a minute, I want this to be a learning experience for Barry, one of our new ASA's." Having an extra person in the room would also enable her to further distance herself from Doug. She hit the speakerphone and dialed an extension. "Barry, are you busy right now?"

Barry's response was sarcastic, as usual. "Is there really a right answer to that question? If I said, 'no I'm not busy' to you, you'll wonder why not. If I said that 'I am,' then I may miss out on something interesting."

"Then why don't you say, 'Yes, I am busy, but I can always make the time for you?'" She teased the young attorney.

"Oh, I didn't think of that. What's up?"

"Do you want me to go over a search warrant with you? Detectives Wescott and Newsome are here about the Witherington murder."

"Sure thing, I'll be right there." You could hear the excitement in his voice. If he stuck with this job, it would only be a matter of time before he would moan at the thought of going over a search warrant with an officer. But for now, he was eager to learn anything and everything. With such a small office, he was fortunate to be able to spend time with all of the more experienced attorneys. In larger circuits, he would have had to fend for himself. It was not unusual for the division chief in larger circuits to only have a few more months experience than the least experienced person in the division because of the high turnover rate. But that wasn't the case at the Third Circuit State Attorney's Office.

Barry walked into Jesse's office with a note pad in hand.

"Pull up a chair beside me." She looked at the tight space. "Well, as best as you can, anyway." With the large executive desk, a credenza and a separate computer desk forming a quasi u-shaped area, it would be a tight fit.

"Sure." He started to pull a chair around but stopped to introduce himself. "Hi, I'm Barry Anderson." He stuck his hand out to Marty first.

"Marty Newsome, detective at the Sheriff's Office. Good to meet you."

"Likewise." Barry offered his hand to Doug also.

"Doug Wescott. Unfortunately, I work with him." He gestured to his partner.

Jesse interjected, "Okay, do you two have driving directions?" While Barry was introducing himself, Jesse had opened up a template for a search warrant.

"We don't have the exact mileage, but we can tell you how to get there."

Jesse was going to use "teaching" Barry as an excuse to also educate the officers, which was a never ending task, even with experienced officers. It never hurt for the officers to know the legal reasoning why she had to word things a certain way. For the most part, she knew Doug understood the ins and outs of warrants, but Marty could sometimes be too quick on the draw.

She turned to Brad, "Okay, you pretty much start the affidavit for the warrant out with this general language." She pointed to the screen. "It just states who the affiant is." She turned to Barry and went on, "As you know, the affiant is the person swearing to the affidavit. It goes on to say that you are appearing in front of the judge. You then state a description of the place where the property to be searched is

47

located. We also put in the driving directions to the place to be searched, starting at a known address, or intersection. Typically we do the main intersection right here by the courthouse." She turned to the detectives. "What is the address of his house and I'll Mapquest it to get distances."

Doug flipped back through his notepad, finally spotting the address. "4997 176th Terrace.

Jesse was familiar with the area and inputted the zip code before Doug even had a chance to say it.

Turning back to Barry, Jesse started to explain, "The purpose behind the driving directions is so that the warrant is very particular about the place to be searched. As you know, the Fourth Amendment gives us an expectation of privacy in our homes. That is where we have the highest level of expectation of privacy. It would be a very bad thing if a warrant was issued based on probable cause and then the wrong house was searched.

Likewise, it would also be bad if the officers searched the right house, but had the driving directions wrong. It may not make sense as to why, but there have been cases where evidence seized was suppressed just because the driving directions were wrong. So, as a matter of practice, always describe the actual driving directions, put in every turn and every direction of travel."

Jesse went on, "Once you get to the part where you describe the residence to be searched, put in details such as the color of the house, the color of the shutters, if there is a fence with a gate, put that. If there are numbers on the mailbox, describe the color of the mailbox and state what the numbers are on it; don't necessarily say that is the address of the residence to be searched, just state the fact that those numbers appear on the mailbox nearest to the house to be searched. If there are numbers on the house, put that down. It is also best to attach a photograph of the house. If you can't see the house from the road, attach a photo of the driveway leading up to the house. There is a Second DCA case, State v. Houser, where they put the wrong physical address in the warrant, but since there were so many other details, the evidence was not suppressed." Jesse didn't typically have DCA case names memorized, but how could you forget *Houser* when it was about a house?

Doug held up his camera bag, gesturing to Jesse, "Here, I've got my camera with me and I actually brought my cable to download the pictures this time. We stopped at the vic's house before coming over, so we have the picture already. Well, actually, we have a picture of the wrought iron fence and a long driveway. But you can see the house up the drive. There is no mistaking this place. It is the only one like it in the county."

While plugging in the appropriate cables to start uploading the photograph of the house, Jesse went on with explaining the affidavit and warrant process to Barry. "When you do your first warrant on your own, go to the brief bank and we have a template for affidavits and search warrants.

Marty interrupted her, "What is a 'brief bank?'"

She looked at Marty and responded, "Oh, that is just a database full of actual motions that our staff have filed in the past. Some people

49

submit it as a template so others can just insert names of defendants and other pertinent information. Other people add to the brief bank with actual motions and legal memorandum without redacting it at all."

"I see. Kind of like not wanting to re-invent the wheel, right?" Marty asked.

"Exactly," Jesse responded. She picked up right where she left off with discussing the affidavit. "It starts off with stating who the affiant is. Typically, your main investigator will swear to the warrant. Sometimes you'll need a co-affiant, but we should be okay without one here. The second paragraph talks about the fact that there is a premise and the curtilage of the premises in our county that are under the control of a certain person."

She saw a puzzled look on Barry's face. "The curtilage is basically the area surrounding the home." Barry's furrowed brow disappeared upon her explanation even though he never would have admitted that he forgot the meaning of curtilage.

Jesse went on, "You need to state the name of the person from whom the items will be seized. We also insert whoever is renting and/or owns the home. It is very important you have the language about the curtilage in there. Later, we go even further and list outbuildings, automobiles and some other things, but we'll get to that.

Then we come to the description of the property and driving directions." She turned to the two detectives after switching her screen over to the Mapquest results. "Okay, I've got the directions based on Mapquest; look at them and tell me if they are any different from what you would have said; sometimes there are quirks with the directions, but since you've been there, you can tell if they are right. We can add in the direction of travel after I get the basics in the warrant."

Doug and Marty came and read over both Jesse's and Barry's shoulders. "Yeah, that looks about right," Marty said.

"Okay, give me a few minutes and I'll get these typed in as we go along. Be thinking about your wording for the probable cause section."

Jesse typed quickly, blocking out the quiet chatter amongst the three men. After a few minutes, she spoke up. "Okay, I've got the directions pretty much done, we'll come back to it later. Barry, the next part is where you indicate the violation of law. The affidavit should indicate what law has been violated. Here, it will be homicide. You also put the statute number.

She went on, "next you put the items to be seized – basically what you are searching for." She turned to the detectives, "So, other than bleach and evidence of blood, what are you looking for?"

"Let's put in there cleaning supplies, to include brushes, towels, mops, bleach, aluminum foil…"

Jesse cut him off, "Aluminum foil? How could that possibly be used to clean up a bloody mess?"

Marty answered this one before his partner could even speak. "We have reason to believe that our victim was hanging out with Kerri Hall quite a bit and that she introduced him to the meth scene. The maid saw behavior in Witherington that is consistent with using meth. He was up for days on end and wouldn't eat. We know Kerri is into that

51

scene. Oh, and also, the maid said that she found an empty roll of aluminum foil in his bedroom; that he had no reason to have it there, or to even venture into the kitchen."

Barry spoke up for the first time, "Okay, call me crazy, but what does aluminum foil have to do with methamphetamine?" He hated sounding unknowledgeable, but he just couldn't help himself.

"Have you ever heard of floating a boat? It's when they take aluminum foil and roll it up to where it is kind of in a boat shape. Then they smoke the meth out of it." Marty looked back at Jesse, "look, we're just trying to throw the kitchen sink in at this point. We just got the name of the girl and we haven't even tried talking to her yet. I have no idea if she had any involvement in his death. He could have just been a sugar daddy to her, not that she needed one. Or they could have just partied together in the weeks leading up to his death."

Doug interjected, "We don't have the toxicology results back on Witherington yet. If he had meth in his system, that is definitely going to make us look a whole lot harder at Kerri Hall."

Jesse looked at the detectives. "You do realize that none of what you have just told me is substantiated, right? You haven't followed up on any of it yet. We're not putting aluminum foil in the warrant. Every household has aluminum foil in it. The basis of the warrant is to see if the murder occurred at the house. Of course, if you come across drugs and something that is obviously drug paraphernalia, you can collect it because it is evidence of illegal activity. Besides, it isn't like we're going to charge Witherington with possession of methamphetamine and possession of drug paraphernalia. It shouldn't be an issue." She closed the discussion and moved on. "So, what else are you looking for?"

"The presence of blood , firearms, ammunition. Do we have to put bullet holes?" Doug asked.

"No. If you see that, then collect it. Actually, are you calling the FDLE crime scene techs in on this to help search?"

"Yes," the detectives said in unison.

"I'd just have them take the whole portion of the wall, assuming it is in a wall. You don't want to put more indentures on the bullet fragments. It could mess it up for future testing."

"Yes, ma'am, thanks for the advice. I never would have thought of that." The sarcasm in Doug's voice bled through.

Barry asked another question since he was already on a roll. "This may sound stupid, but why are you getting a warrant for this in the first place? The guy is dead, right? And he lived by himself?"

Jesse answered, "There is not a general homicide exception to getting a warrant. With that said, there is an exception for police to enter a dwelling if they have a reason to believe a person is dead or dying inside. That will fall under the exigent circumstances exception. But even with that, the officers can't do a thorough search; they can just do a basic walk through, take photographs and collect the body. To do a thorough search, they would have to get a warrant."

Barry responded, "When I first started, I had a motion to suppress that I had to argue. One of the other prosecutors gave me a checklist to go through when responding to a motion to suppress and other than seeing if the motion is facially sufficient, one of the first things I'm supposed to look at is whether or not the defendant has standing to challenge the search. So here, say they searched this house and found the murder weapon. How could the murderer possibly have standing to challenge the search of the victim's house? I mean, I can see it if we searched the murderer's house, but not the victim's house."

"He's got a point, Jesse." Doug threw in his two cents worth.

Jesse shot a look at Doug. She knew he knew better. She proceeded to explain to them both, "You are right to an extent. Let's look at it this way. Say they went and searched the house without a warrant. Say we eventually catch whoever did this. But then let's say we find out that person had been living at the victim's house. Now the murderer has standing to challenge the search. Officers had P.C. to get a warrant and didn't. In my opinion, it is always best to get a warrant. Looking down the road, at a motion to suppress, who has the burden of proof to show the search was valid if you did not have a warrant?"

"Um, the State, right?" Barry was pretty sure he was right.

"Right. Now who has the burden to show the search was invalid when there was a warrant signed by a judge or magistrate?"

"The defense."

"Right, so why wouldn't you get a warrant? In order for evidence to get suppressed when there is a warrant, a judge is going to have to make a finding that another judge made a mistake in signing the warrant. That just isn't going to happen every day. Not around here, anyway." Doug and Marty actually looked like they were listening. Hopefully they also understood what she was saying. Marty had been known to jump the gun in the past and not get a warrant when he

54

should have.

"I see. You're right. I just hadn't thought of it that way."

"That's okay. There is never a stupid question. I'm a big fan of doing the work on the forefront, so you don't have a mess to clean up later." She turned to Doug and Marty, "so have you scratched something out for the probable cause section?"

Marty handed her a legal pad. "If you can read my writing, it'll go something like this. Make whatever grammatical changes you need."

Jesse took the pad and skimmed over it. "This will be fine." She went back to explaining to Barry, "The probable cause section, or P.C. as you will often hear it referred to, basically has to set forth facts that would lead a judge to find that there is a fair probability that the officers will find contraband or evidence of a crime. Remember the 'W's.' Who, What, When and Where. You have to state who observed the facts, what the facts are, when the events which established the P.C. took place and why you believe the items to be seized are located in the place to be searched." She turned back to her computer. "Give me a minute to type all of this up and we can go on."

Jesse copied the probable cause that Marty had written up. She only had to add in a couple of words to make the transitions better. When she was done she looked up. "Okay, Marty, are you the affiant on this one or Doug?"

"Doug spoke up. Let's put me down. Marty was the affiant on the warrant for the cabin, so let's spread the love."

"Okay, what was the name of the last defendant you and I did a search warrant for? I'll just copy your credentials from there."

Doug thought for a moment. "Terrance Tyler, I think."

Jesse looked in her computer under that name. "Yep, you're right." As she copied and pasted, she explained to Barry, "In this section, you are just talking about the training, experience and education of your affiant. I recommend you always save a copy of each search warrant and over time, you'll build up a database of each officer's credentials so you don't have to recreate this part every time. It is usually the same guys that come to us to get warrants, so it isn't too hard to keep up with."

Doug spoke up. "I've had several more schools since the last warrant, should we put that in there?"

"What were they?" Jesse asked. She hoped her face didn't reveal the emotions stirring inside her. She knew good and well about one of the training programs because she had been there, spending time by the pool while he was in class.

"I had one homicide school and an arson investigation school."

"Let's add in the homicide school. How many hours was it?"

"Forty."

"Okay, we don't need the exact name of the school. You have the certificate in case we need it down the road, right?" She asked Doug.

"I sure do."

Jesse added in the information about the homicide school. "That pretty much does it. The last section is standard language, where we pray for the warrant. This part is on the template in the brief bank. One thing you have to be sure of is that the person listed as conducting the search has to actually be present at the search and participate in the search. What we usually put is the Sheriff or any of his duly constituted agents. We haven't been challenged on that, but I think it is ripe for a challenge.

We also include that any person already on the premises or arriving during the search may be detained until the search is completed. All vehicles and outbuildings may be searched. We also state that the search may occur during the daytime or nighttime, or on Sunday as the exigencies of the occasion may demand, to procure the evidence to be used in the prosecution of such persons unlawfully possessing or using them in violation of the laws of the State of Florida. Then, the affiant signs the affidavit in front of the judge." Jesse finished reading from the computer screen.

"Is that it?" Barry asked.

"No, then you have the warrant itself, which is separate from the affidavit. The warrant makes findings of P.C., states who the residence is under the control of, copies the same description of the residence and driving directions and commands the search of the premises and curtilage thereof along with any persons, vehicles, or outbuildings for the property described in the warrant, authorizing the officers to seize and secure the evidence."

She went on, "the officers have to create a property receipt and return it within 10 days of the service of the warrant. The warrant also commands them to leave a copy of the warrant with the person in charge of the premises, or if no one is there, to leave a duplicate there. It may seem strange, but when they show up at the house, they have to read the warrant to the house, even if no one is there. I don't even want to know if they skip this step." She looked purposefully at the two detectives, who just sat there grinning.

Barry turned to the detectives and asked, "Okay, really, do you seriously read a warrant to an empty house?"

Marty started in, "Now what do you –"

Jesse cut him off. "If your answer is anything other than of course we read it, that is what the law requires of us, then do not ever answer that question in my presence. If your answer is something other than what I just said, then I am strongly advising you to change your ways." Usually Jesse joked with officers, but when it came to executing the law correctly and legally, nothing was a joking matter to her.

"Sorry I asked, I didn't mean any harm." Barry was a little embarrassed at his question.

Jesse ignored him and went back to business. "Let's go back through this and add in the direction of travel and then give me the information you have about the victim's phone. I'll go ahead and get the subpoena for his records ready."

They all went back to work. Everything was all business from that point forward.

5

Fortunately, it did not take Doug and Marty long to get the warrant signed by a judge. They had already called FDLE to have the crime scene van meet them at the victim's house. The Sheriff's Office crime scene investigator could handle smaller matters, but the detectives usually called FDLE when it involved a murder. Since FDLE was already involved in the forensic aspect of the case, Doug called them to continue the investigation.

Doug and Marty beat the crime scene van to the Witherington estate by about twenty minutes. That gave them just enough time to figure out a way to get past the wrought iron gate and up the impressive driveway. It also gave them enough time to read the warrant to the unresponsive house. Evidently Jesse's comments had made an impact.

Brad Lanier pulled up to the front of the house and jumped down from the crime scene van, which was more like a semi-truck. "Hey guys, what's going on?"

Everything about Brad's casual demeanor and good looks turned the ladies on. On a certain level that made Doug dislike the guy. But, on the other hand, Doug recognized what a great job Brad did and as much as he hated to admit it, Brad was just a nice guy. "Not much, we just missed you so much from the other day that we thought we'd have you back again."

"What happened here? This is a great house."

"It is actually about the same case you were here about the other day. The floater. This is his house. Actually, I'd more so call it a mansion. Anyway, we have reason to believe he was killed here and transferred to the pond."

"What makes you think that?"

"You know the weights we recovered? Well, after you left, our guys dredged the pond and we found more. According to the maid, all of the weights match the weights the victim had in his home gym. The weights from the home gym also happen to be missing. And another thing, the maid noticed about four gallons of bleach missing."

"Have you been inside at all yet?"

"Nah. We were waiting for you."

"Okay, let's do a complete walk through first so Amy and I can get a feel for the scene. Then just Amy and I will go through and document the whole house." Brad turned to Amy who was still by the van, "Will you grab the video camera too? This place is so big that we'd be better off filming." He turned back to the two detectives, "Unless there is something obvious, I imagine we're going to have to block the windows to try to make it as dark as possible. I'll go through the place with luminol and see if I can detect any blood."

"I doubt we'll see anything obvious. The maid has been here for about a week and didn't notice anything out of place. She seems pretty meticulous, so I'm sure if she had come across a bunch of blood, she would have noticed."

Amy Ross, Brad's partner had been quietly gathering the camera equipment while the men talked. She walked over to the three men. "Hi Doug. Hi Marty." Amy was as perky as ever.

"Hey girl, welcome back to our small town." Doug was fond of the younger crime scene technician. Even though she was fairly new, she was good.

"Thanks. Are you guys going to come with us for the initial walk through?"

"The only time I'm ever going to get a chance to set foot in a house like this one is right now, so let's go." Doug had big dreams, but even his wildest dreams did not include owning a house like this one.

Back to business, Brad said, "Just don't touch anything as we go through guys."

The four of them made their way inside the house. Before going in, Marty made a quick call to Maria Hernandez to find out the alarm code. They certainly didn't want to set off any alarms as they entered the house.

As expected, everything inside the house was magnificent. The foyer had Italian marble floors, with a smaller version of the fountain from the driveway as the centerpiece. It actually had running water bubbling out of the top tier and running down to the lower two tiers. Two elegantly carved staircases formed a semi circle around the perimeter of the room. What they led to was just as grand as the foyer.

Taking a systematic outer perimeter approach, Brad led the group to the first room on the right. The formal dining room had a chandelier hanging from the twelve foot ceiling and must have had over five hundred crystals. A handsome bar sat in the corner with all of the top shelf liquor prominently displayed. The china cabinet held the finest china one could own. Everything in the room was exactly in place.

The tour led the group into the kitchen. All of the appliances were state of the art stainless steel. The cabinetry had such detailed carvings in the dark cherry wood that it had to have taken a master carpenter weeks to have created a single cabinet. Another set of stairs stemmed off of the kitchen. Doug and Marty both took note of them, remembering what Maria had said about her boss's interaction with Kerri Hall in that very spot.

After walking through the rest of the downstairs area, spiraling into the center of the downstairs floor, the four went upstairs, where they found the first room of particular interest. Dean Witherington's home gym had every piece of gym equipment you could possibly want; and then some. In the corner, by a five-gallon water bubbler, sat a rack of weights. As expected, all of the heavy weights were missing. Also as expected, the weights appeared to match the ones that had been used to weigh Dean Witherington's body down in the pond.

Marty spoke up for the first time. "Do you think you can try to get prints off of the racks over there? The shiny metal should be a good surface, don't you think?"

Amy replied, "We'll come back through and process it after we finish the initial walk through. With as clean as this place is, I'd be willing to bet the maid even keeps the weight machines dusted. I can't imagine she would let a latent print that was visible to the eye go by without cleaning it." That would be a safe bet.

The master bedroom hosted a masculine four-poster bed. Each poster was more like a Greek column, rising ten feet in the air. The rest of the furniture was just as ornate as the bed. Solid mahogany appeared to be the Dean Witherington's choice of wood for this room.

The master bathroom also had Italian marble throughout. The shower was unlike any of the four had ever seen. It did not have any walls. It had a rainmaker showerhead hanging from the ceiling and a stainless steel twenty jet massage shower panel. The other corner sat an oval Jacuzzi, with candles bordering its edges. Evidently even Dean Witherington liked to take a leisurely bath. Or have a romantic tryst.

The master closet was just off of the bathroom. Any woman could have died and thought she was in heaven in that closet. The center of the room hosted ten shelves dedicated solely to shoes. Most of the slots went unfilled, however. Also in the center was a dressing area with a full-length mirror. On top of a four foot cabinet sat a tie rack. With the push of a button, it rotated around, enabling the owner to find the perfect tie to go with his suit. Which, there were multiple suits in every color imaginable around the perimeter of the room. There were at least ten black suits alone, some with just the most minute differences in cut to distinguish it from the next one. Also around the perimeter were crisp dress shirts, also in a variety of colors. For some

63

reason the suits did not really seem like they were used that often. The crisp, ironed jeans hanging on solid wood clothes hangers seemed like they were the wardrobe of choice for Dean Witheringron.

The tour continued. The rest of the bedrooms were unremarkable. It was as though they were made up in case a guest ever came over, but were never actually used. The other three upstairs bathrooms were nice, but not as grand as the master bathroom.

The men in the group were particularly impressed with the entertainment room. It hosted state of the art surround sound, a 60 inch HDTV flat screen television, a blue ray DVD player and a high definition DVD player. Without opening cabinets, they could not see what else was there, but whatever it was, it was undoubtedly enviable.

After walking through a variety of other rooms, including a game room with a fifty thousand dollar billiards table, the group concluded its tour and stepped outside to the FDLE van. Brad spoke first, "Other than the home gym, nothing in the house really stood out to me, how about to you guys?"

Marty spoke up first, "I could have sworn I smelled the slightest hint of bleach while going up the stairway."

Amy agreed with him. "I think I did too. I wasn't quite sure where it was coming from though. That area is so spacious."

Brad told the detectives, "Okay, well, Amy and I will go through and film the entire house and then process the gym. I would prefer it if you two stay here. Not to say I don't think you can stay quiet during filming, but it is never a good thing when we play a video of a crime scene in front of a jury and they hear a crude joke or something worse on the video."

It did irritate Doug, but he didn't let on. "Not a problem, we'll wait right here."

Brad and Amy went back inside the house with their camera gear. It was at least an hour before they returned for the materials they would need to gather latent fingerprints. The plan was to process the gym for prints and then go through the entire house with luminol to see if there was any trace amount of blood.

By the time Brad and Amy finished processing the home gym, they were ready for a break.

"Did you find anything?" Doug was hopeful.

"No. Normally, I would say that not finding a single latent print in a room like that is suspicious, but looking at how clean that house is, it really isn't suspicious at all." Amy responded.

"So what is next?" Marty asked.

"Brad wanted to take a few minutes for a break and then he was going to prep the right side of the foyer and stairwell for the luminol testing. I'm going to start mixing up the solution for the testing."

"Why start there?"

"Like Marty said, there was a slight odor of bleach. Both Brad and I smelled it too. It could be nothing, so don't get your hopes up."

Doug watched her pulling various containers out and arranging them. "You have to mix it now? Doesn't it come ready for you already?" Doug asked.

Amy responded, "No, after it is mixed up, it is only good for eight hours at the most."

"This is my first time being around luminol testing. Would you mind explaining the process to me?" Doug knew the basics, but it never hurt to make a pretty lady feel like she was helping a guy out.

"Sure. I'm sure you already know that the luminol test is a presumptive test for the presence of blood. It utilizes hemoglobin's peroxidase-like activity. Before we create the mixture, we go ahead and set the area up that we are going to test. We have to make the room as dark as possible and set the camera up on a tri-pod. That is what Brad is going to do while I mix a bunch of this stuff up."

"Why can't you just hold the camera and snap pictures throughout the room?"

"Because we have to set the camera to a super slow shutter speed. The exposure time is around thirty seconds or so. If you were to hold the camera by hand, then even the slightest movement would blur the photo."

"I see." Doug said.

Amy went on, "Anyway, once you have the room blacked out as much as possible and the camera set up, you prepare the solution. Since there are two of us here, we're combining steps." She paused for a moment, "Do you really want to know what all goes in it?"

"Humor me." He didn't really care, but this was giving him an excuse to talk to an attractive blonde. At this point, any attention he could get made him feel a little better.

"Okay. I use a covered mixing container, to mix distilled water and Sodium Perborate and shake it for about fifteen seconds. Then I add Luminol and Sodium Carbonate. Cover it again and shake. Then

I let the undissolved particles go to the bottom of the container. After that I just pour the solution into the sprayer."

Doug asked, "Then you just spray it all over the room?"

"Not haphazardly. We use special bottles that allow for a super fine spray. We start in a corner so we can back away while spraying. You never want to walk over an area that you have already sprayed. While spraying, we just do it in a sweeping motion from side to side like this." She demonstrated the hand movement.

"Is that it?"

"That's it. If blood is there, then it will light up in a bluish luminescence."

"What makes it light up like that?"

"You really do want to test my knowledge, don't you?"

"Eh, consider it practice for cross examination on the witness stand."

Amy chuckled and continued explaining, "Basically, it is a reaction between the luminol mixture and the iron in the hemoglobin."

"Will it light up even if it was cleaned away with bleach?"

"If there was a large amount of blood, then I can almost guarantee we'll find something. Criminals think that once they have wiped the blood away and cleaned the area with peroxide or bleach or whatever their cleaner of choice is, that you can't see the blood anymore. Well, you can't see it with the naked eye, but the luminol testing allows us to see it. So we just take a swab and hopefully come up with DNA."

Marty jumped into the conversation, "Does anything else make luminol glow?"

67

Amy responded, "You aren't going to like this, especially considering that you suspect your perp cleaned up the area with bleach, but luminol will also react to bleach."

"You're kidding me?" Now Doug wasn't so much concerned with flirting as he was about breaking his case.

"Don't worry about it. We can usually tell if it is blood based on how quickly the reaction occurs. We still take swabs to verify whether it is really human blood."

"What about DNA?" Doug asked. "You said a second ago that you can 'hopefully' get DNA off of the swab."

"The bleach does a good job at breaking down the DNA, but usually we can find an area that wasn't cleaned as well as other areas. In a crime scene like this one, we aren't so concerned about matching the DNA as just locating an area where a large amount of blood pooled up or finding blood splatter. That will help with figuring out the homicide location."

"I guess that is true." Marty said. "Unless more than one person was killed here."

"We still try to get DNA. Oh, and the luminol does not effect the PCR testing for DNA."

Doug and Marty both gave her a blank stare. Now she really was talking over their heads.

She smiled at them, "Don't worry. We'll make the case as strong as forensically possible. Making sense of it and putting it all together will be your job."

Doug took the hint and allowed her to get back to work mixing the chemicals.

The next time Brad and Amy came out of the house, they were smiling. Doug and Marty were optimistic that they had found something.

"What's up?" Doug asked in anticipation.

"I think we found your crime scene." Brad flashed a beaming smile.

"What makes you say that?" Doug said.

"Pooling pattern of what we believe was blood, the way it dripped down the stairs, the apparent splatter on the wall and best of all, an area of the wall where a hole was filled in with fresh joint compound. Whoever made the repair didn't bother to paint the area over. If I were a betting man, I'd bet we have a bullet or at the very least, a fragment in that wall."

"Did you cut it out yet?" Now Doug was excited.

"Not so fast, don't you want us to collect the latent print first?" Brad said with a grin.

"You're kidding me?" Doug was really excited now.

"Not at all. I don't even need my kit to see it. Whoever repaired the damage to the wall left us a nice print to collect and analyze.

Doug said, "That is great. I didn't even notice a repaired area on the wall as we went up the stairs."

"It was on the stairway we went down, not the side we went up.

69

But it was barely noticeable. The wall is almost the same color as the joint compound. We may not have seen it but for the blank spot it left with the blood splatter."

"What do you mean?" Marty asked.

"I'd imagine your perpetrator cleaned all of the blood up first, realized there was a hole in the wall and then repaired the wall. Well, the small spot where there is fresh joint compound on it doesn't have any blood on it. Get it?"

"Yeah, I see."

"So, we're going to go back in and cut out that portion of the wall. Hopefully we'll find a bullet or a fragment in the wall. We've already taken all of the swabs we need for analysis at the lab. If we find a bullet, I don't really see any need to go through the rest of the house with luminol, do you?"

Marty answered, "No. We do want you to check the cleaning supplies though. I imagine they used a mop, sponge, bucket or whatever, basically stuff that was already here to clean up the blood."

Brad was two steps ahead, "Absolutely. There is a supply closet just off of the kitchen. We'll process that room next. Other than that, I don't really see how you'll need us for anything else here."

"I think that will be it. Let's see what is behind that wall." Doug was anxious to see if they could find a fragment that matched the one found in the victim's body.

With that, Brad and Amy went back to work. Doug and Marty stayed outside to give the crime scene specialists their space. The detectives were quite pleased to see Brad and Amy return with an evidence bag labeled, 'metal fragment recovered from east interior stairway' as well as an entire mop and bucket that they collected as evidence. It would take a couple of weeks for them to learn that the fragment in the wall was consistent with the bullet recovered from the victim's body and to find out that the mop had the victim's DNA all over it. It only took twenty minutes after uploading the latent print to IAFIS to put a name to the partial print that was left in the joint compound. Robert Sessions was officially a suspect.

6

Doug knew he was walking a tight rope dealing with Jesse. He still loved her and wanted to be with her whether she believed him or not. The problem was that he also wanted to be with his ex-wife, Alice. Not because of Alice, but because of his son, Jake. By hanging around Alice's house so much, one thing led to another and he wound up back in bed with his ex.

He was able to keep the secret from Jesse for about eight months, but then his worlds collided and everything he ever cared about came crashing down. But, despite all of the personal problems going on, he had to put his feelings aside and call Jesse about the case. She answered the call on the fourth ring.

He put on a false bravado. "How about lunch? I'd like to catch you up on the Witherington murder, if you'd like." Doug had not talked to Jesse since she helped prepare the search warrant for the Witherington Estate two weeks prior.

Jesse's stomach had immediately gone into a knot when she heard Doug's personalized ringtone on her cell phone. A sound that once was so frequent now sounded foreign. She had a busy schedule that day, but she quickly weighed the pros and cons of actually leaving the office for lunch and finally opted to go with him. Despite her better sense, she yearned to see him again. She would just have to be all business and only discuss the case even though there were still so many unanswered questions between them. "Umm…okay. Where do you want to meet?"

"How about Mel's? The one on Main?"

"Okay. I can leave in about five minutes, so I'll see you then?"

"Sure thing." The truth was that Doug was already in the parking lot of his favorite restaurant. Whether Jesse was coming or not, he was dying for one of Mel's famous cheeseburgers. Having her company again would make it all the better.

By the time Jesse breezed into the restaurant, Doug was half finished with his large sweet tea. He stood up and waved his arm in the air to grab her attention.

"Sorry it took me so long. There was an accident on main, right by the courthouse. I had to circumvent my way around it."

"Not a problem. I was just enjoying my tea here and going over some notes."

She sat down and a waitress was at the table immediately, "What would you like to drink?"

"I'll have a Diet Coke, please." She knew she needed to drink more water, but right now her head was screaming for caffeine. The waitress walked away, after depositing a menu on the table. Jesse immediately asked Doug, "So, do you have any leads?" She didn't want to even hint at their personal issues.

"Actually, yes. Several things have happened. Let me first start

73

with the results of the search warrant at the house. FDLE found where Witherington was shot. It happened on the main stairway. They took a bunch of swabs of the area and the DNA was Witherington's."

"Was there still blood visible?"

"No. Brad and Amy used luminol and then took swabs for further testing. The reason why we are quite certain that was the spot he was shot is because there was a portion of the wall that had been repaired with joint compound but not repainted. Guess what was behind that part of the wall when Brad and Amy removed it?"

"I don't know, but I have a feeling you are going to tell me."

"A bullet fragment." He waited for a smile to flash across her face, which it did. "But that isn't the best part."

"Okay, do tell. What is the best part because that is pretty good!"

"The person that repaired the wall left us a calling card."

"Don't tell me – "

He interrupted her, "you guessed it. He left us a perfect partial."

"Was it enough to make an ID?"

"Yes. Robert Sessions is our number one suspect at this point."

"That name sounds familiar." She stopped to think for a moment. "Isn't he big into the meth scene around here?"

The waitress returned with Jesse's Diet Coke before Doug could respond. "Ya'll decided what you're havin' yet?" The waitress asked.

Doug answered immediately, "I'll have a double cheeseburger, medium well, all the way with fries."

Jesse had been good all week and she knew she would have food envy if she didn't get the same thing. Giving in to her craving, she

74

ordered, "I'll have the same, only I don't want it all the way. Just lettuce on the side for me. Oh, and a single, not a double."

"It'll be right out folks." The waitress walked away, taking Jesse's menu with her.

Doug picked up where they left off. "Yes, he is. We've been able to put together some intel that he and Kerri Hall were hanging out an awful lot. We think he is the one that got her into the drug scene, not that it took much to convince her to do it."

"Kerri Hall? Isn't she the daughter of Thomas Hall, the big time realtor?"

"Yes, she is our local version of Lyndsey Lohan."

"Meaning party hard?"

"Yes." He took a gulp of tea and continued, "Anyway, we think Kerri is involved in this also."

"Why?"

"When Marty and I talked to Maria, the maid, she remembered seeing a thin blonde that drove a yellow Mustang at the house with Dean Witherington. And the blonde had a black streak in her hair. From the maid's description of what happened, it sounds as though Witherington was hitting the juice too. Anyway, this encounter took place a couple of weeks before he ended up dead."

"So how does that make Kerri involved in the murder?"

"It doesn't. Not so far from what I've told you."

"So what else is there?"

"I got Witherington's cell phone records back. Once I got those numbers, I got the subscriber information from the numbers that he called and the numbers that called him. Kerri Hall's number is all over the place until Saturday at 3:21 in the afternoon. After that, she never calls him again and he doesn't make any more outgoing calls."

"Does Saturday jive with when the medical examiner thinks Witherington died?"

"Yes. So, my question to you is, 'why would Kerri Hall, who up until Saturday at 3:21 p.m. used to call Witheringron all of the time, suddenly stop calling him?'"

"She knew he wasn't taking calls anymore." Jesse answered.

"Bingo. So, I went ahead and subpoenaed Kerri Hall's phone records. I also had them ping her phone and was not too shocked to find out that she is in another state right now."

"Wait a minute, you pinged it?"

"Yeah, that's just a way to figure out a person's location using the GPS on their phone."

"I know what ping means, but there is recent case law about obtaining historical cell site data – is that all you did? You didn't get the content of any text messages or anything, did you?"

"No, just past and present location."

Jesse was relieved. "Good. Where is she?"

"Kentucky. We started mutual aid already. The locals are looking for her as we speak. I know she is there, so after lunch, I'm going to head up there myself."

"Why do you want to be there?"

"We don't have enough to arrest her at this point. She is just a person of interest and I don't want somebody I don't know screwing up the interview."

"Do you have any reason to believe that Sessions is up there too?"

"Yes, but I'm getting ahead of myself." Jesse noticed that all too familiar sparkle in his eyes. "It turns out that one of Witherington's credit cards has been used all the way up I-75, I-24 and I-65, through Georgia, Tennessee and into Kentucky. One of the places it was used was at a gas station in Forsyth, Georgia. I know a deputy up there and he was able to get the video surveillance for me. Guess who was filling up their tank?"

"Hall and Sessions." It was an obvious answer for Jesse.

"Yes. But, it gets even better. They weren't in their own vehicle."

"Could you tell whose vehicle they were in?"

"Witherington's!"

"Really?" Already her mind was ticking. She knew that Witherington had been shot twice. Once in the chest and once execution style in the head. She didn't know which one killed him, but assuming he was shot in the chest first and was still alive before the execution shot, then that meant he saw the execution shot coming. That alone could be an enhancer to make this into a death penalty case. Combine that with capital gain because of the theft of the vehicle and use of credit cards and it sounded more and more like it was going to be a death penalty case.

"Yes. Witherington has several vehicles, but it looks like Hall and Sessions took his Excursion. My guess is that they used it to move the body to the pond and then just took off in it. I know Hall drives a Mustang convertible, which isn't exactly conducive to moving a body."

"That sounds reasonable. Have you tried to see if his Excursion has OnStar or some other navigational system?"

"I like the way you think. I'm one step ahead of you though." He took another gulp of his tea. "It does. Well, it did, anyway."

"What do you mean, 'it did?'"

"It had OnStar FMV. From what we can tell, after they dumped the body, they fled in the vehicle and dumped it at a chop shop just outside of Atlanta. We were able to subpoena the navigation records going back to two days before he was killed. They couldn't give me a detailed account of where the vehicle was within the county, but they could tell me that the vehicle traveled north and then their signal ended on Sunday, just outside of Atlanta."

"Meaning the day after Witherington was killed?"

"Yes."

"So what makes you think chop shop? Why don't you think they just discovered how to turn the navigation system off?"

"That is possible, but Sessions rap sheet is covered with dealing in stolen cars, so I'm thinking he was just sticking to what he knows. We've linked him in the past to a whole ring of chop shops that are spread throughout the southeast. Based on the timeline, we think he dumped the Excursion and got a new ride in Atlanta. The shop people must have gotten to work on it Sunday and disabled the OnStar FMV system."

"It sounds like things are coming along nicely. Is there anything else I can do to help?"

"Not at this point. Marty is throwing together some clothes right now. When we're done here, I'll swing by his place to pick him up. It will be a long drive, but I expect to make it to Kentucky just after nightfall if we push it."

"That is going to make it a long day for you."

Her comment could be construed on either a personal level or professional level, but Jesse didn't get a chance to see how Doug would interpret it because the waitress walked up to the table carrying two plates brimming with fries. Somewhere underneath lay two cheeseburgers. "Can I get you two anything else?" She asked after laying the plates on the table.

"Not right now, thank you." Doug sent the waitress on her way and answered Jesse, "That's okay. We won't make it to where we think Hall and Sessions are. I just want to make it into the state. That way we can get an early start in the morning." He obviously chose to treat her comment as professional.

Jesse reciprocated the professional approach. "Are they still using his credit card in Kentucky?"

"Yes. They've been going to a lot of pharmacies, so I'm willing to bet they are buying up a bunch of ephedrine."

"Isn't that kept behind the counter nowadays?"

"In some places, but not all. I don't know what they are doing about ephedrine sales in Kentucky. They have a worse meth problem there than we do here." He stopped talking long enough to take a big bite but continued talking while chewing. "I don't know this for sure, but it would not surprise me to find out that Sessions either has a

79

supplier in Kentucky or that he originally learned to cook meth up there."

"Why is that?"

"Actually, no, let me rethink that. If he had a supplier up there, then he wouldn't be buying the precursors to make his own meth. He'd just go straight to his supplier to get some."

"Unless his supplier was out of ephedrine, which is necessary to make methamphetamine. He could just be buying the supplies and letting someone else do the cooking." Jesse suggested.

"Either way, I bet he is involved with meth up there also. We don't have enough to get a warrant for where he was staying down here, but from what I hear on the street, he was dealing meth big time. I don't know if he was making runs up to Kentucky on a regular basis or not. It is so simple to make that it wouldn't surprise me if he was just cooking it himself. You know you can just look the recipe up on the Internet now, don't you?"

"Yes, unfortunately, I did know that. I went to a Clandestine Laboratories seminar a while back. I was shocked to find out how easy it is to make meth. I was even more shocked that the instructor gave us the exact recipe. That is, I was shocked until he also told us about numerous websites that give you step-by-step directions."

"You aren't kidding. The drug task force is getting more and more information about meth labs being set up in the woods. I guess these meth heads figure if there is an explosion, it is better to be outside than in a house or trailer."

"Who knows? I just always remember how lethal the cook sites can be. They told us a story about an officer that walked into a meth house without protective clothing. He supposedly went home and held his three month old baby without changing clothes or cleaning up. They told us the baby died due the exposure to the methamphetamine."

"Yeah, I've heard that story too. Back in the day, it wasn't unusual for us to just walk into a meth house. Nowadays if there is a full-out lab in the house, we call in the guys with Hazmet suits. It costs hundreds of thousands of dollars to clean one of those places up."

"I just wonder how many places go untreated. Just think about all of the motel rooms that have been used to cook. Do you really think the motel manager puts the money into sanitizing the room? There is no way."

"I agree with you. All we can do is report the busts we make to the EPA. We just let them follow up on it from there."

"It is still bothersome. I certainly wouldn't want to stay in a room that had been used to cook meth."

"Jesse, really. Do you really think you would be staying in some shabby motel where a drugged out meth head was staying to cook his meth?"

She answered, "Probably not, but they don't necessarily always use the dives."

He kidded her, "I have never heard of a meth lab at a Hilton."

"Let me remind you, I'm a State employee. I don't have the money to stay at a Hilton."

"Okay, well I've never heard about a meth lab at a Holiday Inn either."

81

She continued the familiar friendly banter, "I'm more of a Comfort Inn and Suites kind of girl, actually."

"Whatever." He rolled his eyes at her. A hint of the flirtation that they used to have came through.

She smiled at him and wondered if this conversation was going to turn personal after all. "I know you are probably right."

"I know I'm right." Doug's Nextel beeped at him. After seeing who it was, he turned it off of speaker and put it on private "Go ahead, Marty." He listened for a moment and responded, "All right, man. I'm just about done here. I'll be at your house in about twenty minutes. You want me to bring you a Coke or anything from Mel's?"

"Is everything okay?" Jesse asked after Doug finished his conversation with Marty.

"Yeah, he was just letting me know that he's ready and that Sessions has been spotted in Elizabethtown, Kentucky. The locals are trying to keep tabs on him for us."

"That's great that they've found him. They aren't going to actually make contact, are they?" Jesse asked.

"That isn't the plan. So far Marty is the one that has been keeping in touch with the Sheriff up there. Marty told their Sheriff that we just want to know where they are so we can do a consensual interview when we get up there."

"What if they won't talk?"

"Well, what do you think? At this point, I could go ahead and get an arrest warrant for Sessions for the homicide. He also absconded from probation, so there isn't really an issue about getting a warrant.

But what about the girl? I can't put her at the murder scene yet."

Jesse thought for a moment before throwing out suggestions. "What about accessory after the fact? Or grand theft? Or unauthorized use of credit card? Wait, no, that charge would be in Georgia, unless they used it here too."

"No, they didn't use it here, but do you think I have enough for accessory?"

"You know I can't tell you that. If I were to tell you that you have enough to make an arrest, then that oversteps my role as a prosecutor and I lose my prosecutorial immunity. Now, if you were to ask me if I would charge her based on what we have so far, then that is a whole different story."

"Okay, Ms. Semantics, if I arrested her, would your office prosecute it based on what we have so far?"

"Probably. But she sounds like the type to sell out whomever she has to sell out in order to get what she wants, so it wouldn't surprise me if she talks when you catch up with her. She'll probably fill in a lot of holes that we have now."

"And if she doesn't?"

"With a little more investigation, I think you have enough for at least the grand theft of the Excursion. I'll need more information about how much time she spent with Witherington, someone to be able to say that Hall knew the Excursion belonged to Witherington. I just wouldn't want her to be able to say that Sessions told her he had permission to take the Excursion or told her it belonged to him. I can bring into evidence the fact that they used the credit card since they were using it to put gas into the Excursion."

"I thought there was some rule against using evidence of other wrongdoings?"

"Usually yes, but here it is all inextricably intertwined."

"Excuse me?"

"It boils down to the fact that one act of wrongdoing, meaning the theft of the vehicle, is so intertwined with using the same victim's credit card that you can't separate the two." Not to mention pecuniary gain is an aggravating factor if we go for the death penalty.

"Works for me. Listen, I've got to go. If I need to get a warrant, can we do it over the phone?"

"Just call me and I'll get one prepared. We'll have to talk further about how you get it signed. The judge will need you present to be the affiant for the warrant. But just see how things play out."

With that, Doug and Jesse each got take out boxes, paid their bill and went their separate ways. Jesse went back to the office to prepare a *Motion in Limine* on a child sex case and Doug went to pick up Marty to head to Kentucky. Little did he know what chaos would be awaiting him.

7

The drive to Bowling Green, Kentucky took eight hours. If they had gone the speed limit, it would have taken closer to nine and a half hours. The original plan was to stay in Bowling Green, since it was just inside the state line and then travel the last seventy miles to Elizabethtown the next morning, but while the Florida detectives were making the drive, the local sheriff's office in Elizabethtown had quite a day following Sessions and Hall.

It all started when Glen Summers, a young deputy who had just been released from his field training officer, was assigned to keep tabs on Sessions, the Florida fugitive, who was now driving a Jeep Wrangler. Elizabethtown was large enough to have all of the chain restaurants, but small enough to where local law enforcement was able to recognize almost everyone, if not know the person on a first name basis. Glen was instructed by the local Sheriff himself to not pull Sessions over unless he broke a serious law. Even if there was some sort of traffic infraction or non-moving violation, Glen was under strict orders to not have contact with the people the Florida detectives wanted to speak with.

Everything was fine for the first five hours of the surveillance.

Glen was in an unmarked vehicle, so it made the job much easier than if he were in a marked unit. He was actually enjoying riding around in the nearly new Avalanche his agency had recently seized as part of a drug bust.

Glen thought that it was quite strange that the Florida man and woman went to every pharmacy in town. They seemed to be driving the streets aimlessly until they found the next one. All of the U-turns the man did in the roads made it difficult for Glen to follow him without being detected, but his truck blended in quite well with the rest of the traffic.

After the man driving the Jeep established a pattern of turning back to go to a pharmacy, Glen relaxed a little and started anticipating where the next stop would be. Glen was quite proud that he had learned every road name and pretty much knew where each and every store was located. That included all of the local pharmacies.

This haphazard hunt went on for about five hours before the Florida duo finally stopped for food at a McDonalds. Even though McDonald's was not one of Glen's favorite fast food restaurants, he would have settled for it based on how hungry he was feeling at the moment; yet, he didn't give in to the temptation. Instead, he popped the top on a bottle of water and opened up an energy bar. He parked across the street at a Sonic parking lot and waited for the couple to emerge from the restaurant. He slowly munched on his snack, trying to make it last longer. Unfortunately for Glen, the Florida couple stayed inside the restaurant for nearly an hour.

Finally, the man and woman came out. They both walked out

quickly. The man made a beeline for the Jeep. He didn't even look before crossing through the path of an oncoming car in the parking lot. The woman, however, was looking all around her, as though she knew someone was watching her, but just didn't know from where.

Glen involuntarily slunk lower in his seat. He knew the woman wouldn't be able to see him through the dark tinted windows of the Avalanche, but he didn't want to risk being seen. He thought to himself, *I did park far enough down, didn't I? Surely they didn't notice me across the street in this parking lot, did they?* He quickly thought through all of the surveillance techniques he had been taught.

The woman seemed to stop mid stride as she looked across the street to the Sonic parking lot. Glen's own paranoia kicked in. He had done everything just as he had been trained. There was no way they could have realized they were being followed. Was there?

With one last look around her, the woman jumped into the passenger seat of the Jeep. Without speaking to one another, the man cranked the engine and squealed out of the parking lot. He ran through a stop sign, which was only the first of many traffic laws he was about to break. He peeled out onto West Dixie Highway, forcing the driver of a Honda Celica to slam on her brakes to avoid hitting the side of the Jeep.

Glen was at a loss as to what was happening. All he knew was that he had to get across that street or he may lose his targets. There was no way he was going to screw up an assignment as simple as this one. Glen wanted to turn on his lights and siren to stop traffic so he could get across the street, but if he did, he would blow his cover, if there was even any cover left. The blue and red lights were on the inside of the vehicle, attached to the sun visors, not on the top of the vehicle, so there was no way the Florida people could have made him that way. Resisting the temptation to turn the lights on, he waited, hearing the trail of honking cars that the Florida duo left behind in their wake.

Finally, with a break in traffic, Glen spun out and entered the line of vehicles on West Dixie Highway. He weaved in and out of traffic, hoping to catch sight of the Jeep. Finally, he saw the tail end of the Jeep down a cross street. They had turned left on Coonce. Glen could not make the turn onto Coonce, so he took a chance of losing sight of the Jeep again and went one block down before making a left onto Mayberry. Fortunately he caught the light to make the turn, so he stood a chance at catching up with the Jeep.

Glen sped down the road, only slowing as he came to the first intersection. He made a sharp left, traveled down the block and made a quick right onto Coonce. He didn't see the Jeep. He was starting to panic, but was able to maintain his cool. He called dispatch to let them know what was going on. He told the dispatcher the last intersection that he had seen the Jeep, as well as a description of the vehicle and the tag number.

He wasn't in hot pursuit, so there was no reason to call out other units for assistance. No reason other than the fact that he did not want to screw up this assignment. He did not want to look bad in front of the Sheriff. All he had to do was tail a Jeep. How hard could that be? Though Glen didn't know the details of why these two were of interest he knew it had something to do with a murder in Florida. How could he have screwed up such a simple assignment?

Finally, Glen spotted the Jeep. The driver had already made the block and was headed in the opposite direction back to West Dixie Highway. Rather than turning to follow behind the Jeep, Glen made a quick three point turn and drove parallel to the Jeep. The trick would be figuring out which way the Jeep was going to go once it got back to West Dixie Highway.

Glen didn't have to worry about that for too long. The sound of a blaring horn, screeching tires and the unmistakable sound of metal crashing into metal told Glen exactly what happened. The Jeep pulled out in front of oncoming traffic, forcing a light pickup truck to brake so hard that the car behind the truck rear ended the pickup truck. Even though the pickup truck tried to avoid colliding with the Jeep, he did knick the left rear corner. Not having serious damage, Sessions sped away in the Jeep. Unfortunately for the pickup truck driver, the line of traffic behind him had been moving at a pretty brisk pace, so there were multiple cars following too closely. By the time it was all said and done, the Jeep's driver had caused a four car pile up.

That was problematic for Glen. He only had a split second to decide whether to turn on the lights and siren. He did. Then he called in the multi-car crash to dispatch, adding in that he was in hot pursuit of the Jeep that caused the crash and then fled the scene. The Florida man had now violated Kentucky law. He just left the scene of an accident that he caused. Hopefully that would be a major enough incident so that the Sheriff would not have his head for blowing his cover.

Glen sped by the crash while driving in the turn lane in the middle of the road. He could see that at least one woman was bleeding from her forehead. Glen was racking up all of the possible charges against this man in his mind – he also had leaving the scene of an accident with bodily injury. Glen would have to wait to see how badly the person was injured to determine whether or not it was serious bodily injury.

The chase was on. The Jeep still had about a one block lead over Glen's Avalanche. Glen, however, had the advantage of lights and a siren. Not to mention, the Jeep was leaving quite a wake with cars veering out of its path. Most of the shocked drivers had not started driving again by the time Glen sped past them.

The Jeep hit the curb as its driver made a hard right on Esplande Avenue. Glen knew this road choice would lead them through a residential neighborhood and eventually intersect with a highway that would lead out into the countryside. Glen suspected that was where the two were headed. He only hoped there would not be any kids playing ball in the road as the two vehicles sped past.

The Jeep did not slow down as it flew past house after house. Glen could see the residents sticking their heads out to see what was going on. After all, it was not every day that a police chase with lights and sirens took place in their neighborhood.

Being familiar with this street, Glen knew that a speed bump was just ahead. The Jeep was easily running eighty miles an hour as it raced towards the obstacle. If the Jeep didn't slow down at all, it would surely scrape the pavement.

Running at such high speeds, the warning sign for the speed bump did not come quick enough for the Jeep's driver. Even though his vehicle was pretty high off of the ground, he slammed on his brakes, causing the rubber on his tires to burn into the pavement. With smoke rising from the tires, he hit the speed bump. The Jeep's undercarriage made a screeching noise as it scraped across the raised pavement. From behind, Glen could see numerous sparks flying. Then the Jeep launched into the air, crashing down as it landed. The suspension nearly gave out, but the driver pushed the Jeep for all it was worth. With the speed bump behind him, the driver slammed the pedal to the metal once again.

Glen saw the way the Jeep handled the speed bump and did not want to suffer the same fate. Slowing in advance for the bump, he scraped a little, but did not have the difficulty going over the hump like the Jeep did. After all, Glen's vehicle was much newer and had a much better suspension.

Glen accelerated as fast as he could. He had no doubt that he would be able to overtake the Jeep. The question was what would he do when he caught up? This guy obviously was not going to pull over. Glen took an evasive driving course while in the law enforcement academy. He had also heard about the PIT maneuver, but had never done it before. Growing up, Glen had always wanted to be a cop and always enjoyed watching car chases on television. It was an especially great thrill to see it when the officers would clip the rear of the suspect's car and "put it in the trees," thus the slang name, "PIT."

There was no way he could do a PIT on this road. The Jeep would most assuredly spiral into a house. Not only was that too dangerous, it would be career suicide. Even the current Sheriff, who had excellent popularity ratings, would have a difficult time overcoming a publicity disaster like that.

The speeding vehicles were quickly approaching the highway. Glen called his location into dispatch once again. Where was his back up? Why hadn't they arrived yet? It was looking more and more like Glen was going to have to take matters into his own hands. Smoldering in the back of his mind was the fact that he was possibly dealing with a couple of murderers. If they had already killed one person, what was one more?

The Jeep's brake lights suddenly came on, which brought Glen's attention back into focus. The only question now was which way they were going to turn. That question did not hang in the air for long. The Jeep's driver turned left, nearly causing the Jeep to roll over in the process. Though Glen couldn't hear it, he imagined the woman screaming during the turn, as she reached up and grabbed the Jeep's roll bar above her head to steady herself.

All Glen had to do now was catch back up to the Jeep. It was obvious that the driver was not going to stop, so Glen was already thinking ahead of where the best place to do the PIT maneuver would be. There was a pasture up ahead on the right, but Glen was afraid if he ran the Jeep off the road into the pasture, that the driver would just put it into four wheel drive and be able to take off again.

Then again, if he knocked the Jeep off of the road into a stand of pine trees, then it was possible that he could kill the occupants. No matter what kind of evil things they may have done, he certainly did not want to do that – for multiple reasons.

Glen decided his best option was the pasture. If the maneuver did not work the first time, he could always try again. The only bad thing was that in the interest of keeping the Avalanche anonymous, the Sheriff had opted to not install a push bar on the front of the vehicle. Glen was not entirely sure how the Avalanche would handle the crash it was about to endure.

Accelerating steadily, Glen approached the left rear bumper of the Jeep with his front right fender. Gliding in, almost as if on air, Glen nudged the smaller vehicle's rear bumper. After a slight fishtail, the driver was able to regain control and accelerated harder. The Florida man kept both hands on the wheel as he looked over his left shoulder. If looks could kill, Glen would have been dead.

Glen recalculated what he would have to do. Whatever he did, it would have to be quick because not only was the pasture about to end with a large stand of pine trees beginning, but they were coming up on a curve. They had been fortunate so far to not encounter any oncoming traffic, but that luck could end at any moment.

Glen sped up again, with determination in his mind. It was going to work this time. Glen fell in behind the Jeep and even to its right a little bit. Perhaps if he hit the Jeep's bumper at more of an angle, from right to left, the PIT would actually work. With seconds remaining to act, Glen stomped on the gas and launched forward.

This time, there was a solid impact. Glen lunged forward, causing his seat belt to lock up and throw him back against the seat. The

Avalanche started swerving, but Glen was able to regain control. By the grace of God nobody was driving towards them, or else Glen would have had a head on collision since he was driving in the oncoming lane.

The Jeep's driver did not have the ability to maintain control this time. He frantically spun the wheel, trying to keep the Jeep from spinning in a circular motion, but it was no use. The Jeep spun one hundred and eighty degrees in less than three seconds. Time was standing still for everyone involved as the Jeep started to roll over. If the driver had not been turning the wheel so much, it may have stayed upright, but that was not what destiny had in store for the Florida duo.

Glen watched as the Jeep took its first roll, the driver's side hitting the ground first, then rolling onto the top and the other side before becoming upright again. Then it hit into a slight embankment, which sent it up into the air and into its second roll. This time it rolled end over end. The Jeep crashed down, with the momentum of the crash keeping it going forward on the front and back passenger side wheels. Finally, the Jeep made its final roll, landing with the passenger's side on the grass and the driver's side wheels spinning uselessly in the air.

Glen was speechless with all that had just happened. Could anyone have survived that crash? He had not seen the man or woman ejected from the Jeep, so it was still possible that they were alive. Glen quickly turned the Avalanche around and drove off the road at the same place the Jeep had crashed through just moments before.

The young deputy called the crash into dispatch, requesting fire and rescue to be sent to the scene. The field was extremely dry, so dust was flying everywhere; so much so that Glen could not fully see the Jeep until he was almost on top of it.

Glen jumped out of his vehicle and with his gun drawn, ran up to the crashed Jeep. He heard a moan and then he saw where it was coming from. A young woman's arm was trapped under the bent frame of the Jeep. At least she was alive. Glen ran to her side, momentarily forgetting that there was another possibly armed person nearby. "Ma'am, are you all right? Can you hear me?"

The woman winced in pain, but managed to curse, "What the fuck – How the fuck do you think I am? You just fucking ran us off the road."

That answered Glen's question. If she could talk like that, then she was well enough that he could focus his attention on finding the driver. The dust was beginning to settle so Glen barely caught sight of the driver before he disappeared into the pine trees. Glen heard sirens approaching as he used his portable radio to call in a description of the driver, "56 to dispatch, over"

The dispatcher chirped back, "Dispatch to 56, go ahead."

"Suspect's vehicle is inoperable. Suspect one fled the scene. Whiskey mike, white male, with dark hair, wearing a white T-shirt. Travel is on foot, traveling west into a stand of pine trees. Second occupant is whiskey foxtrot, white female, trapped in the vehicle. Rescue is needed immediately." With the exception of a few ten codes and signals, the department had recently switched to plain language for the officers to call into dispatch.

"Ten-four. Be advised fire rescue is on the way. Units 27 and 32

95

are en route."

Not being able to help the female, Glen started to jog over to the tree line to see if he could see where the driver went after running into the trees. Meanwhile, Keith Simpson, the department's K9 officer pulled up. Glen had never worked with the K-9 officer before. The K-9 currently assigned to Keith was a Black and Tan German Shepherd named Max. The K-9 was certified in apprehension, drug detection and tracking.

"Hey man, did he head that way?" Keith got out of his car with a leash looped over his arm and yelled to the junior officer.

"The dust was flying after the crash, but I caught a glimpse of him running into the trees."

Keith yelled to the junior officer, "Go back over to your vehicle, I don't want you to contaminate the track. I'll pick up his scent at the Jeep and go from there."

"Sure." Glen was already upset at himself for losing the suspect and now he may have made it worse by messing up the scent that had just been left. If he had known more about dogs, then he would have known that Max could easily distinguish between the scent of the person he was tracking and the scent of a cross track left by another person, but it would be later in his career before Glen learned such things.

While Keith was putting a 30 foot tracking line on his dog, the other backup officer, Morgan Lawson, showed up on scene as did the fire rescue truck which drove right out onto the pasture next to the overturned Jeep. Two men got out and immediately went to work.

Not being able to rescue her, the EMT's got the firemen to use the Jaws of Life to cut the woman free. All the while, the woman cursed at everyone trying to help her. In the meantime, Keith and Max had already gone to the Jeep, where Keith pointed to the driver's area and commanded the dog to "Suche," which is the German word for search.

While helping the woman stuck in the Jeep, Jason, one of the EMT's asked, "Ma'am, I need you to calm down for me, okay?"

She just glared at him.

"Ma'am I need to ask you a few questions. Work with me here, all right? We're going to get you patched up just fine. What is your name?"

"I don't have a name." She snapped back.

"Ma'am, I'm just trying to help you here, okay. Just tell me your name so I can talk to you. My name is Jason, now what is yours?"

"Fuck off."

"Fine. If that is how you want to play this, then have it your way. I'm just trying to help you lady." He waited a moment to give her a chance to cooperate. She wouldn't. "All right, if you want to be that way, you'll be Jane Doe. Now Jane, this is important, do you have any allergies?

"No."

"Are you taking any medications right now?"

She just glared at him.

"Jane, listen to me now, I'm asking you these questions so I can help you better. I need to know if you are taking any medications so we don't give you something that will make you have a reaction."

97

Her response was the same – just a hateful glare.

Meanwhile, Glen was searching the perimeter of the Jeep in case there was any evidence ejected from it. "Hey guys, I found a purse that flew out of the Jeep, I can look and see if her identification is in it." Near the purse, Glen also found at least two hundred packs of cold medicine. His earlier suspicions of why the two had been to all of the pharmacies in town were confirmed. They were getting cold pills with ephedrine in them so they could make methamphetamine.

Jason yelled back to Glen, "Yeah, why don't you do that. Maybe she'll have an emergency information card and we can see if she has any allergies or someone to call."

Though he didn't know that it was an expensive Kate Spade bag, Glen opened the purse up and started going through the contents. Spotting a wallet, he opened it up. He expected to find a driver's license looking back at him. What he found instead was a clear plastic baggie of crystal methamphetamine commonly known as ICE on the street. Not letting on to what he had found, Glen continued to look in the wallet until he came to a Florida driver's license. "Her name is Kerri Hall."

Jason turned to his patient, "All right, Kerri, we are going to take you to the hospital now. Your arm is going to have to be X-rayed and set by a doctor. Do you think you can handle that?"

Now Kerri wouldn't even look up at her rescuer. The extent of Kerri's cooperation with Jason had expired. The two EMT's loaded the stretcher onto their truck. Before Jason could get into the back with the patient, Glen took him to the side. "Look, don't let her know

98

this, but as I was going through her purse, I came across some crystal meth. I'm going to charge her with it, but I don't want her to know that I found it yet. It may make it harder for you guys to treat her."

"All right. I won't tell her. I'll just let the hospital know to notify you before she is released, okay?"

"Sure, that will be fine."

With that said and done, the EMT's left for the hospital. Eventually the fire truck and remaining deputies left, leaving Glen at the scene to wait for the tow truck by himself. Surveying the mess, he was going to have a lot of explaining to do to the Sheriff.

8

For Doug and Marty, the sign welcoming them to Elizabethtown did not come soon enough. They were both anxious to talk to Kerri Hall, who by now was resting comfortably in the Hardin County Jail. The drive gave the Florida detectives plenty of time to get up to speed with all of the events of the day.

Since Hall's broken arm was a relatively clean break, she did not require surgery. The emergency room doctor gave her pain medication and put a secure splint on her arm so a cast could be applied after the swelling went down. She was given instructions to keep her arm elevated and was then transported to the jail for booking.

Unfortunately, Sessions had not been apprehended yet. Keith, the K-9 officer, lost Session's track about two miles from the crash site. Since the track was lost at a cross road, they suspected that Sessions had called someone to pick him up or hitched a ride.

Even without Sessions being available to interview, the detectives were anxious to speak with Kerri so they drove straight to the jail. Doug and Marty did not speak to one another as they were escorted into an interview room at the jail. After waiting for about ten minutes, a corrections officer escorted Kerri Hall into the small room. Both detectives stood up as she entered the room. The orange jump suit swallowed the young woman's small frame.

"Kerri, I'm Detective Doug Wescott and this is Detective Marty Newsome. We're here to ask you a few questions, okay?" He did not want to tell her that he was from Florida, preferring to get her to open up to him and talk about seemingly innocuous things first.

Kerri looked at him and slowly replied, "Okay," in a childlike voice.

"Before we get into all of that, how are you feeling? I see you got banged up pretty good."

She replied, "I'm fine," she paused and exhaled slowly. "My arm is broken, but it will get better. I have good bones."

"Was it a clean break?"

"That's what the doctor told me. I'll have to go back for a cast because they took me to jail." Kerri's demeanor was drastically different than it had been at the crash scene. Probably because the illicit drugs in her system had worn off or, perhaps it was because of the pain medication the doctor had given her.

"Well, Kerri, that is what we are here to talk to you about. Before we do that, there is a formality that I have to go through. Let me pull this card out and read it to you, okay? Now listen closely as I read it to you."

"Okay." She yawned.

"You have the right to remain silent. Anything you say can and will be used against you in the court of law. You have the right to an attorney. If you cannot afford an attorney, one will be appointed to you. You have a right to stop answering questions at any time. You have a right to consult with an attorney at any time." He looked up from the card. "Do you understand these rights as I have read them to you?"

"Sure."

"Do you have any questions before we continue talking?"

"This is like what they call my Miranda Rights, right?"

"Yes, ma'am, it is known as the Miranda Warning."

"Now I'm just going to have you sign this form acknowledging that I read you your rights, okay?

"I'm not signing that."

That wasn't the response Doug was hoping for. "All I'm asking you to do is to sign this form. All it says is that I read you your rights. Just read through the form."

"I just told you I'm not signing that."

"May I ask why not?" He suspected she was trying to be coy so he decided to indulge her.

She giggled, "Because, Silly, I'm right handed. I kind of can't write anything right now." She motioned towards her bandaged arm. "Duh."

Doug relaxed a little. "I see. You got me there, Kerri. I've got to admit you got me there." He wanted to make her feel like she was outsmarting him. "Tell you what, do you think you could try to write with your other hand. At least make an 'X' where it has the signature line?"

"Okay." She was back to the little girl voice again. She picked up

102

the pen that was offered to her and scribbled her name. The writing definitely matched the voice, but then again she was not using her dominant hand.

"Thank you, Kerri. So tell me a little about yourself. You don't sound like you're from here."

"I ain't no hick, that's for sure."

From the grammar she used in answering him, her statement sure seemed far from the truth.

Doug asked, "A girl like you? No way. So where are you from?"

"They already asked me these questions when they took my picture. Why do we have to go through it again?"

"I'm just trying to get to know you, Kerri. Is that okay? I could go read it from your booking sheet, but I'd rather hear it from you. I like talking to you."

That was all it took to make her feminine wiles start kicking into full throttle. She didn't know how much trouble she was in but she wanted to take advantage of every asset she had. "So you'd like to hear it from my lips?" She leaned towards him.

"Exactly. I think you know exactly what I want. So the question now is: Are you going to give it to me?" He knew at that point that she would talk. Stroke her ego a little and she would be singing like a Jay Bird in no time.

"I guess so." She giggled again and ran her left hand through her hair, which wasn't quite as neat as she normally kept it. Understandably so.

"So, let's start over again. Where are you from, Kerri?"

"Florida."

"Well that explains it."

"What?" She looked perplexed.

"How your tan is so nice. It's completely natural, isn't it?"

"Ohhh. Of course, of course. I would have nothing less."

"I wouldn't imagine. You seem to have a lot of class, Kerri. Am I just making that up, or are you pretty sophisticated?"

"My father is very wealthy. I'm his only little girl. That should explain it." It certainly did.

"If I had a daughter like you, I'd sure give her the world. Does your dad give you lots of things?"

"Not really. For my last birthday, he only gave me a Mustang convertible. He should have at the very least given me a Lexus convertible. A Mustang is like nothing."

"Oh, I bet you look great in it. What color is it?" Doug was playing it up for her. He already knew exactly what color the car was.

"Yellow with a black racing stripe."

"Now you know what my next question is going to be, right?"

"No, what?"

"Really, you don't know?" She shook her head no. "Which did you do first, the black racing stripe on the car, or the black streak in your hair?"

She chuckled and responded, "That is like the age old question, isn't it? You know, like which came first, the chicken or the egg?"

"Oh, I see. Yeah, I guess so." Doug thought to himself that the blonde hair was completely natural and didn't come from a bottle.

104

"I hate to say that I copied a car, but that is kind of what happened. Daddy brought the car home and I just did my hair like it the same day."

"I bet you look awesome riding in it, don't you? Did you drive it all the way to Kentucky? I would have known about it if you had, because there would have been national news about wrecks all the way from there to here because of truck drivers breaking their necks trying to get a look at you."

"No, I didn't drive it up here. I rode with a friend in um," she hesitated, "well, a friend's SUV." She seemed unsure of how to phrase it.

That statement was good. She had just admitted to being in a SUV. Hall and Sessions had taken the victim's SUV, but he wanted to shore up the admission. "Yeah, that Jeep that you were in when you hurt your arm? That what you're talking about?" He knew it was not.

She hesitated before answering. "Um, no." She paused and then said, "I mean yeah."

"You two must have had the sides on it then, because even in that, you could stop traffic." He had to relax her again to get her talking. She had already given up many small details that he would be able to use against her later.

"Yeah, I guess so."

He decided to change course slightly. "So how long have you been up here?"

"I don't know. Around a week or so." It was actually more like two weeks, but Doug wasn't ready to push her yet.

Doug went on, "It's beautiful up here, isn't it? That what brought you up here? The countryside?"

"Well, my friend and I just wanted to get away for a few days and we started driving."

"That's always nice to be able to do that. I remember the days when I could do that. I can't do it anymore. I certainly miss it though." He leaned back in his seat and tapped his finger on the table. "So, this friend of yours that you came up here with, what's his name?"

"Rob."

"That short for Robert or something?"

"I don't know. I've always just called him Rob."

"Everyone calls me Doug. There isn't really any way to shorten that, now is there?"

"No, I guess not."

"So tell me, how do you know Rob? Is he your boyfriend or what?"

"I guess you could say that. We're close, you know. But, we're each our own person. We do what we want." The translation in Doug's mind was booty call.

"That's cool. How'd you two meet?"

"He's just a guy from my hometown. I ran into him at a pool hall one night and we hit it off."

"Yeah? Just like that, huh? How far back was it that you met him?"

"What does it matter? Why are you asking me all of these

106

questions about Rob?"

"Listen, Kerri, I'm just trying to get to know you. When we find Rob, I'm going to go talk to him too. I get to talk to you first, okay?" He liked to lay the most subtle hints – if she talked first, then they might go easier on her.

She bowed up at the officers. "Why do you need to talk to Rob? He didn't do anything wrong." She was being defensive of Rob.

"Now, Kerri, you and I both know that isn't true. For one thing, he caused a big wreck where people were hurt. Then he fled from officers."

"Oh." She leaned back in her chair and seemed relieved. She still did not know that the detectives knew all about the crime in Florida.

"So tell me, where are you and Rob staying up here? Did you get a hotel room?"

"No."

"Staying with friends?"

"I guess you could say that."

"What do you mean?"

She snapped at him, "Why does it matter where we are staying? You have me in jail, so it looks like I'm staying here, right?"

"That is one way of looking at it, but Kerri, you know we are going to be looking for Rob, right?"

"You already made that clear to me."

"So you can choose to help us or you can choose to not help us. That is up to you."

"What's in it for me?"

Bingo. Now she was starting to think the way he wanted her to. "You know the other officer found some Ice in your pocketbook, right?"

"So I've been told." Maybe she was smarter than she appeared. Typically at this point in an interview, suspects slip up and admit to the drug possession charge, not turn the statement around on the officer. At least she confirmed she knew what Ice was.

"Up here, that is a felony. It isn't like just having a little bit of weed on you. You could go to prison for meth."

"That is ludicrous. I'm not going to prison. I've never been in trouble before in my whole life." She giggled, "Well, nothing that stuck, anyway."

"My point is that we aren't talking fun and games. This is serious." She looked down at her feet that were clad in rubber jail slippers. "Kerri, listen to me. The more you talk to us, the more you help yourself. Don't think for a minute that Rob won't throw you under the bus to save his own skin."

She looked up with tears nearly brimming over her lower eyelids. "What do you want to know?"

"Where have you been staying since you've been up here?"

"A friend of mine has a place up here that he is letting us stay at."

"Does your friend have a name?"

"Yes."

"Kerri, don't do this the hard way. What is your friend's name?"

"Dean."

That took both Doug and Marty aback, but neither one showed any

108

reaction. Could it possibly be Dean Witherington? There was no way there could be such a coincidence that it wasn't the same person. "What is Dean's last name?"

"Witherington, I think." She confirmed it.

Jackpot. Doug came up with a new tactic off the cuff and decided to roll with it. He turned to his partner and said, "Dean Witherington, does that name sound familiar to you? I swear I've heard that name before."

Marty played along, "Yeah, I've definitely heard it before. Give me a second and it will come to me."

Kerri quickly chimed in, "Uhh. He has his own business. He's a very savvy businessman, so maybe that is why?" Kerri was worried; the fact that the two detectives recognized Dean Witherington's name was not a good sign for her.

"Yeah, maybe that's it." Doug stopped talking and pretended to be in deep thought. His silence made Kerri nervous. All of the sudden Doug looked up and snapped his fingers as he waved his hand in the air. "I know why I know that name." He stopped and turned to Kerri with a look of concern on his face. "Oh, my. Kerri, when is the last time you spoke to Dean?"

She got a deer in the headlights look, "I don't know, why?"

"Think back for me, okay? When did you get permission from him to stay at his place up here? Was it when you left Florida? So that would have been, what? A couple of weeks ago?" He was trying to trip her up on her dates.

She started to panic. "Ummm, I'm not sure. I think it was before that. Yes. Yes it was definitely before that. It's not the type of situation where I have to ask for permission to use his place." She was starting to get her groove. "It is an open invitation, so I didn't ask him right before coming up here. He's always told me that I'd be welcome, so I just came. I don't remember exactly when the last time I spoke to him was."

"Kerri, I don't think you are being truthful with us."

"What?" She looked panicked. "Why would you say that?"

"Kerri, we know about Dean, it is all over the news."

"What? What has happened to Dean? I haven't seen the news!" She was doing her best to act genuinely concerned.

"Kerri, Dean Witherington is dead. His body was found in a pond."

She turned white and just sat there. Finally, she asked, "Are you sure? Are you sure the body was Dean's?"

"We're absolutely sure, Kerri. And I think you know that."

"What?" She looked taken aback. "What do you mean?"

"You know exactly what I mean, Kerri." It was time to turn up the heat.

"No, I don't. Dean was fine when I talked to him last week. I just came up here to get away from it all." With nearly every sentence, Kerri was slipping up with statements that would eventually be used against her in trial.

It was too soon to push her all of the way, so Doug decided to lock her story in about the SUV. "You know, I was wondering about something you said earlier about how you got up here. Where is the

110

SUV that you drove up here in? Why did you switch to the Jeep? I would think a girl like you would rather ride in style in a big Excursion than in a rough and tough Jeep."

"The Excursion broke down, so we bought the Jeep." Another point for Doug; she had just admitted to being in the Excursion. Apparently jumping from subject to subject was the way to have a successful interview with this girl.

"Wow, when a vehicle breaks down, you just dump it and get another one? With a vehicle as nice as an Excursion, I would stop and get it fixed rather than going out and buying a new car."

"We didn't have time."

"What was the rush, Kerri? I thought you and Rob were just taking a leisurely get away road trip."

"That's right, we were." Now she was getting confused in what she had previously told the detectives.

"So why didn't you have the time to get the Excursion fixed?"

"It wasn't my vehicle, so why should I pay to get it fixed?"

"Oh, that's right, you said it was a friend's SUV. Who was that friend exactly?" He used the past tense on purpose.

She moaned and swooned forward before taking a deep breath, sitting back and slowly saying, "Dean Witherington."

"Dean again, huh? So you left Florida about two weeks ago in Dean Witherington's Excursion and as you were driving, his new SUV broke down, so rather than getting it repaired, you dumped it and bought an older model Jeep. Then you came to Kentucky and went to stay in Dean Witherington's house up here. Do I have that about right?"

"Yes, but it's not what you think." Now she admitted to the correct timeline.

"What do I think, Kerri? You tell me."

"You think I killed Dean!" She shrieked at him. The tears started pouring down her cheeks.

He didn't want to give her a chance to lose the emotion of the moment. "Well, Kerri, tell me what happened. You can obviously see what it looks like to me. Tell me what really happened."

"I don't know what to tell you."

"Kerri, let's take it slowly then. Tell me about the last time you saw Dean alive."

"I think I should talk to a lawyer."

He was treading on dangerous territory. She didn't actually ask for a lawyer. Her request was equivocal, but it was still risky to keep going with the interrogation; whatever she said from this point forward could possibly be suppressed. Doug decided to push on. "Kerri, this is your chance to help yourself out. I know you were involved in Dean's death. I know he was shot. I know he was wrapped up and weighed down in his pond on his hunting land. I know the Excursion was used to move the body."

Her head hung low as she sobbed.

Doug went on, "I know you and Sessions used Dean's credit card to buy gas. I know you dumped the Excursion outside of Atlanta. I know Sessions and you are involved in the meth scene. This is your only chance to help yourself, Kerri. Look at me, now. Do you want to help yourself, or are you going to let Sessions come in here and talk to us first?"

She squeaked out, "I don't know what to do."

"Help yourself, Kerri and maybe we can help you out. I think Sessions is the bad guy in all of this. Don't ruin your life to protect a low life like him."

She shuddered and solemnly asked, "What do you want to know?"

"I want to know everything, Kerri. Take us through all of it."

After a long pause, Kerri looked up and past the detectives, as though they were no longer in the room. Then she began, "I met Dean at the grocery store of all places. It was just like in the movies. He held a melon out to me and asked me how to tell if it was a good one or not. I thought he was kind of cute, in an older guy kind of way. I could tell by his clothing that he had money, so I took the melon from him, squeezed it, inhaled deeply and told him he already had the perfect melon. I didn't know how to select produce, but I knew how to flirt with him.

From there, we just started talking. I genuinely liked him. We started hanging out with one another from time to time. He would have me over to his house whenever the maid was out doing the shopping. For some reason he wanted to keep me a secret. I don't know why. It wasn't long before we started having sex. It made me think he was getting it on with the maid too and just didn't want her to know about me."

"How long ago was it that you met him?"

"I'm not sure. Maybe two months or so."

113

"Go on. How did Sessions come into the picture?"

"I had been seeing him on and off for about a year. You were right about the meth. He's the one that got me hooked. It started because I heard it was a good way to keep the weight off. It was the hottest trend with the soccer moms even. These crazy soccer moms just kept going and going and going. And they were skinny. So, Rob gave me some and it was incredible. Ever since that first high, I've tried to get back to it again. It never works. My dad put me into rehab and I learned all about my addiction. It was awful there. But my dad made me stick it out."

"How long ago were you in rehab?"

"I had just gotten out when I met Dean."

"Were you still seeing Sessions?"

"It's hard not to. There is something about him that is just so captivating. I think I was as addicted to him as I am to the meth."

He noticed she used the present tense when addressing her addiction yet the past tense when addressing her relationship with Rob Sessions. Perhaps she was distancing herself and was willing to spill everything she knew about him.

"I tried to leave him alone. I knew that if I saw him again, I'd go back to using. I was good at first. And Dean was a good distraction for me. I even started thinking Dean and I could have a future together."

"So what happened?"

"I ran into Rob. He convinced me to go hang out with him. It all went downhill from there. He gave me some Ice and I forgot

114

everything that I had learned in rehab. I just wanted to get back to that feeling I had after my first bump. I stayed with Rob for four days straight. We partied night and day. Then Rob just left. I was crushed. Then I started Jonesing. I went to Dean's place."

Doug didn't need her to explain that 'Jonesing' meant an intense craving for drugs so she could get her high back. "Did Dean know about your drug use?"

"No. Not until that day. Little did I know that he used to use too. I think inwardly I went to him to have him save me, but he ended up enabling me."

"How so?" Doug asked.

"I was so desperate for a bump by the time that I got to his place. He figured out what was going on and he sent out for some meth. I don't know how he knew who to contact." She paused for a moment and then looked at Doug. "It is kind of like that song, you know? Having your drug dealer on speed dial. Dean could do anything and make anything happen at the drop of a dime. So, he scored for me and ended up smoking it with me."

Based on what Maria had told the detectives, Doug believed Kerri so far. "How long ago was it that you two smoked together?

"I think it was about two weeks ago. Maybe a little more, I'm not sure. Anyway, Rob came back into the picture. He found out about Dean and he was pissed. He's always had a quick temper, but the way he was acting about Dean was like nothing I'd ever seen out of him."

"Why do you say that?"

"By this point, I had already left Dean's house. I don't know how

Rob found out about Dean. I suspect whoever Dean called to score saw my car at Dean's house and told Rob. The meth scene is like an underground network. Everybody kind of knows everybody that is doing it.

So I don't know. Anyway, I hooked up with Rob later that same week and he kept my high going. I don't really remember everything that happened. After I was cranked, I remember Rob pumping me for information about Dean, but it isn't completely clear to me now."

"Tell me exactly what you do remember."

"We were low on cash. My dad had cut me off. My dad has some stupid rules. I had to be living in his house to get any money from him. Since I had run off again, he canceled all of my credit cards and everything. Rob didn't have a job. All he did was sell drugs. Anyway, we were both hurting for money. Dean had plenty of money, so I went to him."

"Why?"

"I just wanted to borrow some from him. Really, that is all I wanted, I swear." She started to tear up again. "I went into his house. It was all quiet. The lights were off everywhere. I called out to him, but he didn't answer. So I went upstairs and I found him in his bedroom."

"Was he okay?"

"He was fine. He was meditating. I asked him what was going on and the first words out of his mouth were that he couldn't see me anymore. I was shocked."

"What else did he say?"

116

"He glared at me and then said that he had a dark side to him that he had laid to rest a long time ago. That I brought it back out of him and he didn't like that. He wouldn't go back to who he was before. He had come too far. I went to him, but he lashed out at me."

"How do you mean that he lashed out at you?"

"He hit me. I yelled back at him. I think that is when Rob first heard me. I started to run away from Dean and he chased me. I was able to make it to the top of the stairs before he grabbed a hold of me. He ripped the back of my dress when he snatched me back to him."

"What did you do?"

"What could I do? I screamed and I slapped him. I scratched him pretty good across his face, which only enraged him more. I somehow got away and started running down the stairs. I was about half way down when I saw Rob standing in the doorway. I just kept running. The next thing I know I saw a gun in Rob's hand. Rob yelled at Dean to stop where he was or he would shoot, but Dean kept coming after me. Then Rob fired the gun. Dean fell down the stairs and that was it."

Doug knew she wasn't telling the truth now, but he wanted to lock her into her flimsy self-defense story. "So, if I have this right, you are almost all the way down the stairs when Rob fires the gun?"

"Yes, Dean was right behind me."

"Where is Rob? At the front door?"

"Yes, he was just barely inside the threshold."

"How many times did Rob fire the gun?"

She stopped to think. "Twice. It happened so quick. Rob was just trying to warn Dean, but he accidentally hit him."

"What did you do?"

"Well, Dean fell down and started bleeding all over the stairs. I started freaking out. Rob was freaking out. We didn't know what to do." She clammed up all of the sudden and wouldn't say anything else.

Doug tried to get her talking again, "Kerri, if you were acting in self-defense, everything is fine. Worst case scenario, it is a misdemeanor to not properly transport a dead human body." While it is true that it is a misdemeanor to not transport a dead human body properly, Doug was not completely forthcoming with the extent of the trouble that she was actually facing.

"Really?" She looked at him. "So all I am facing is a misdemeanor?"

"At this point, I don't know, Kerri. Based on what you have said so far it might not even be that much."

She sat there for a moment and chewed on her lower lip. Finally, she started talking again, "We couldn't leave Dean there like that, so we decided to hide the body."

"Why would you hide the body? You were acting in self-defense." He didn't want to point out to her that he knew that Dean had been shot in the head execution style.

"You don't understand. No one would have believed me or Rob. You might find this hard to believe, but this isn't Rob's first rodeo. He's already on state probation and this would have sent him to prison."

118

"So tell us exactly what you did."

"Rob went out to the barn and found a tarp. He brought it back in and put Dean's body in it and wrapped it up. He moved all of it to the garage where the Excursion was. While he was taking care of that, I went and got a bucket, bleach and a mop and started cleaning."

"Were you able to get all of the blood cleaned up?"

"It took forever, but I did. I had to keep dumping the water and getting fresh bleach water, but I got it all up. Rob found the keys to the Excursion and we left."

"Now, Kerri, I know that isn't everything you did at the house. Tell me about the money you took."

She didn't miss a beat, "Dean didn't keep cash on him so I got his credit cards. We had to run, but didn't have any way to go. My Mustang was at Rob's house. We had ridden to Dean's in Rob's Oldsmobile. So I drove Rob's car and parked it at Rob's place. Rob followed me in the Excursion, picked me up and we decided where to take the body."

"So how did you decide where to go?"

"I had never been out there before, but Dean had talked to me about his hunting land, or haven as he liked to call it. He was going to take me out there, but I guess I ended up taking him, didn't I?" She looked off into the distance before going on with her story. "Anyway, we found the land and Rob took the body back to the pond and dumped it."

"That's all he did, just drop it in the water?"

"Yeah. We had to get out of there. We were both freaked out and

119

afraid no one would believe us. I guess I was right about that, huh? You don't believe me."

"What I believe isn't relevant Kerri. I just want you to tell us the truth. Have you told us the truth?"

She looked him dead in the eye. "Absolutely."

9

Jesse was hiding from her captor. Moments earlier, she escaped by barreling out of the trunk of the car and blindly running along the lake's edge. She sought refuge amongst the moss covered limbs of a fallen tree. It was so dark out, there was no way her captor could find her, could he?

She could no longer hear his footsteps, but his heavy breathing filled the ominous void. And then there was whistling – the tune from *Kill Bill* overtook the sounds of her captor's raspy breath. She also felt dampness on her cheek. How could the water from the lake be getting her wet? It seemed like time stood still, but then she finally awoke from her dream.

Doug was calling her – his ringtone was the whistling tune from *Kill Bill* and her faithful dog, Xander was licking her face to wake her up. She answered the phone and only took a moment to wake up and start comprehending everything that Doug just told her over the phone. "So she is trying to make this into a self-defense case?" she asked. Her voice was still thick with lingering sleep.

"Yes, but she left holes in it big enough to drive a semi truck through."

"Can you go back and interview her again? I want to lock her into more details before she has time to think it through. Or before she decides to lawyer up."

"Oh yeah, I left that out," Doug said.

The pit of her stomach dropped. If she wasn't already completely awake, she was now. "Left what out?"

"She kind of did mention wanting a lawyer."

Jesse immediately thought of the worst case scenario: Kerri lawyered up and the detectives continued to interview her. "Doug, tell me exactly what she said."

"She didn't exactly say she wanted to talk to a lawyer, she said she *thought* she wanted to talk to a lawyer."

"Doug, this is very important. Depending on how she phrased it, her whole statement could get thrown out."

"Look, I remember what you taught us about an equivocal versus unequivocal request for a lawyer. She didn't flat out say that she wanted a lawyer. Her exact words were, 'I think I should talk to a lawyer.'"

She let out a sigh of relief. "Okay, that should be all right. Just make sure no other officers have talked to her. I don't want her to be able to say that she requested an attorney with someone else and then talked when you came to see her. That is another way it can get thrown out. Can you still get in to see her again tonight?"

"Yeah, that shouldn't be a problem. Everyone here has been really helpful to us so far."

"See if you can lock her into more details. What do you think about confronting her about the weights from the house that they used?"

"That's fine. It's a detail that doesn't hurt her self-defense story, so she may roll with it even though she already left out the fact that weights were used."

"You got all of this on tape, right?"

Doug let a deep breath out. "No. I'm sorry Jess, we screwed up. We drove all this way and went straight in there and didn't even think about a recorder. We're just so used to it automatically recording when we walk into the interview room like it does at home."

Jesse was not happy. The judges in her circuit had chastised law enforcement for not recording confessions in the past. "Okay. I'm not happy about it, but there is nothing that can be done now. Why don't you both go take a bunch of notes about what she said? Recreate the interview to the best of your ability, but keep in mind whatever you write down may be discoverable."

"I thought they couldn't get our notes." By 'they,' Doug meant defense attorneys.

"Normally they can't, but this is going to be a death penalty case and I try not to hold anything back that could possibly lead to a reversal. I like to lay all of my cards on the table."

"All right, no problem. We'll get it done."

"Also, I'd like you to video the next interview and have her demonstrate where Witherington was and how he was standing when Sessions shot him. If we lock her into those types of details, we can disprove them with forensics."

"That will work. What do you think about going back in the

morning to interview her? It is pretty late. I don't want to run into suppression issues because of depriving her of sleep. What are the key words? A statement to law enforcement has to be knowingly, voluntarily and intelligently made?"

"Yes those are the magic words. You may have a point about the late hour. Plus, do you know if they gave her pain medication at the hospital?"

"They did. She seemed okay though. Well, considering I don't know how she is normally. She acted like a normal blonde."

Jesse let that comment pass. There was a brief period that Jesse had gone overboard with the highlights in her hair and she had a feeling that was what Doug was referring to. He certainly liked her switch up in hair color at the time. "Let's play it safe. Worst case scenario, she doesn't talk anymore. That isn't so bad. You already have a good statement from her. All we can do from here is make it better."

"Sounds good to me. Frankly, I'm kind of glad you opted for the morning. I'm beat."

"Get some rest, Doug. Thanks for calling me and keeping me up to speed."

"No problem." He hesitated. It would be so easy to slip back to the way they were before he screwed everything up. "Jesse?"

Her heart started pounding even harder than it had been during her dream. "Yes?"

He thought better of it. He knew she deserved better and before he opened that door again, he had to be willing to commit. "It's nothing.

Go back to sleep."

She felt disappointed. Why wouldn't he just say something? She quietly responded, "I will. Good night."

"G'night."

****

The next morning came too soon for Doug and Marty. But, with an investigation hot under way, they got up, grabbed a cup of coffee from the continental breakfast bar and drove back to the jail.

A new person was at the security checkpoint, so they had to produce their credentials again. "Detectives Wescott and Newsome from Florida to see inmate Kerri Hall again."

The corrections officer barely looked at the detective's ID cards.

Marty interjected, "Last night we were in one of the secure attorney client rooms. Do you have an interview room that has a hidden camera set up in it?"

"Nah. Those are all down at the criminal division. You can probably use the Intoxilyzer room though. It has a camera in there."

"Yeah? You don't think it would be too small? I know ours back home is only big enough for the Intoxilyzer operator and the subject."

"Oh no, ours has plenty of space. All three of you will fit just fine."

"That would be great then. Who do we need to talk to, to make sure the camera is running?"

"It automatically starts running as soon as the lights come on."

125

That process was similar to the in-car cameras the sheriff's office had back home. They would come on as soon as the blue lights were turned on.

"Great." Doug started to walk towards the secure steel door and then stopped to ask, "Hey, one more thing, does anyone keep a log of who has interviewed each inmate? I just want to make sure this woman hasn't invoked her rights with someone else."

The blank stare on the correction officer's face told Doug not to even bother explaining. "You know what, never mind; if you could just point us in the right direction, please."

With that, the steel door to their right clicked and then rolled open. "Just go through that door and turn to your left. Walk straight and you'll come to the control room. They'll be able to help you out from there."

It only took a couple of minutes for the two visitors to be shown to the Intoxilyzer room. Like their agency in Florida, the Kentucky department had switched from the Intoxilyzer 5000 to the Intoxilyzer 8000. The instrument was a lot smaller than its predecessor. Though it had quite a few kinks in the beginning that resulted in hundreds of cases getting thrown out, it was now functioning smoothly.

Kerri was escorted into the room but before the corrections officer even left, Kerri started in on the two detectives, "So, you aren't done with me yet? You come in here yesterday talking to me about a little Ice that I had on me and then get me talking about Dean, huh? Where are you two from, exactly? You never did say." Evidently she had done some thinking during the night.

"Columbia County. You're a smart girl. I think you probably already figured that out, didn't you?"

"I figured. You sound like a different kind of redneck than the rednecks around here. So what was it that made you come up here to talk to me? I didn't do nothing wrong." Both detectives thought she had used interesting word choice for her derogatory comment.

Doug decided to still play along with her version of events. "Well, Kerri, look at it from our perspective. We found a body. We discovered who the body was. Then we look into that person's finances and discover that his credit cards are still being used. The problem is that a dead guy can't use his credit cards throughout the Southeast. That means somebody took them. We just followed the paper trail, really. It led us right to you."

"Is that why that guy was following Rob and me yesterday?"

"Yes, the local authorities put a tail on you for us. All we wanted to do was talk to you. We weren't going to arrest you or anything."

"Are you going to arrest me now?"

"Kerri, at this point, your only charges are for possession of methamphetamine. Those charges are being brought in the Ninth Judicial District of Kentucky." That was the truth; at least for now.

"You aren't charging me with anything?"

He needed to gain her complete trust. "Kerri, from what you told us, you didn't do anything wrong. You acted in self-defense and Rob came to your aid."

"So he won't be charged either?"

"We don't have enough to charge either of you for Witherington's

127

death." It was well-established law in Florida that law enforcement could lie to a suspect during an interrogation.

"Okay. So why are you back today?"

"We're going to get to that, but before we start talking in detail, I just want to remind you of your rights, okay? Remember our conversation about the Miranda Warning yesterday?"

"Yes."

"I'm going to go back through those rights with you, okay? It is just a formality. It doesn't mean you are under arrest for anything dealing with Witherington. I just have to do my job, okay?"

"Skip it. I know my rights. I know I don't have to talk to you. I know I can have an attorney even if I can't afford one. But since you two are so smart, I know you know who my father is, so you know I can afford the best. So let's get this show on the road. I've got nothing to hide."

"Okay, it seems as though you understand your rights. But before we talk to you, have you invoked your rights with any other officer?"

"No. Now let's get this over with."

"That's fine, Kerri. Now yesterday you told us that Witherington was chasing you down the stairs, right?"

"Yes."

"Tell us exactly where he was when Rob fired the gun."

She had the tiniest micro expression of being dumbfounded by the question, but covered it up with deliberate thought before answering. "I'm not sure exactly. We were close to the bottom of the stairs. I probably had about ten steps left or so. He was reaching out for me. It

128

is a wonder that Rob didn't hit me with the gun."

"Okay, so Witherington was chasing you and about to grab you when Rob fired the gun. Where was Rob standing?"

"In the doorway. He had just come in when he heard me screaming."

"How many times did he fire the gun?"

"Twice."

"Did he fire both shots from the doorway, or did he walk into the house at all?"

"Both from the doorway. Rob didn't mean to hit him. It was an accident. Rob was just trying to get him away from me."

"I understand. I'm sure you must have been terrified." Doug was trying to make her think that he empathized with her.

"I was. I was absolutely stunned. And then there was all of the blood. And well, you know the rest of the story."

"Actually, I don't think you told me everything yesterday, did you?"

"What do you mean? I did tell you everything." She managed to sound offended.

"How did you two weigh the body down in the pond?"

This time her micro expression showed terror before she regained her composure. "Oh, that. I forgot about that. Rob went and got some of the weights from Dean's home gym."

"Whose idea was it to hide the body?"

"Rob's. Like I told you, he is on state probation. From what he tells me, it is a first degree felony. He got busted a few years back for dealing within a thousand feet of a church. He said that he could get sent off for thirty years, that no one would believe that this was all just an accident. So, the best way for us to handle it was to get rid of the body and make a run for it.

Dean was always talking about how he could do business from anywhere. It wouldn't have been strange for him to just pick up and go. By the time anyone realized that he was actually missing . . . his body. . . well, you know."

"No, what?"

"I've said enough. It was Rob's idea to hide the body, okay? I just did as I was told. I was scared." She was trying her best to sound genuine, but it all came off as an act.

"Tell me what you were wearing the day it happened."

"I had on a little sundress."

"Do you still have it?"

"Obviously, I don't." She gestured towards her orange jumpsuit.

"Do you know where it is?"

"Yeah, it is in the house we were crashing at."

"The one here in Elizabethtown?"

"Yes."

"To be clear, we're talking about the same dress you had on when Rob shot Dean?"

"Yes. How much clearer can I be?"

He ignored her. "Where is the house?"

"I don't know the road names around here. I can show you though."

130

He wasn't biting. There was no way he was going to take her outside of the jail's walls. "How did you find it to begin with?"

"Dean had a GPS in the Excursion. There was an onboard one and he also had an external one that he had bought. When we left the Excursion, we took the external GPS because it had the Kentucky home's address programmed into it."

"How did you know Dean had a place up here?"

"He told me about it once. I figured he wouldn't need it, so it would give Rob and me a place to lay low, you know? Until we could go back home. The GPS thingy led us straight here."

"Tell me again why you left the Excursion in Atlanta." Again, Doug was adding details that Keri had never supplied.

"I don't know. Rob wanted to get a different ride. You have my statement already." She was starting to get testy; probably because she couldn't remember exactly what she had said before. She obviously didn't remember that she had not told the officers that the vehicle was left in Atlanta.

"Okay, one last thing, will you show me how Dean was positioned as he was chasing you down the stairs. Was he standing, falling, or what?"

"He was behind me, how should I know what he was doing?"

"Well, you said that he was about to grab you, how did you know that?"

She thought about her options for a split second. "I think I turned around." She looked off as if in deep thought. "You know what? I did turn around. He was running down after me. I was against the

131

wall and he was against the banister. Because of the curve of the stairs, the way I was going down the stairs against the wall had bigger steps. I guess that is how he was able to catch me."

"So he was on the inside rail, the side that opened into the foyer area?" Doug asked.

"Yes, and I was against the wall and he was coming down the inside of the stairs."

"Where did he fall?"

"Down the stairs." She responded.

"Do you remember exactly where he was when he began falling?"

"You know what; I'm not sure where he was exactly. He ended up right against the wall. I might be wrong about that. It just happened so quickly." She had realized her mistake about Dean's final resting position and tried to correct it.

"That's okay, I understand." Doug leaned in ever so slightly, "Listen, is there anything else about this that you want to tell us? Now is your chance."

"No, I can't think of anything."

"Other than what you have told us, did Rob do anything else?"

"No."

"So he didn't try to hide any evidence left at the house?"

"What do you mean?" She asked.

"Well, you said that you cleaned the blood up, did he do anything like that?"

"No. He just moved the body."

"Did he do anything to the wall?" Doug actually wanted to know

132

if she knew about Rob's repair job.

"I don't know what you are talking about." For once, she appeared genuine.

"Do you know where Rob may have gone after yesterday's chase?"

"I imagine he went back to Dean's house . . . at least to gather his stuff. I don't know beyond that."

"Speaking of Dean's house, tell me more about it. Did you leave everything you brought with you from Florida at Dean's?"

"Yes."

"Including the dress you were wearing when Dean was shot?"

"Yes. It is trashed. The blood won't come out. Not that it matters since it is ripped now," she added as an afterthought.

"What does the house look like?" Doug asked.

"It's actually like a cabin. It has a wraparound porch that overlooks a lake. It's real pretty. Kind of quaint."

"Okay, Kerri. If you think of anything else, let one of the guards know and we'll come back to talk to you."

"Wait, don't go yet. How do I get out of here?"

"If Kentucky is anything like Florida, then you should be seeing a judge today for your first appearance. He'll set your bond. Either you pay cash for the full amount, or you put up a percentage with a bondsman."

"But I don't have any money with me."

"I'm sure they'll let you make a call. I don't think your dad will leave you up here in Kentucky." With that, the detectives left her all alone.

"This is Jesse, may I help you?" Darby had not told her who was on the line.

"Hey Jess, it's me, do you have a minute?"

Jesse swallowed hard, "Sure Doug, how did it go? Did she talk to you again?"

"Yeah, she did. It went pretty well. She told us that she left the dress that she was wearing when they killed Witherington in Witherington's house up here. How do I go about getting a search warrant for the house up here?"

"Check with the local officers and see if they do their own warrants and take them to the judge or if they go to the District Attorney's office or whatever it is called up there."

"The equivalent to the State Attorney's Office up here is called the Commonwealth. Do you think her word alone is good enough to get a warrant for the house?"

"Sure, it is evidence of a crime. Her statement has been corroborated to an extent. Look at it like this. We have a dead body, she admits to how the body became dead. She admitted to where they took the body and that is where we found the body. She admitted to him being shot on the stairs and we have proof that he was shot on the stairs. You'll need to put all of that in the warrant as your probable cause, but you should be fine. All of the states operate under the same

134

Fourth Amendment."

"Okay. What about arresting her? I'm leaving it up to you. Do you want us to do an arrest warrant or do you want to take it to the Grand Jury and get an Indictment first?"

"We better walk an arrest warrant through pretty quickly. I don't want her to bond out on the meth charges and disappear on us. I'm sure her father has enough money to keep her hidden."

"All right. I'll call Wes and have him walk the arrest warrant through. I'm thinking First Degree Premeditated Murder, how about you?"

"I think so. Let's also add on the grand theft of the motor vehicle. If we end up seeking the death penalty, I'll use that and the credit card usage as an aggravator – that the murder was committed for pecuniary gain."

"Do you mind typing the warrant up and I'll have Wes come and get it?"

"No, not at all. I'll make sure the judge makes the warrant extraditable." She paused for a moment, "Hey, are you okay?" She asked Doug. "You sound strained." She wanted to say so much more but had vowed to herself that he had to make the first move.

"I'm fine. I'm just tired, I guess. We rushed up here and then didn't get much sleep last night. We'll join in on the man hunt until we get the warrant pushed through." What he didn't tell her is how much it still hurt to talk to her; how much he wanted to be with her. Being worn out lowered his defenses and let some of the emotion come out. He hoped he had covered it up well enough.

She lowered her voice, "Okay, I just . . . well, I'm just worried about you."

"Jesse, I'm fine. Let's leave it at that, okay?"

"All right. If you need anything let me know." She purposely left it ambiguous as to whether she meant personally or professionally.

"Thanks. I'll call Wes and have him up there within the half hour. I don't think he has ever walked a warrant through, so will you help him?"

"Of course. I trained you, didn't I?"

"In many ways." He caught himself getting too personal again and stopped himself. "Thanks again. I'll let you know if she is going to waive extradition."

"Okay. Take care of yourself, you hear?" She started to hang up but then remembered what Sessions' probation officer had told her earlier, "Oh, and Doug?"

"Yeah?"

"I spoke with Sessions' probation officer. They went ahead and put a warrant out for him for violating his probation. Right now it is just for absconding, but if you can fax a copy of Kentucky's affidavit for the leaving the scene and the fleeing to elude, they'll add it on as additional substantive violations of his probation."

"Sure thing. I'll go track it down."

"Oh, and one more strategy idea. Hold off on arresting him for the murder. Since he is on probation, they already had him sign extradition papers, so we can just arrest him on the violation of probation and he'll be held no bond. That will give me a chance to take it to the Grand Jury and get an Indictment."

"Sounds good, but we have to find him first."

"Of course. I just wanted to let you know there was a warrant out for him already. Hopefully he'll talk to you. His probation officer seems to think Sessions will talk."

"We'll see as soon as we catch him. I'm going to go work on getting that search warrant now."

"Okay, bye."

"Bye, Jesse."

Both of them ended the conversation with words unsaid.

****

Checking with the local officers was no problem; they were very helpful. Peter Sims was the problem. Peter was an Assistant Commonwealth Attorney. He was the equivalent to an Assistant District Attorney or Assistant State Attorney as they are called in most states. Peter was in court, so he was busy and certainly didn't want to be bothered by the two detectives from Florida. If it didn't involve a case he was going to be prosecuting, he didn't want to be involved in helping – a typical state employee attitude.

Doug and Marty finally cornered the attorney. Doug quickly said to the man, "Look, I know you are busy, but we have probable cause to go into the house. I've got the address, I've driven by and taken photographs of the place and I've written the warrant. I'm just asking you to review it and tell us what judge to go see to get it signed."

"Listen Mr. Wescott, I'm in the middle of court and have to get back in there. From what you've told me, all you have are the statements of a woman who is in jail on drug charges telling you where some alleged evidence of a crime is located. It's not enough. She is not a credible witness."

Doug decided to let the undercutting of calling him "Mr." instead of "Detective" slide. "But that is what I'm telling you, everything she told us is corroborated. She told us how the murder went down in Florida. She told us where it took place in the house, that it was with a gun, that they moved the body and that they weighed the body down in a pond."

"Yes and you also believe she is lying to you about how it happened. You can't have it both ways – either she is credible or she isn't."

"The only thing she is lying about is the self-defense aspect of things. Everything else is pretty accurate. We've investigated the house and where the body was found. The dress will help us prove that she is lying about how she was positioned when the victim was shot. Or, you know what, she may be telling the truth. We may be able to further corroborate her statement."

"I don't know how you do it in Florida, but it isn't enough. Now if you'll excuse me, I've got to get back to court." He turned to walk back through the double doors that led into the courtroom."

Doug reached out and grabbed the young attorney's arm and through gritted teeth said, "Now listen here. I don't know if you don't

138

follow the Fourth Amendment in this Godforsaken place, but the last time I checked, it was in the Constitution of the United States. The highest God-Damn law, buddy. I will guarandamntee you that I know more about search and seizure than you do. I've studied it and have been teaching it for years. In all of my career, I've never had a case suppressed. Now all I am asking of you is to grant us the courtesy of reading through this and directing us to the judge."

Peter had a slight hint of resentment in his eyes, but it passed quickly as he regained his composure. "Fine." He snipped, "I'll read through it. We'll see if Judge Jolinger will sign off on it. You say you've never had a case suppressed before, well there is always a first."

With that, he snapped the papers out of Doug's hand and quickly read through them, or at least he pretended to. "Judge Jolinger is on a recess for another five minutes. Go to the second floor and down the hall to room 248. There should be a bailiff outside. Tell him what you want and maybe he will see you. I can do nothing else for you."

****

Contrary to the attitude that Assistant Commonwealth Attorney Sims gave the detectives, Judge Jolinger happily agreed to read the warrant and even signed off on it with no changes. The only thing he did was warn the detectives that local law enforcement had to be present during the search.

So, with that in mind, they went to the Sheriff's Office and rounded up a couple of the deputies to go to the house and conduct the search. The drive to the house was uneventful. Once they found out the house belonged to Witherington, it was as simple as looking his name up on the property appraiser's website to find out the address. Upon arrival, Marty immediately got out of the vehicle and knocked on the door, announcing who he was. Not surprisingly, no one answered. So, he read the warrant to the house.

While he was doing so, the local deputies started turning over stones in front of the house. "I found it!" One of them called.

Doug looked on with mild curiosity at what they were doing.

"What kind of hidey hole was it in?" Allen, a short pudgy deputy asked.

"It was right here under this fake rock. It's a pretty good one too. The top part is made of actual stone, but it has the hollowed out compartment to hide the key." Bart let out a low whistle, "I bet this one sure cost a pretty penny."

Doug wasn't going to tell them that money was of no consequence to the late owner of the house they were about to search. But, watching their antics was mildly amusing. Actually, it was pretty clever. At least they would not have to break into the house now.

Once Marty was done reading the warrant, Bart walked up to the front door and with a beaming smile, unlocked it and waltzed right in. Allen, Marty and Doug followed.

What greeted them was in stark contrast to the luxurious mansion in Florida. Everything in the quaint country home was obviously expensive, but it had a homey feel to it, right down to childhood photos framed on the walls.

"How do you two want to do this? A complete walk through first?" Allen seemed excited. This was his first search warrant for all Doug and Marty knew.

"That will be fine. We've got a camera, but we'll walk through first."

So it began, the four men walked through each room and did not find a single thing that was obviously disturbed until they came to the master bedroom. The bed had clearly been slept in, but what was of more importance was the pile of dirty laundry. Lying right on top was a woman's white and yellow sundress. From the way it was crumpled on the floor, they could not tell if there was any blood on it or not.

"You guys can go on, but before I leave this room, I'm going to go ahead and take photos before we process the room." Marty was ready to get to work.

"Okay, we're just going to peek into the bathroom first and go on through the rest of the place. It should only take a couple of minutes." Doug could tell that Marty was tired and wanted to get the show on the road. Plus he probably didn't want the two young local deputies breathing down his neck the entire time.

Doug, Allen and Bart saw nothing of interest in the bathroom other than crumpled towels on the floor, so they continued their walk-through of the house. Meanwhile, Marty stood in the doorway of the master bedroom and started taking photos. He took them systematically so that they could be pieced together at a later time.

After he was done with taking the photos from that viewpoint,

Marty walked to the closet. But as he reached for door's handle, the door flew open and a white male jumped out, grabbing Marty by the throat with both hands. They both fell to the ground. "Who the fuck do you think you are coming in here like this?" The assailant growled at Marty.

Marty, being surprised by the assailant, dropped the camera and went into self-defense mode. Marty immediately went for the man's eyes. He placed his fingers on both sides of the man's temples and dug his thumbs into the assailant's eyes. The man let out a blood curdling scream as he let go of Marty's throat and reached for his own face.

As the man rocked back on his heels, Marty leapt up and pulled his service weapon on the man. "On the floor, now!" He yelled.

The man did not listen. Instead he twisted around, half on his knees and half on his feet and started running blindly to the door. Just as he reached the doorway, Doug appeared and shoved a gun right against the assailant's forehead. "Stop where you are right now!" Doug shouted at the man, causing his own veins to bulge on the sides of his neck.

This time, seeing he had nowhere to go, the man stopped and placed his hands behind his head. "Don't shoot, just don't shoot me." He started to bend his knees to go to the floor.

Allen and Bart came running up after all of the excitement had passed. Seeing that neither Doug nor Marty had handcuffs on them, Bart stepped up and cuffed the young white male assailant.

"Who are you?" Doug demanded of the man.

"Fuck you." Was the only response.

"You want to play that way, fine." He turned to Bart, "lock him up in your car. We've got work to do here."

It took less than an hour for the remaining three men to process the entire house. As suspected, Kerri's dress did have blood on it. Not surprisingly, it wasn't on the back of the dress as it should have been according to Kerri's story. They also found a man's shirt with blood all over the front of it.

With the search of the house completed, it would only be minutes before Doug and Marty would get to go and have a nice little chat with none other than Robert Sessions.

10

The local corrections officer led the newest addition to the jail into the same room that the Florida detectives had interviewed Kerri Hall in during her first interview. Armed with a micro camera they borrowed from the local drug task force, Marty started talking to the murder suspect before he even sat down, "So, Robert, we've been looking for you. You gave me quite the scare back there. Don't worry, I'm not upset at you about it. In fact, I'll ask the local folks to not even press charges on you for it. I can see how things were from your perspective."

"What do you mean?" Robert Sessions looked Marty Newsome right in the eye.

"Well, you're just up here on vacation and then some strange people come into the house and you were just defending yourself, right?"

Sessions thought about what the detective had just said. "Yeah, that's right."

"Now all of that stuff about running from the local officers in your Jeep, that's another story. I can put a word in for you though, how about that?"

"How so?"

"Well, why would Kentucky want to spend money prosecuting you when you have a violation of probation pending in Florida? You know there is a warrant out for you, right?"

"I figured there was."

"Yeah, about that. You know what? I need to go through a couple of formalities here for a minute, okay? I'm going to advise you of your rights. I know you've been through this before, but just hear me out, okay?" Marty pulled a standardized card from his wallet.

"Sure." This was nothing new for Sessions, it certainly wasn't his first rodeo with the cops.

"You have the right to remain silent. Anything you say can and will be used against you in the court of law. You have the right to an attorney. If you cannot afford an attorney, one will be appointed to you. You have a right to stop answering questions at any time. You have a right to consult with an attorney at any time." He looked up from the card. "Do you understand these rights as I have read them to you?"

"Yep. I sure do. I could have recited them to you myself."

"Do you have any questions before we continue talking?"

"Nope." Sessions' lips popped as he said the consonant, "p" in the word.

"I'm just going to have you sign this form acknowledging that I read you your rights, okay?

"I'll sign away. Whatever I have to do to go back to my cell." He signed the form and asked, "So do you think they'll send me back to

Florida today?"

"Well, it all depends on whether they want to pick up charges here. You may have noticed that you caused quite a pile-up yesterday. Then you fled from the scene of where you crashed the Jeep. Kerri was pretty banged up."

"Yeah, how is she?" His phony attempt at concern was transparent.

"She'll be fine. We've already talked to her about what happened to Dean."

Sessions was able to keep a straight face but inside he started to panic. "Yeah, what did she have to say about that?" His last statement by itself was a good start – Sessions already admitted to knowing the victim's name.

"You know that isn't how this works. We're going to give you a chance to talk and tell us how it actually went down. Let me warn you though. This is your one and only chance to set things straight."

"And if I don't talk?"

"That's completely up to you. But I'm telling you, this is your chance to help yourself."

"Fine. Then I want a deal."

"You know I can't promise you anything. I can sit here and lie to you and say you won't get more than ten years prison, but you and I both know it is the State Attorney that makes the final call."

"Then get him on the phone. I want a deal."

"Look, I've dealt with this prosecutor before. If you cooperate with us, she'll take that into consideration in any plea deal she gives you."

"She? Which one will be prosecuting me this time?"

"Well, you've moved up in the world. You're going to have Jesse Bradshaw herself prosecuting you."

"Shee-it." The way Sessions pronounced the word created two distinct syllables.

Marty told him, "Seriously man, she's all right. Just come clean and she'll do what's right." What he didn't say is that what was right was more than likely the death penalty.

"Dude, I've heard about her. She'll send me to the chair."

"That's not likely." The electric chair hadn't been in use in years. Lethal injection was the method for executions now, but Marty didn't need to let this murderer in on his game of semantics.

"I need a minute to think, all right?"

"Sure, take your time, we'll wait on you." Marty leaned back and laced his fingers behind his head.

Robert Sessions stared off into space. He was physically still located in the small interrogation room, but his mind was beyond any walls. The small undercover camera on Doug's shirt was capturing every movement and word uttered by Sessions.

"All right, here is how it went down." He looked at Marty to make sure he was on the same page.

"I'm listening," Marty said.

"That chick is fucking crazy. She killed the dude in cold blood."

Neither Detective expected Sessions to go straight into the murder. They figured he would fish a little to see how much the detectives

147

already knew, but this was a great turn of events. "How did she kill him?" Marty asked.

"She just shot his ass."

"What type of gun did she use?"

"Umm…I think it was a .45 caliber handgun."

"That's kind of a big gun for such a small girl, isn't it?" Marty was taking the lead in this interview.

"Dude, she knows her way around guns, believe me."

"Where did she get it?"

"I don't know man, but she sure knew how to use it. She even had me scared a little bit."

"So how did it happen? Why were you both at Mr. Witherington's house?"

"The guy called Kerri. You see me and Kerri split up for a while. She was out of town, you dig?" What he really meant is that she went into rehab to clean up her act.

"Okay."

"When she came back, we didn't really hang, you know? Anyway, she got herself a sugar daddy in that Dean dude. Not that she needed it; her daddy has more money than God himself."

"So did you talk to her when she came back into town?"

"Nah. We each rolled our own ways. But then we ran into each other and I tell you it was like meeting each other for the first time all over again. We were hot for each other and well, I guess it goes without saying, we were back into each other."

"What about her new relationship with Dean Witherington?"

"She just dumped him cold, man. She was back with me like twenty-four seven."

"How long ago was this?"

"I don't know. I guess about two and a half, three weeks ago, maybe."

"So are you saying she has stayed with you that entire time? From two and half to three weeks ago to now, she's been with you?"

"Yeah man, she was living with me."

"She never went back to Witherington even for an afternoon?"

"Dude, I'm telling you, she was stuck on me. Never left me at all. That Witherington dude kept calling her all the time. Finally, after he left a message saying something about killing himself if she didn't come see him, she gave in and went over there."

"When was that?"

"The day it happened."

"Did she go by herself?"

"No. I went with her. No way I was going to send my bitch to that man alone. He'd brain wash her or something into coming back to him."

"Did he know that you were with her?"

"Nah. I stayed in the car. We had a code worked out. She was supposed to call me and let it ring three times if she needed help. She was just going to talk the guy down from killing himself and then we would bounce."

"So you were outside the whole time?"

"Up until I heard the dude yelling at her."

149

"Could you tell what he was saying?"

"Not until I went into the house."

"How did you enter the house?"

"Through the front door. She left it unlocked."

"What happened when you went inside?"

"They were upstairs. I couldn't hear her or nothing. Just him. I don't know what he was saying, but I took off up the stairs. When I got to the top, I heard her telling him to be quiet that he was just making it worse for himself. He didn't have a choice in the matter, that she was going to do it."

"Do what?"

"I guess kill him 'cuz that's what the crazy bitch ended up doing."

"Go ahead and tell us exactly what you heard after you came upstairs. Pick up where you left off."

"The dude was begging for his life, asking her why and all that shit. She just told him to act like a man and take it. Next thing I know, she shot the dude."

"How many times did she shoot him?"

"I don't know, maybe three or four. It all happened so fast, you know?"

"Where were they upstairs?"

"In the gym. It took a minute to really digest what had just happened and then I ran into the room and pretended like I didn't know what went down. I asked her what happened and she ran over to me and started crying that he tried to rape her or some shit like that and she grabbed the gun and shot him."

150

"Did she still have the gun in her hands?"

"She dropped it as soon as she saw me."

"Where was the body?"

"Over by the Elliptical machine."

"Was he dead?"

"As a doornail."

"What did you do?"

"I just held her and let her cry it out. After a few minutes she stopped crying and looked up at me and said, 'We've got to get rid of the body.'"

"So she didn't know that you saw her shoot Mr. Witherington?"

"Nah, man. She was so intense when she had the gun on him. She never even heard me coming."

Doug interjected, "What did she do with the gun?"

"Dude, I don't know. She just went and grabbed a bunch of stuff to wrap the dude up in and I helped her put him in the back of the Excursion."

"Why didn't you just walk away?" Marty wanted to give Sessions a chance to explain away all of his defenses.

"Look at me and look at her. There is no question that I'd be the one taking the ride for the shit that she pulled. I've been in trouble before. Hell, I'm on probation right now. Just by being here in another state, they are going to send me to prison."

"But that doesn't explain why you didn't walk away and call the cops."

"That bitch had just killed one man in cold blood. I didn't want to

151

make it two." Sessions managed to look indignant.

"I imagine there was a lot of blood. What did you do to clean that up?" Marty wanted to cover all of the territory they had covered with Kerri.

"I didn't do nothing. That was all on Kerri. She found some bleach and a mop and she cleaned it up. All I did was carry the dude's body down stairs and put it in the ride."

Doug followed up, "So, what did you do while Kerri did all of that cleaning? I imagine there was quite a bit to clean up and that it took her a while to clean it."

"Dude, I didn't do nothing. I was flipping out as it was. What was I supposed to do? At that point, all I could do was help her get rid of the body. She told me about a hunting camp that wasn't going to be used, so we took the body there."

"Did Kerri tell you how to get there?" Marty asked, which cued Doug to back off with his questions.

"Yeah, she got me headed in the right direction. Then she found the address programmed into the dude's GPS."

"So where was this place that you dumped the body?"

"It was the dude's own hunting camp. That sick bitch wanted to dump him on his own land."

"Had you ever been there before?"

"Nah, man."

"Who actually took the body and dumped it? Kerri is a pretty small lady to do something like that by herself."

Sessions quickly weighed his options. A little bit of truth would make the whole story more believable. "I did it for her. I had no choice. I didn't know if she still had the gun or not, but I wasn't going to take no chances. She said to take the body into the woods and get rid of it, so that is what I did."

Marty asked, "How exactly did you get rid of it in the woods, Rob?"

"Dude, I just carried him out there. There was a path that went straight back and I dumped the body into a pond."

"Weren't you worried about the body floating and being discovered?"

A flash of realization came across Sessions' face. Perhaps he really had forgotten about the weights. After all, he was stoned at the time. "Yeah, yeah, that's right. Kerri had told me that there was a pond when we were back at the house. She told me to grab the weights and we could weigh the body down so it wouldn't float."

"So you didn't make two trips to the hunting land? You brought the weights with you while you were still at the house the first time?"

"Yeah, that's right. In fact, now that you mention it, that was what I was doing while she was cleaning up the blood. I was carrying the weights down to the Excursion."

Doug wanted to know, "So who got Witheringron's credit cards?"

"She did, man. She grabbed the dude's entire wallet and went through his drawers to find some cash. The dude didn't have cash in the house, so she took his wallet."

"Did Kerri help you carry the body to the pond?"

"No. She stayed in the ride."

Marty, with a hit of skepticism asked, "Now surely you didn't carry the body and all of those weights in one trip, did you?"

Sessions rolled with it. "Um, no. It took a few trips back and forth to get everything down there. Yeah," he paused, "yeah that's it. You know, actually, Kerri did come down there now that I think of it. She was the one that thought of the weights, so while I carried everything back and forth, she tied the weights to his body. Then once I was done bringing all of the weights down there, we both rolled him into the water."

"Why did you two take off? It sounds like you had the perfect way to hide the body and no one would have been able to connect you two to the disappearance." Doug asked.

"Dude, I told you already. The chick is crazy. I didn't know if she had the gun still or not, so I just did as she said. She said we had to bounce so we bounced."

Marty didn't want Sessions to leave anything out, so he asked, "What about your car? What happened to it in all of this?"

"Uh, yeah, we just drove it back over to the place where I was crashing and left it there. She drove the Excursion and picked me up and then we went to the hunting camp and dumped the body."

"So where did you go from there? Did you have a plan or were you just doing as she told you?" Doug asked.

"We took 41 north until we hit the Interstate. From there, we were on open road. As we were driving, I told her that I was worried about driving in the dude's SUV. If we got pulled over, and they ran my name, I was going to get arrested since I'm not allowed out of state without permission from my probation officer. Anyway, I convinced her to dump the Excursion in Atlanta."

"Did you just leave it there or did you sell it to some of your old friends?" Doug asked.

"Hmph. You know about that, huh?"

"We know that you used to be tied up with a chop shop ring that goes all over the eastern seaboard." Doug just stared at Sessions before going on, "So is that what happened?" Doug asked.

Sessions didn't have a plausible story so he opted to admit to the small stuff. "Yeah, I hit up an old friend of a friend, if you know what I mean. He didn't want to give top dollar on it though." He looked off into space, "I don't know what was up with that. Anyway, I went and bought that Jeep with the money he gave me for the SUV."

"Does this guy have a name?" Marty wanted to collect as many witnesses as possible against this scum bag. The problem was that the person who bought the SUV also committed a crime, so it would be hard to make him talk, nevertheless to testify.

"Nah. I don't know who he was. Like I said, man, he was a friend of a friend."

"So why Kentucky of all places? How did you end up here?" Doug wanted to make sure he made Sessions commit to a full time line.

"Kerri was playing with the dude's GPS and came across a setting to go to 'Kentucky Home.' It seemed as good as anywhere else to go since we didn't really have anywhere to go, so we just kept driving and ended up here."

Doug and Marty both noticed that he left out the fact that he had drug ties to the area also. Marty tried to bring him to the present, "So why did you flee from the local cop?"

"I didn't know who that was, man. All I know is that some guy was following me around. There weren't no stripes or lights on that truck. There are all kinds of crazy people out there and that guy was on me like white on rice. I didn't know what he was planning to do to me. It wasn't until later that I realized he was a cop. By then it was too late."

"Why was it too late?" Doug asked.

"Because I was going to end up right where I am now. At least the way it played, I had a chance until you showed up at the new crib."

Marty was tired of dealing with Sessions and really didn't think they would be able to get anything else of value out of him. "Is there anything else you want to add to your story?"

Sessions went on the defensive. "It ain't no story, man! It's the truth. Just like I told you. That chick is crazy. She killed that dude in cold blood." Sessions leaned forward, placed his elbows on the table and laid his palms faced down on the table. "Now we need to talk about a deal. I know I was wrong in helping her hide the body, but like I told you, I had no choice. She had a gun and I knew she wasn't afraid to use it."

Doug put him off, "Like we told you before you started talking to us, the deals aren't up to us. It's up to the State Attorney. If everything is like you said, then you shouldn't have any problems. You seem like a truthful guy, so it should all check out."

156

"There ain't no way you can check my story out. She cleaned that room with so much bleach there is no way that there is any blood left in that room. And I looked for bullet holes and there weren't none."

Doug and Marty both stood up to leave. "We'll see about that. Don't you watch CSI? It is amazing what kind of technology is out there to test these types of things. I bet the crime lab will be able to corroborate your story no problem." Marty paused for a moment before continuing, "They will have something to corroborate, won't they? Everything you told us was the truth, right?"

Sessions looked Marty straight in the eye and said, "I swear, man. I swear on my mother's grave."

****

As soon as the detectives walked outside, Doug turned off the hidden camera and asked his partner, "So, what do you think?"

"He is cocky. He doesn't think we found the area where Witherington was actually shot. Yet, at the same time, he is pretty smart."

"Yeah, there are bits and pieces of truth to both of their stories. Who do you think did the actual shooting?"

"My gut says Sessions. But it doesn't really matter, does it? The State will probably go for the death penalty on both of them. No matter how you look at it, the one who didn't pull the trigger is a principal to the one that did pull the trigger. That makes the other just as culpable."

Doug asked, "You really think the State will go for death on both of them? I mean, think about it; Kerri Hall's father is a prominent person in the community. I'm sure he pulls some sort of political weight."

"You may be right. But if I had any say in the matter, I'd say put the needle in both of them."

"Me too. If Jesse is allowed to make the decision, she'll do the right thing. She has never let politics stop her from doing what was right before."

Marty said, "I know, but since when does the elected State Attorney not have a say in whether a person gets the death penalty? It just won't go down like that. Anyway, speaking of Jesse, we should give her a call and update her."

"Yeah, let's get in the car so there aren't any ears around us."

****

Jesse immediately picked up the phone when Darby told her who was calling, "Hey, what is happening on your end?"

"Well, we have Sessions," Doug told her, while holding the phone out so Marty could hear her on speakerphone too.

"That is great! Did he talk at all?"

"Yes, we have a great recorded interview with him. Their jail doesn't have the greatest place to interview people and record it, other than the intoxilyzer room, so we borrowed an undercover camera to hook up to my shirt. It should all be on tape."

158

"That is music to my ears." There was once a time when most officers insisted on not recording interviews with detainees. It took a local judge "strongly encouraging" the agency to utilize resources that were so easily available to them during the course of an investigation before the officers started using recording devices on a regular basis. "What did he say?"

Doug answered, "He committed to Kerri being the triggerman. Well, triggerwoman, I guess. He said that it happened in the gym upstairs, which we know isn't true. He basically laid it all on Kerri and said he only went along because she had a gun and she had already killed in cold blood once. He didn't want to be her second victim of the day."

"Doug, that's great. We'll be able to contradict everything he says. I've already been working on getting the grand jury convened. They are already in session, so it is just a matter of the foreman contacting all of the jurors and getting them in here. I'm looking at Monday of next week. Does that work for you two? I need you both here."

"We can get there no problem. Our work here is done, but what about giving Hall and Sessions an invitation to come to the grand jury? Aren't you supposed to do that?"

"I don't have to, no. I will, but I don't have to. That brings up another point; do you two want to drive Sessions back with you? That way we know for sure that he is back in our jurisdiction."

"I have no problem with that, but he has charges up here too." Doug reminded her.

"I know, but murder trumps fleeing a law enforcement officer.

159

They can put a detainer on him."

Marty spoke up for the first time, "Aren't you getting ahead of yourself? He isn't charged with murder yet. All he has is a violation of probation."

Jesse smiled and responded, "Yes, that is true, but every D.A. in this country knows that the grand jury is just a rubber stamp for the charges that we want to press. I'll have my indictment for murder, no problem."

"I'm sure you will, but we can't just waltz the guy out of the jail here. How are we supposed to get him out?" Marty asked.

"I'll have my boss give the elected Commonwealth Attorney a call. I'm sure they will be able to work something out."

"Well as soon as some arrangements are made, let us know and we'll be more than happy to run transport back to Florida." Marty went on, "What about Hall? We haven't checked with her today."

"Oh yeah, we got the warrant walked through. It was teletyped to the jail up there. From my understanding, it was just in the nick of time too. She was about to bond out on the possession charge up there, so it was a good thing we did the arrest warrant."

Doug asked, "Any word on whether she will waive extradition?"

"I believe she is going to. Her dad hired an attorney up there to consult with her on that very issue. The only thing they would be able to use to fight extradition is identity. I've already talked to the hired gun up there and he knows that you two are there and would be able to prove identity without a problem, so I think he is going to save all of us the hassle and advise her to waive extradition."

160

"Would it do any good if we went and talked to this attorney?"

"No. I told him that the lead detectives from the investigation down here were up there and had already interviewed her. I also told him that we had other officers that have had prior dealings with her, so we wouldn't have any problem proving it is really her on the arrest warrant. Plus, I'm sure he signed a non-refundable retainer, which is earned upon receipt, so he has no incentive to advise her to fight extradition. It just makes more work for him and he knows that he will lose."

"Well, that is good. Hopefully we won't run into any problems with getting her back down there," Doug said.

"I really don't expect there to be any problems. Once extradition is waived, they'll just transport her with other inmates through interstate transport. How about the evidence that was collected at the house? Are you going to have it sent to FDLE?"

Marty was responsible for the evidence, so he chimed in, "Yeah, it is in the local sheriff's office secure storage right now. As soon as we leave, we're just going to take it with us."

"Will you have enough room for the evidence, your luggage and Sessions?"

"Sure, it shouldn't be any problem. We just have a few bags of evidence from the search warrant and each of us just carried an overnight bag, so there shouldn't be a problem."

"Please tell me that you aren't going to put any of the evidence in the back seat with Sessions."

Doug knew she was teasing, so he gave her a dose back, "Yeah, we'll be sure to put everything there so he can tamper with it and then you'll have to prove up the whole chain of custody for all of the evidence." He chuckled out loud, "I guess that would mean you'd have to call Sessions to testify!"

"You are so full of it. Just let me know if you need anything from my end. If I hear anything from the Kentucky attorney that Hall's dad hired, I'll let you know."

"Sure thing. We should be wrapping things up here. We may even head home tonight." Both detectives were anxious to return home.

"Just let me make some phone calls and make sure Kentucky will release Sessions so you can go ahead and bring him home."

"We'll wait to hear from you." Doug started to hang up, but thought of one more thing, "you don't want us to do anything about Kerri Hall now, do you? Since she lawyered up, we can't really talk to her anymore, right?"

"No, we got everything that we need from her from your last two interviews. You guys did a great job with that, by the way. Actually, you've done great with this whole investigation."

"Thanks, Jess. I think I can speak for the both of us when I say that I appreciate that. We're both tired, but I can see the light at the end of the tunnel. The only thing that sucks is that we have to write all of this up in reports when we get back." Doug hated typing out his reports.

"Well, make them good reports. Just keep in mind that we're likely going before the Grand Jury on Monday."

"Yeah, that shouldn't be a problem. I don't think I'll have my portion of the reports done by then, but you can ask us questions based on what we've talked about, can't you?"

"Sure. I feel confident there is enough for an indictment even without all of the results of the forensic evidence. I certainly don't need all of your reports. Besides, all of the testimony is secret. There are very limited circumstances in which the defense can get a copy of a transcript from the Grand Jury testimony and I have never actually seen that happen."

"Okay, well, we'll let you know if anything happens here. We're really just hanging tight until we can pick up Sessions and come home."

"All right, I'll let you know if anything changes here."

"Same here. Bye."

"Bye you guys, drive safe."

11

Everything worked out relatively smoothly over the next few days. Hunter Robinson, Jesse's boss, knew the Commonwealth Attorney in Elizabethtown. Needless to say, both elected officials agreed that state resources would be better spent on prosecuting Sessions and Hall in Florida rather than on their relatively minor crimes in Kentucky.

Because Sessions had an open warrant for absconding from probation, the Florida detectives were able to drive the murder suspect back to his familiar home at the Columbia County Detention Facility. Kerri Hall got to ride in a van via a standard interstate transport of prisoners. The ride for Sessions and the detectives was uneventful with the exception that Sessions finally came down off of his meth high. Fortunately for the detectives, their detainee mostly slept the whole way home.

Since Marty and Doug brought the evidence collected from Witherington's Kentucky home with them, they made a detour to stop by the Florida Department of Law Enforcement Office, also known as FDLE, in Tallahassee. Dropping off the evidence themselves would eliminate one more person in the chain of custody, which would make Jesse happy. Plus, in the grand scheme of things, it did not add that much more time to their ride back home.

The detectives spent the remainder of the week and weekend typing reports. They had an appointment with Jesse at 3:30 on Sunday afternoon to go over the questions she would be asking them before the Grand Jury the next day. That appointment time came too quickly for both of them.

Jesse met the two detectives at the secure employee entrance at the northwest corner of the courthouse. Only certain courthouse employees had a key to enter the courthouse outside of normal business hours; since she was the lead attorney in the office, she of course had one. She greeted them with a smile, "Hey you guys, how's it going?"

Marty was the first one to respond with a smart remark, "How do you think it is going? It is Sunday and instead of sitting on the couch watching a game and drinking a beer, we're up here living and breathing this case day after day."

Doug was quick to follow up with, "But just seeing your bright and smiling face makes it all worth it, Jesse." Even with their history, he could still joke around with her. Plus, they both were making efforts to make it seem as though nothing had changed between them.

"Yeah, right." She pushed the door open for the two men. "This shouldn't take long. I've got all of your questions typed up, so I'm just going to let you read through them and see what your answers will be. I don't expect anything unexpected, so we should be in and out in no time."

Doug volunteered, "Jesse, you should know better than to not expect the unexpected."

"If this were a trial, then I'd agree with you. But I've never had a problem with a Grand Jury. Hearsay is admissible, so I can put the whole case on with just you two. I don't even need to call Brad or Amy to talk about the crime scene."

"Don't you think they would be better to talk about where the blood was found in the house and how it was found?" Marty didn't want to be questioned about a subject that he didn't feel qualified to talk about. "And to also explain the presumptive tests. I don't even know if the blood has been analyzed for DNA yet."

"All I said is that I can put the case on with just you two. I didn't say that I was going to." She put her hand on Marty's arm to reassure him, "Don't worry, I'm not going to ask you anything that you don't have direct knowledge about. I'm going to have Amy come and testify about the Luminol testing. It would be unnecessarily duplicative to have her talk about the crime scene dump site, so I'm going to have one of you talk about that instead.

While I think it was cruel and unusual punishment for you guys to send Wes to the M.E.'s office to observe the autopsy he is the lucky guy that I'm going to use to testify about the autopsy findings. It is always a pain to get the M.E.'s to cooperate with us and schedule their testimony. Plus, they charge us a fortune. So, I'm using Wes. Unfortunately, he is going to have to look at photos of poor Mr. Witherington again." She chuckled, "Hopefully he won't lose his breakfast like he did at the scene."

That brought a smirk from both of the detectives. It had been a mutual decision between the two of them to send Wes to the Medical Examiner's office. They both felt Wes needed to toughen up if he was going to make it as a detective. Plus, it gave them lots of material to tease him about.

The trio exited the elevator and Jesse unlocked the first of two secure wood doors to the State Attorney's Office. "Come on in. Do either of you want me to put on a pot of coffee? That is all I can offer you other than Diet Coke and I know you don't drink diet drinks, Doug."

"I'm fine, let's just get this show on the road, if you don't mind." Marty kept on walking towards Jesse's office.

"I'm good too, Jesse. Thanks for the offer though." Doug smiled at her behind Marty's back.

The small group headed down the hall and after entering Jesse' pleasantly decorated office, the men settled into their respective chairs. Jesse went directly to a cart filled with plastic boxes which in turn contained manila folders inside the boxes. She thumbed through the files and pulled two out. "Let's see, Marty, here is your set of questions." She pulled out a set of stapled papers and handed them to Marty, leaving a set for herself inside the folder. "And here is your set of questions, Doug." She opened the other folder and handed Doug his set of questions.

"Do you just want us to read through this and see if we have any questions, or do you want to actually go through them?" Marty asked.

"Why don't you go ahead and read through them and see if you have any questions for me or if there are any areas that I didn't cover.

Then, when you're done, I'll ask you the questions one by one." With the look that the two detectives gave her, she added, "don't worry, it won't take long."

"What's the big deal with getting this to the Grand Jury so quickly? I mean, we just arrested them and got them back to Florida," Doug asked.

"For Sessions, it doesn't really matter since he is being held no bond on his violation of probation and hasn't been arrested for the murder yet. But for Kerri Hall, we only have twenty-one days after her arrest for the murder to get an Indictment otherwise the defense is entitled to an adversary preliminary hearing."

Doug asked, "What is an adversary preliminary hearing?"

"It is kind of like a trial. The State has to put on enough testimony for the judge to find that there is probable cause to hold the defendant in custody. The problem is that the defense gets to cross examine my witnesses and they always treat it like an extra deposition."

"So, what's the problem with the defense having an extra deposition?" Marty asked.

"Look, how many times have you been on the stand and the defense attorney tries to impeach you based on your prior sworn deposition or based off of your sworn report?"

The men looked at each other, shrugged and Doug said, "I don't know, it seems like they try to do it at least every other trial."

"That's exactly right. The problem with the defense having another transcript of sworn testimony is that it gives them more fertile ground to try and find an inconsistent statement. You may be giving a consistent statement, but if you don't phrase it exactly the same way, that may give some crafty defense attorney an opening to attack you."

"But we shouldn't have any inconsistent statements," Marty said.

"Seriously?" Jesse just looked at him, not knowing for sure if he was serious or not. "Yes, you are right. You shouldn't have any inconsistent statements, but I can't count the number of times that the defense attorney was able to impeach the officer because of some minute difference in the way the officer answered the question on the stand versus the way the officer answered the question during the deposition."

"Why haven't I ever heard of these adversarial hearings before? I thought I was pretty up to speed on the way things go down in the courtroom." Doug asked.

"The defense only gets the hearing if we don't file the Information or get the Indictment within twenty-one days of arrest. As long as we file it in time, then they don't get the hearing. The reason why you have never seen it happen here is because I make sure all of my attorneys stay caught up on their intake so that never happens to us. For a while there, when one of the prior elected State Attorneys was in office, the defense did adversary preliminary hearings all of the time because the State kept dropping the ball. That simply is not going to happen on my watch"

"I see. Well, I'm glad you're looking out for us." Doug started to read his questions, but then asked, "Who all is going to be in there tomorrow, anyway?"

"Well, as you know, the Grand Jury proceeding is secret. The

169

judge won't even be in there as we present evidence and as the jury deliberates. It will just be me, my boss, a court reporter and between fifteen and twenty-one Grand Jury members. They have all been contacted, but they may not all show up. As long as we have at least fifteen, then we'll be fine."

"What is the procedure, exactly?" Doug asked.

"Well, after the jury is seated, I'll give a summation of what I expect to present in the form of testimony. It is similar to an opening statement in an actual trial. I'll go ahead and tell them up front what I expect them to Indict each person for. Ultimately, I want both Sessions and Hall to be indicted in the same Indictment.

But, I'm getting ahead of myself. I'll start calling witnesses. I plan on starting with you, Doug, to go through the initial investigation at the hunting camp, the search there, the dredging of the pond and discovery of the weights, the interview with the maid, that the credit cards have been used and the fact that you two went up to Kentucky and found Sessions and Hall crashing at Witherington's house up there."

"If he's testifying to all of that, what do you need me for?" Marty asked.

"Don't worry, I'm going to use you for everything that took place up there. The car chase, the interview with Hall, the search of the house up there, Sessions attacking you, everything you found in the house and the interview with Sessions."

"You putting me on right after Doug?"

"No, I'm going to go chronologically. I'll have Amy go second

170

and tell about the search of Witherington's house here in Florida. She has photos of the weights from the house and I'll have her compare them in front of the jury to the photos of the weights found in the pond."

"So is it just going to be us three that testify?" Doug asked.

"No, after Amy, I'll put Marty on and then I'll close with Wes. He's going to go through the Medical Examiner's preliminary findings. We don't have the final report yet, but it is good enough to get us through the Grand Jury."

Doug said, "It sounds like you've got everything planned out. Do you know if Hall and Sessions are going to testify or not?"

"Well, Hall's dad retained a high priced attorney out of Gainesville. I spoke with him on Friday and to quote him, 'Ms. Hall respectfully declines to join us.' Sessions has the Public Defender's office representing him and as a policy, they never let their clients testify at the Grand Jury."

"Who is the attorney from the PD's office?" Doug asked.

Jesse involuntarily blushed a little as she said, "Mark McCullers." It was an uncomfortable situation for her because there was definitely a lot of heavy flirtation directed her way from Mark. Jesse didn't want to repeat her last blunder; just like her relationship with Doug, everything with Mark was secretive. But the problems with being in a relationship with Mark were even worse because bar ethics would likely frown on a prosecutor carrying on a relationship with a defense attorney that has a case directly opposing her. They certainly were not to the point of a sexual relationship, but if things continued on, it might end up that way.

The whole thing was extremely confusing for Jesse – she certainly wasn't over her feelings for Doug, yet she recognized that she had to move on. Doug made his choice – she just had to accept that his actions spoke louder than his words. When she discovered his betrayal, he told her he wanted to be with her and not Alice, but he just couldn't live with himself being a part-time dad.

Jesse tried telling him that they could make it work and she really did try to make it work. Even after discovering Doug's tremendous betrayal, Jesse tried giving Doug another chance. But, she ultimately discovered that Doug was still 'trying to make things work with Alice' at the same time he was trying to work things out with her. So, she cut things off. The problem was that they didn't have any closure. Both of them continued to have feelings for one another, but neither would say anything.

Doug picked up on her uneasiness and prodded, "Hmm…do I know him? It seems like his name is familiar."

"I'm sure you two have met before. He is one of the up and comers in their office. They are trying to get him death qualified."

"What do you mean death qualified?" Marty asked.

"Oh, sorry, I didn't even think about talking in the lingo. Defense attorney's have to second chair a certain number of death penalty cases before they are qualified to sit first chair on a death case. The PD's office only has two people that are death qualified in the entire circuit, so they are trying to train some fresh blood. Actually, I think there is a statute that says that if you are a public defender, you do not have to be

172

death qualified, but it is better for their office if the person that handles the case is death qualified. Plus, it helps the PD's when they leave and go into private practice. "

Doug started to ask Jesse another question about Mark, but Marty broke in and said, "I guess we better get to reading these questions so we can get out of here."

"Yes, I guess so." Jesse purposefully would not look at Doug, who was giving her a curious look.

****

After the Grand Jury indicted Robert Sessions and Kerri Hall for First Degree Premeditated Murder, the next few weeks passed by in a blurry haze for Jesse. She was still maintaining her normal case load, which included preparing a Capital Sexual Battery case for trial in less than a month, as well as supervising the office and making sure she received all of the reports and evidence lists that she needed for the Witherington murder.

In order to cut Robert Sessions' defense off at the knees, Jesse requested that FDLE come back and analyze Witherington's gym in order to disprove Robert Sessions' claim that the shooting took place in the gym. Jesse knew that if she did not have the room analyzed, it would be a ripe area for Mark McCullers to argue before the jury.

Jesse could see it in her mind - Mark would argue that reasonable doubt existed because Robert Sessions told the officers exactly how everything happened; that Kerri Hall shot the victim in cold blood. All

173

his client did was try to save his own life by doing what his crazy, gun-carrying, girlfriend said to do. The legal argument would be that he was coerced into doing everything that he did. The blood on the stairway could be explained away because the body bled as Sessions and Hall carried it down to the awaiting Excursion. The bullet hole and fingerprint along the stairway would be problematic, but Mark was very crafty and would surely come up with something.

But, due to Jesse's offensive strategy, that argument would never come to light. As expected, the FDLE analysts did not find any traces of blood in the gym. But even better than that, there was another problem with Sessions' story - the bullet fragment in the wall. While no weapon had been recovered so far, the firearms section at the lab was able to compare the bullet fragment recovered from Witherington's body to the metal fragment that was recovered from the stairwell wall. Unfortunately, the analyst was not able to be one hundred percent certain that it was the same type of ammunition, but he could say that the piece of metal in the wall came from a bullet.

If comparing the two bullet fragments was all of the evidence that Jesse had, then it may be problematic, but the fact that she also had Robert Sessions' fingerprint on the joint compound that covered the hole in the wall sealed the deal. Jesse was very confident about her case. If you put all of the evidence together, it definitely pointed to the guilt of both Kerri Hall and Robert Sessions. Her most troubling question now was whether the case warranted the death penalty.

In Florida, a person that commits a Capital Felony may be punished by death. There are two phases in a Capital case: the guilt phase and the penalty phase. If the jury finds the defendant guilty, the jury is then charged with making a recommendation to the judge of either life in prison or the death penalty. In order to reach that decision, the jury has to weigh all of the statutory aggravating factors against the statutory and non-statutory mitigating factors. The jury then makes a recommendation to the judge, who then imposes the sentence.

Jesse felt certain that she would seek the death penalty on Robert Sessions. He had four strong aggravators against him: he had previously been convicted of a felony and was placed on felony probation; the capital felony was committed during the commission of a robbery; the capital felony was committed for pecuniary gain; and the capital felony was especially heinous, atrocious, or cruel.

Jesse knew that she may have a hard time proving that the murder was committed during the commission of a robbery, but her theory of the case was that Sessions and Hall went to Witherington's house to get money from him; whether Witherington would willingly give the money or not. The only other aggravator that may be difficult to prove was that the crime was especially heinous, atrocious, or cruel. But, based on the Medical Examiner's report, Witherington was still alive when the execution shot came to the head. Case law supported a finding of heinous, atrocious or cruel when the victim saw the fatal shot coming.

Whether to seek the death penalty on Kerri Hall was another thing. Jesse chalked a lot of Hall's actions up to being young and stupid. The girl had everything handed to her on a silver platter and was just showing out to get attention. Combine that with being hooked on drugs and it was a recipe for disaster. Jesse felt confident that Kerri Hall never would have done something like this on her own. But, Jesse could not look at it that way. The law required Jesse to weigh the aggravating and mitigating circumstances against one another.

The biggest mitigator going in Kerri Hall's defense was that she was not the primary responsible party. No matter how you looked at the case, Sessions looked like the worst person in all of this. Jesse was considering taking death off of the table for Kerri if she would turn on her co-defendant and testify against him. It was something to think about, but not something she was ready to offer to Ronald Dasher, Kerri Hall's high priced attorney.

Jesse was lost in thought when Darby buzzed her, "Jesse, you have a call on line one."

"Who is it?"

"I didn't ask, but I'm pretty sure it is Mr. McCullers. Do you want me to check?"

Jesse's pulse quickened at the sound of his name. Things between them had definitely been heating up over the last few weeks. "No, that's all right, I'll just pick up."

"Okay, thanks, I've got another call to answer."

"Thanks, Darby." She took a deep breath to steady herself before picking up the line. "This is Jesse, may I help you?"

"Wow, that is quite the formal greeting, is there someone in there with you?" Sure enough, it was Mark.

She tried to play it cool. "No, not at all. I just didn't know who was on the phone. You never know when it is some slimy defense attorney calling after all."

"Ooohh, that hurts, Jess, that really hurts. So what are you doing?"

"Pursuing justice. What are you doing?"

"Thinking about how hungry I am and how nice it would be to have lunch with you."

Jesse automatically looked at her doorway to make sure no one was near. She lowered her voice as she said into the phone, "Mark, if we keep this up, we're going to get caught."

"Keep what up? We haven't done anything wrong. We're just two colleagues that happen to dine together from time to time."

"Oh really? Do colleagues also meet each other in neighboring towns and go on hikes together, or have the occasional kiss in the witness room outside the courtroom?"

"Jesse, my dear, I don't know what you are talking about." He chuckled, "as you know, I am a defense attorney. A large part of my job is boldly asserting a statement. As long as my bold assertion is plausibly maintained, then I'm golden in my defense. I am also a state worker on a state phone that has many lines that can be monitored by anyone unbeknownst to me." His hint was well taken. "Now, back to the reason for my call; would you like to go grab a bite to eat?"

She looked at the clock and quickly thought through her calendar for the rest of the day. Without another moment's hesitation, she answered "Sure, I'd love to have lunch with you."

"See you at the Cuban Café in ten."

"Okay, see you there."

Spending time with Mark McCullers was like having a breath of fresh air for Jesse. Somehow he was able to maintain a passion for the law and life in general like no other person that Jesse knew. While Mark's main business was his job at the public defender's office, he also ran a small online organic coffee roasting business.

The fact that he was able to do his job at the Public Defender's office so well while also maintaining an independent business never ceased to amaze Jesse. She also loved the fact that he was always coming up with innovative business ideas. Sometimes it was all Jesse could do just to keep up with his thought process. She wondered how he had any time just to relax in life; though she wasn't too good at finding relaxation time either.

Jesse arrived at the restaurant first and ordered the drinks for both of them. A Diet Coke for her and a sweet tea for Mark. The dangling bells on the front door caught Jesse's attention. She looked up in time to see Mark coming straight towards her.

"Hey you, how are you?" As he sat down, he flashed her a smile, which revealed a set of perfect teeth.

She smiled back at him, "I'm doing all right, how about yourself?"

"Ahhh," he let out a breath of air, "I'm busy. I'm trying to get out of here so I can go to the warehouse tonight to meet with Tom, but I still haven't made it out to the jail to see clients today. There are a bunch of new arrests and the new guy is backed up on his work, so I

178

told him I'd go see the new arrestees for him."

"Well that was nice of you to offer that to him."

"I'm a nice guy, what can I say?" He picked up his menu and aimlessly opened it, flipping through the pages. "So are we both having a Cuban sandwich today?"

"I don't know about you, but I am going to have a Cuban sandwich. Please don't feel like you have to order the same thing as me," she said with a gleam in her eye.

"Believe me, honey, I don't."

Jesse didn't quite know how to take that comment but she just smiled and waved the waitress over to their table so they could order. After all, since the restaurant was across town, the driving time took up a large portion of her lunch hour and she was a conscientious state employee.

After placing their orders, both attorneys waited for the waitress to leave before talking to one another again. Mark was the first to speak, "So, what are you up to today?"

"Well, I'm just going through everything on the Witherington murder. Making sure all of the evidence has come back and that we've received all of the reports from FDLE."

"Have they gotten the Jeep back into Florida yet?"

"It should be here by this time next week. It was already sealed off in Kentucky so it can be loaded onto a flat bed and transported to FDLE for analysis in the same condition that it was in when taken into custody in Kentucky."

"I want my expert to look at it too."

"What is there to look at? It is a mangled Jeep. All I care about are the contents. I want to make sure there wasn't anything in the Jeep that I'll need at trial."

"Look, when I come in on a case, the facts are already decided for me. I have to play with the hand that was already dealt to me. In this situation, I'm playing with the hand that I was dealt, but I get to investigate at the same time as you because there is still evidence being analyzed."

"Are you asking if your investigator can go through the Jeep first, or are you asking if your investigator can be present while the FDLE analysts go through the Jeep?"

"Just having him there at the same time will work for me. I may want to have my own analysis done later."

"Well, the Jeep will remain in state custody until the trial is over, so it will be available for anything you want done."

"Don't get testy, I'm just asking for a fair shake, okay?" He reached his hand across the table and lightly touched the back of her hand.

Jesse immediately looked the room over to make sure she did not know anyone in the restaurant. "I'm sorry. I'm not upset at all. I didn't mean to give the impression that I was. I just have a lot going on right now and not enough time to deal with it all."

"Want to talk about it?" His hand was within an inch of hers.

"It's just work stuff. I have all of those child hearsay motions and Williams Rule motions in my child sex case that I have to deal with before the trial." Williams Rule dealt with the State being able to present evidence of prior bad acts of a defendant as long as the prior acts were similar in nature to the current charges. In regular cases, the motions were rarely granted, but in child sex cases, a Rule of Procedure made it to where the motions were more likely to be granted.

He interjected, "yeah, but isn't that all pretty standard stuff? You've handled those motions before in other cases.

"Yes, I just need to Shepardize my case law and create some charts to show how the prior bad acts are similar enough to this case." Shepardizing was a way of looking into the procedural history of a case to make sure it was still good law and had not been overturned.

"That isn't so bad." He hesitated, but is there something else going on with you?"

She just looked at him before responding. How could she possibly tell him the truth; which was that she was falling for him romantically while they were in the middle of a death penalty case as opposing counsel but she wasn't even sure about that because of how things ended with Doug? She smiled and responded, "Nothing for you to worry about. At least not now, anyway."

"What do you mean?"

She hesitated and said, "Oh, just that there are a lot of motions that need to be done on this case too. I don't know if you want to do a motion to sever, or if Ronald Dasher is going to move to sever your client. There are so many Bruton issues that I was expecting that motion. I'm surprised it hasn't come already."

"It's funny you should say that. I was just talking to Mr. Dasher about that very issue. We're trying to strategize to see what would be best for each of our clients. My guy says that Hall did it all and Hall says that my guy did it while defending her."

"Well, I'm sure you are considering all of the forensic evidence in this case. Even though Hall doesn't quite get it right, at least she put the shooting as occurring on the stairway."

"Yes, but according to the FDLE report you just disclosed last week, she didn't have any blood on the back of her dress like there should have been if she were telling the truth."

"Yes, that is true. But the other reports put the victim's blood on the front of a male's shirt that was recovered from the house in Kentucky. We're just waiting on the DNA section to analyze the epithelials on the inside of the shirt to confirm that Sessions was wearing the shirt."

Mark bolstered, "Yeah, yeah, yeah. The best you will have is that the DNA might show that Sessions had that shirt on at some point in time. You don't know when he put it on. And so what if it does show that Sessions wore the shirt; the shirt was found in a home that is owned by your victim. Who is to say that the victim didn't cut himself while shaving and that is where the blood came from?"

"So how would that explain Sessions having worn the shirt?"

"He traveled lightly when he went to Kentucky. He didn't bring his own shirt to change into, so he grabbed what was there."

"So you are telling me that you would argue to the jury that he picked up a shirt with blood all over it and wore it?"

"Who is to say that Mr. Witherington had paid his electric bill?

182

Maybe my client was just feeling his way around in the dark and came across a shirt and put it on."

She grinned at him, "You know, it is amazing that your eyes aren't brown with how much sh-"

He interrupted her, "Hey now, be nice. You have to throw me a bone here. I don't have a lot to work with, okay?"

"I am being nice." She thought about it and rephrased, "that was me being nice. You just haven't seen me being mean yet."

"Yet?" He teased.

"Oh yes, I'm sure there will be a time and place when you see me be dirty." She quickly realized her slip-up and stammered, "I – I mean be mean."

He smiled at her slyly, "I think I'd rather see you be dirty."

"Well, that will just have to wait until. . ."

"Until what?"

"Our food is coming." Jesse smiled at the waitress as she approached with the two Cuban sandwiches. The waitress' timing could not have been any better.

"We're going to have to continue this conversation later." He got one last word in before the food hit the table.

12

Like most of her career, the next several months flew by for Jesse.
She won her Capital Sexual Battery case against a three time child
molester and he was sentenced to multiple life sentences. The
Witherington case had also progressed nicely. All of the police reports
were in and all of the witnesses had already been deposed. Nothing
terribly damaging occurred during the depositions, so all in all, Jesse
was pleased with the progression of the case. The only remaining
things to do before trial were pre-trial motions.

The first motion of a long line of pre-trial motions was a motion to
suppress filed by Ronald Dasher, Kerri Hall's attorney. Jesse had all
of her research ready and neatly filed in her trial folders. She had
never dealt with Ronald Dasher prior to this case, but so far, she was
impressed. He was definitely worth the six figures he was being paid
to defend Kerri Hall.

The elevator opened and Jesse put her game face on, which went
with the rest of her appearance. Jesse was always amused when
people told her how prim and proper they thought she was. Just
because she almost always wore her hair in a French twist for court did
not mean she was uptight. Nor did her tailored suits mean she was

vain. The truth of the matter was that the updo kept her neck cool because her hair was so thick. And the suits? Most people would be shocked that her designer looking suits cost less than $40.00 per suit. Jesse was definitely a bargain shopper.

Jesse had even been told that she looked like the type of person that would carry a Chihuahua in an oversized pocket book. Jesse laughed at that and proceeded to brag on Xander, her muscle-bound, 85 pound German Shepherd that she loved with all of her heart and competitively trained nearly every weekend.

But, for now, it was time to go defeat Kerri Hall's *Motion to Suppress Statement to Police*. The hearing was on a specially scheduled day, so the hallway was not crowded like it normally was on a regular felony court day. Jesse wheeled her cart with all of her case files and research for the current motion down to courtroom two.

The bailiffs already had the room unlocked, so she just went straight through the two sets of double doors and started setting up her files and case law so she would be ready as soon as the judge walked in. The defense attorney was not there yet, which was typical. Apparently it was typical even for high priced attorneys.

About ten minutes passed before Ronald Dasher came into the courtroom. He walked up to Jesse and greeted her with a slight bow of his head while saying, "Good morning, madam prosecutor. I hope this day finds you well."

Jesse smiled back at him and responded, "Yes, Mr. Dasher. I'm doing very well today. I hope you are also."

"But of course. I couldn't be better. The law and facts are on my side today; a combination that does not often happen for a defense attorney, so I could not be better."

Jesse just smirked at the gameplay that he was employing. "Ahh, yes. I know the exact feeling that you are talking about. I know exactly what it is like to have the law and the facts on my side. In fact, I am having that very same feeling that you are having right now."

"Tsk tsk, madam prosecutor. We cannot both be right."

"Ahh yes," Jesse responded, "that is why we have a judge to settle our differences."

"And that he will. From my understanding, motions to suppress are not often granted in your circuit. Is that correct?"

Jesse carefully considered her answer, "As you know, cases have a way of working themselves out. If there is a problem with a case, such as a potential suppression issue, then the case may be No Information'ed in the first place or be plea bargained down." There was no need to explain to him that a "No Information" meant the State was dropping the case.

He quickly interjected with a gleam in his eye, "Ah yes, then misdemeanor battery it is for Ms. Hall. Credit for time served!"

Jesse couldn't help but to chuckle at his brazen attempt to knock her off her game. "No, unfortunately for you, no plea bargaining here. As I was saying, when there are *valid* suppression issues, I encourage my attorneys to do the right thing. That starts with the filing decision. If there is even a hint of a suppression issue, my prosecutors research the issue before filing an Information. So, once an Information is filed, the defense may file a motion to suppress, but the prosecutor has already evaluated the likelihood of the motion being granted; therefore very few Motions to Suppress are ever granted around here. It isn't because the judges are partial to the State, it is because the State has already vetted the case."

"So, Ms. Bradshaw, is that your gentle way of telling me that you are five steps ahead of me?

"Oh no, Mr. Dasher. We are on an even playing field. Yes, it is true that the thought of a motion to suppress such as the one that you filed here today did cross my mind. However, I did exactly what I expect my staff attorneys to do – I evaluated it, researched it and went forward with the case. I feel just fine with my odds here today."

She wasn't going to go any further into her legal argument because Ronald Dasher was as slick as they come. He was trying to chat her up and get her to reveal her case strategy. It was not going to work. As some would say, this wasn't her first rodeo.

"It's true what they say about her, Ron," Mark McCullers, Robert Sessions' attorney had snuck into the courtroom during the banter between the attorneys. "Don't let her fool you. She may act all innocent and sweet, but once you get her going in a motion or trial, she is as feisty as they come."

"Mark, so glad you could make it." The two men shook hands.

"I wouldn't miss this for the world. I just wish we had scheduled the Bruton hearing and *Motion to Sever* today too. That way, once your motion to suppress is over, we can both take a shot at her on the Bruton motion. If nothing else, we could have worn her down by tag teaming her." He winked at Jesse while Ronald Dasher was looking

187

away.

Jesse addressed Mark, "Hardy, har, har. Very funny, Mark. But you should know better than that. It would take a whole lot more than two defense attorneys to wear me down." Her mind instantly slipped into thinking about her last time alone with Mark. He certainly had one proven method of wearing her down; and it wasn't in the courtroom.

Mark just grinned at her like a Cheshire cat. "Well, I guess we won't get that opportunity to find out, now will we?"

Jesse responded, "Not today, but how about next week? We already have your *Motion in Limine* scheduled about the defendant's flight away from the scene, but there is no reason we can't stack the *Motion to Sever* and <u>Bruton</u> motion all together during the same hearing. In fact, it would probably work better to have the <u>Bruton</u> and severance motions heard together. What do you think, gentlemen?"

Ronald Dasher answered first, "Well, I think you are right about it making more sense to have them heard together. I already have the entire afternoon blocked off to travel here and have the motions heard. We may go past five o'clock, but I'm paid by the hour, so it doesn't matter to me."

Mark smiled, "Great, it's settled then. After I watch the blood bath that is about to ensue between the two of you, I'll go down to my office and prepare the notice of hearing. I just need to clear the whole afternoon with the J.A. to make sure the judge is available for the entire afternoon." Every judge has a judicial assistant, which is just a dolled up name for secretary. One of the J.A.'s roles is to keep the judge's calendar running smoothly.

"Fine by me. I'm ready to go at anytime." Jesse wasn't worried about the motion today, but she did have some concerns about the motions that were just agreed on to be heard next week.

The bailiff stood up from where he was sitting and put his hand to his ear, presumably listening to what another bailiff was saying in the ear com device. "Court will come to order, the Honorable Benjamin Doverman presiding." Since it was just a hearing, the bailiff didn't instruct everyone to rise, though they did anyway.

The esteemed Judge Doverman walked in from the private entrance behind the bench and waved at everyone to sit down. "Good morning, everyone. I see that we have a *Motion to Suppress* scheduled today. Are you ready to proceed?"

Ronald Dasher stood and said, "Yes, Your Honor, however my client has not been brought out from the holding cell yet." He held his hands in such a way as to seem helpless while trying to score pity points with the judge.

Judge Doverman quickly looked at the bailiff but before he said anything, the bailiff piped up, "Sorry, Judge." They have her coming down the back hallway right now. We have a new person working in transport and he didn't want to bring the defendant down the hallway at the same time that you would be back there."

It was a lame excuse and everyone knew it. Judge Doverman would speak to the Sergeant over courthouse security later to make sure the bailiffs always had the defendants present and ready to go prior to him taking the bench. "Very well, are there any preliminary matters that can be taken care of while we wait for Mr. Dasher's client?"

"Yes, Your Honor." Jesse stood up to address the Court. The State will be calling several witnesses, would you like to swear them in all at once so as to move along more smoothly?" Jesse knew very good and well that Judge Doverman always swore witnesses in en masse during motions such as this one. One thing about Judge Doverman is that he liked to be efficient.

"Yes, absolutely." The Judge turned to Ronald Dasher and asked, "other than potentially having your client testify, do you have any witnesses you would like to have sworn?"

Ronald Dasher stood to address the Judge, "No, Your Honor. I would, however, like to invoke the Rule of Sequestration."

Without being asked, Jesse interjected, "No objection to that, Your Honor. I have already spoken to all of my witnesses and told them that the Rule of Sequestration would be invoked. They are all very familiar with the Rule." Jesse was trying to even the ground by showing the Judge that her witnesses were regular attendees at court hearings and familiar with what is commonly simply referred to as, "*The Rule*."

"Very well, have them all come in and I will swear them in and also advise them of the Rule."

"Yes, Your Honor. They are sitting outside. May I step out to bring them in?"

"Yes." The Judge responded.

Jesse pushed her chair back further with the back of her knees and stepped over to the swinging double gate that was the only doorway that separated the court room from the gallery. She quickly stepped through the two sets of double doors and found Detectives Westcott and Newsome sitting on the bench in the hallway. They both looked uncomfortable wearing a suit and tie rather than their normal casual wear. "Hey, guys. It is time to get this show on the road. The Deputy Clerk is going to swear you in like I told you and then the Rule is going to be invoked. They are bringing Kerri in right now, so she may walk through the courtroom while you are being sworn in."

Both men nodded and followed Jesse back into the courtroom. They both stood behind the bar, as was their normal place to stand while being sworn in as a group. Judge Doverman looked up and saw that the two detectives were present and ready to be sworn in. "State please call your witnesses names."

"Your Honor, the State will be calling Detective Doug Wescott and Detective Marty Newsome." She gestured to the two men standing behind her.

The Judge looked at the Deputy Clerk, who then stood and faced the detectives with her right hand raised and read from a card, "Please raise your right hand. Do you solemnly swear or affirm that everything you testify to here today will be the truth, the whole truth and nothing but the truth?"

"Yes." The men said in unison.

The Judge took over, "Very well. Gentlemen, the Rule has been invoked. Counsel informed me that she has already explained the Rule to you, but I like to keep a clean and clear record as well." The Judge looked down to his right at the court reporter who was typing away everything that was said. "From this point forward, I do not want either one of you to talk about the case that we are here about today. Do not talk about this case to one another or anyone else other than the attorneys. Also, do not talk to anyone, especially each other, about your testimony. Any questions about that?"

"No, Your Honor." Both men answered in unison.

"Good." The Judge turned to the attorneys before him. "We'll take a moment so the bailiffs can get Mr. Dasher's client seated and then start the proceeding. Are either of you wanting to make an opening or just get straight to it?" The emphasis was on, "straight to it."

Ronald Dasher stood and said, "Yes, Your Honor, I would like to make a very brief opening statement. More so as to lay a road map for where we are heading with this motion."

Jesse thought to herself, that the phrase "road map" was usually reserved for explaining an opening statement to a jury and was not effective on a judge, especially one as seasoned as Judge Doverman. She also knew that the Judge did not like opening statements on this type of motion, but depending on what was said, she may be forced to make one as well.

"Very well, Mr. Dasher. Ms. Bradshaw, do you wish to be heard as well?"

"No, Your Honor." Jesse sat back down as the bailiffs brought the defendant into the courtroom. She mused about how such a diminutive girl could have participated in such an atrocious act. Kerri

Hall had the world handed to her on a silver platter and had wasted her life. In situations like this, Jesse was often reminded of the expression, 'There but for the grace of God, go I.' Jesse had worked hard her whole life to get where she was today. She certainly had not had anything handed to her, but hard work and dedication paid off.

The bailiff left Hall's handcuffs on her as he helped her sit down in the blue roll chair at defense counsel's table.

Ronald Dasher stood and addressed the Court, "Your Honor, I would like to request that the handcuffs be removed from my client so she can better aid me in this matter. She can hardly reach the table since her handcuffs are attached to the waist iron."

Jesse quickly stood, "Your Honor, the State objects to the defendant's handcuffs being removed. The chain that connects the handcuffs to the waist chain is more than long enough to accommodate the defendant reaching the table to take notes. There is not a jury here, so the defendant is not prejudiced in any way by remaining handcuffed." She barely took a breath before adding, "The defendant is charged with a very serious crime, Premeditated First Degree Murder, and should not have the handcuffs removed. This is an issue of safety, even for defense counsel." Jesse knew the Judge was familiar with the defendant that stabbed his own attorney a few years back.

Ronald Dasher remained standing the whole time Jesse addressed the Court and started to argue back, but the Judge cut him off. "Bailiff, go see if Mr. Dasher's client can reach the table." The Judge then addressed Ronald Dasher, "Mr. Dasher, your client can use a writing utensil to take notes, but it has to be one of those soft sided pens. I know you are not from here, but we had a defendant stab a defense attorney a few years back with a pen and ever since then I do not take chances. The handcuffs will remain in place." Jesse inwardly smirked at the Judge's comment

"But Judge – " Dasher started to argue.

The Judge raised his hand, palm out, a universal tactic used by attorneys and judges alike to stop someone from talking. "I will hear no further argument on the matter. This is my courtroom and I will run it the way I want to."

Rather than risk getting on the Judge's bad side even further, Ronald Dasher graciously said, "Yes, Your Honor."

The bailiff announced to Judge Doverman, "She can reach the table, Judge."

Judge Doverman proceeded in an efficient all-business tone, "Okay, with that settled, we are here on the *Defendant's Motion to Suppress Statements Made*. Who has the burden and who is going first?"

Ronald Dasher began, "Your Honor, if I may?"

"Proceed," the Judge responded.

"Your Honor, Florida Rule of Criminal Procedure 3.190(h) addresses a Motion to Suppress a Confession or Admission Illegally Obtained. Subparagraph one states, 'On motion of the defendant or on its own motion, the court shall suppress any confession or admission obtained illegally from the defendant.' The rule goes on to state in paragraph four, 'The court shall receive evidence on any issue of fact necessary to be decided to rule on the motion.'

Thus, we are here today. The statement that should be suppressed occurred in Kentucky, where the two detectives followed my client and then interrogated her after she had just been medicated at the hospital after breaking her arm. The interrogation occurred in the late hours of the day to where, not only was my client naturally tired because of a long day but she also had the added pain medication which, for lack of better words, left her out of sorts to where she did not know what she was saying to the detectives. Being under the influence of pain medication made it to where my client's statements to police were not knowingly, voluntarily and intelligently made.

Additionally, these statements should be suppressed because the police made direct and implied promises, which rose to the level of improper influence. The way the officers interrogated my client made her have hope that she would only be charged with a misdemeanor or even let off completely from being charged at all.

Furthermore and perhaps most importantly, my client requested an attorney and the detectives kept questioning her, despite her constitutional request for counsel.

At the conclusion of today's hearing, I will present case law to you on all of the fronts that I have just mentioned that supports the Defense's contention that the statements made by Ms. Hall were not knowingly, voluntarily and intelligently made and therefore should be suppressed. The officers made promises and offered "fruits of hope" to my client to get her to make a statement and continued to interrogate my client despite her request for an attorney. At the

195

conclusion of this hearing, the Court should find that the statements may be suppressed on either one of those grounds independently, but most certainly suppressible on all of those grounds under the totality of the circumstances."

"Thank you, Mr. Dasher. Now as to the burden?" The Judge asked.

Ronald Dasher responded, "Yes, Your Honor. The burden is on the State to prove that the statement by my client was voluntarily given. However, the defense must make an initial showing that the statement was not valid. At that time, the burden shifts to the State to prove that the statement was valid."

"Ms. Bradshaw, do you agree?" The Judge asked Jesse.

"Yes, Your Honor. I agree as to the burden and the shifting burden, at which time the State must prove by at least a preponderance of the evidence both a Miranda Waiver and voluntariness of the confession. However, I do not agree with the rest of what Mr. Dasher said."

"Yes, counselor, that is understood. Do you wish to make any sort of opening?"

Apparently he had forgotten that she had already said, 'No.'

Jesse responded, "No, Your Honor. The evidence will more than speak for itself, an opening is not needed." She glanced at Ronald Dasher as she sat down and saw him shooting daggers at her with his eyes.

The Judge did not make any facial gestures after Jesse's comment, but instead turned to Ronald Dasher and said, "Call your first witness."

13

It was always a difficult decision for a defense attorney to call his own client, but Ronald Dasher had no choice at the moment. He knew the two detectives would not testify the way he wanted them to, based on the deposition testimony that they previously provided. Since there were only three people in the room when his client was interrogated and two of them were adverse witnesses, he had to call Kerri as a witness before the burden would shift to the prosecution. Ronald Dasher stood and said,"Your Honor, I call, Kerri Hall."

As soon as the defense attorney said the defendant's name, the bailiff seated to Kerri's right stood up and moved closer to her. While her flight risk was at a minimum, the fact remained that there still was a flight risk. After all, she was facing a capital charge.

Kerri Hall stood up, causing her chair to roll back with the motion. She shuffled her shackled feet and headed towards the witness stand diagonally across the courtroom from where she was sitting at counsel's table. The bailiff that had been sitting next to Hall walked along behind her until they reached the step leading to the witness stand. The bailiff then grabbed Hall's elbow and guided her up the step and turned Hall's body to face the Deputy Clerk so she could be sworn in.

Hall started to sit, not realizing what was happening, so the Judge broke in, "Ms. Hall, please remain standing while the Deputy Clerk swears you in."

"Yes, Your Honor." Hall responded in a small voice.

The Deputy Clerk stood and faced the defendant. She read from a card once again, "Please raise your right hand. Do you solemnly swear or affirm that everything you testify to here today will be the truth, the whole truth and nothing but the truth?"

"Yes, ma'am," Hall responded. Again, she used a small, child-like voice.

"Please be seated." The Judge instructed Hall.

The bailiff continued to expertly place his body between Hall and the court reporter, who was sitting in a similar boxed-in area adjacent to the witness stand, with only a three foot space between the two seating areas. The bailiff pushed Hall's rolling chair up to the microphone and bent the microphone down to her mouth.

Even Jesse almost felt sorry for the diminutive girl who was facing the rest of her life in prison, if not the death penalty. Her boss had instructed her to wait to file the formal *Waiver of Death Penalty* in Kerri Hall's case until after the pre-trial motions were heard. Jesse did not think the death penalty was appropriate for Hall, but she was definitely going after the death penalty for Sessions. Putting aside the appearance of the cold blooded murderer, Jesse came back to reality and knew that Kerri Hall deserved to go away to prison for the rest of her natural life.

Ronald Dasher had already made his way over to the lectern, which was directly to Jesse's left. He pushed it forward so he would be closer to his client. Some judges did not allow counsel to move courtroom furniture around without permission. In fact, in some courtrooms, judges required counsel to make such a request as a formal request prior to any hearing, to be addressed as a preliminary matter. Judge Doverman was certainly a stickler for rules, but he was not over the top.

"Kerri, I'm going to ask you a few questions and I want you to answer them to the best of your ability, okay?" Dasher used his client's first name in an attempt to personalize her with the Judge. Jesse inwardly smiled as she realized that Dasher was once again using jury trial tactics with Judge Doverman.

"Okay." Hall responded. Jesse knew she was going to get tired of the '*poor me, I'm a vulnerable young girl that is scared in this courtroom*' act real soon.

"Okay, Kerri, I need you to speak a little louder for me. It might not feel real natural for you to speak so loud, but you have to speak up for us older folks." He gestured between himself and the Judge.

Jesse nearly laughed out loud when she saw Judge Doverman's eyebrow arch in response to Dasher's gesture.

"Yes, Sir." Kerri responded. She was a little louder this time, but still used a child like voice.

"Okay, Kerri, please turn to the Judge and introduce yourself."

Kerri turned her knees towards the judge's bench as her attorney had previously instructed her when they rehearsed her testimony. "My name is Kerri Hall. I was born and raised here, in Lake City. My father is Montgomery Hall. He owns Hall's Land Acquisitions and Hall Real Estate Agency."

Jesse knew that Hall's father's status was an impediment, but it was not insurmountable. Judges were human and worried about re-election, even though no one ever seemed to run against the judges in the Third Circuit. But, the Hall family was an old time Columbia County family, as was Judge Doverman's. Jesse was sure their families were probably at least acquaintances, if not friends or even related by marriage. It would certainly make it awkward for the Judge to run into any of the Hall family at the Country Club after being the judge on this case.

"What do you do for a living, Kerri?"

"Well, before I got dragged into this whole mess, I was a student." She faltered momentarily, "At least I was going to be a student. I was getting my applications together and was about to apply for college."

Jesse made a quick note. It was a small point to cross examine and probably not one that she would address because pointing out that Kerri lived off of her father and was not a student would not really help her with the legal issues at hand. If they were in front of a jury, she might ask a question or two but not during a suppression motion.

"What do you want to be?" He used the future tense, rather than past tense as a subliminal message to the Judge – *let my client go free*.

"I wanted to become a nurse." She caught herself. "I mean, I want to become a nurse. I like helping people and I thought that would be a

200

great way to help people."

Jesse was close to objecting as to relevance with the line of questioning, but Dasher moved on. "Kerri, you know why we are here today, right?"

"Yes." She looked down as her eyes started to well up with tears.

"Kerri, I need you to be strong for me, okay?" Dasher waited nearly ten seconds before proceeding. He wanted to capitalize on his client's rehearsed tears. "Can you do that?" He asked in a gentle tone.

"I'll try." Her lower lip quivered as a big round tear cascaded down her right cheek.

"Kerri, because we are here for a Motion to Suppress, I'm not going to ask you background questions about the alleged crime. I am going to limit my questions to when the police interrogated you, okay?"

"Okay." Her crocodile tears were already starting to dry up.

"Do you remember two officers coming and interrogating you after you were involved in a traffic crash?"

"Yes."

"Were you hurt in that traffic crash?"

"Yes."

"What happened to you?"

"I broke my right arm."

Jesse could already guess why Hall specifically said her right arm. "Did it hurt?"

"Yes, very much so."

"Did you go to the hospital?"

"Yes. They took me in an ambulance."

"Did the doctors give you pain medication?" Jesse was considering objecting to all of the leading questions, but ultimately it did not matter because this information was going to come out anyway.

"Yes."

"Did the pain medication help you?"

"Well," she faltered, "it helped some, but I was still in a lot of pain. I don't remember a whole lot because the pain medicine kind of put me out of it."

"What do you mean, 'put you out of it?'"

"Well, I was real sleepy and kind of just in a fog. I didn't really know what was going on."

"What happened when you were discharged from the hospital?"

"They took me to jail."

"Did you get to have a full night's rest?"

"No."

"Why not?"

"Because two police men came and talked to me."

"So, you had just been in a traffic crash, where you broke your arm and had been loaded up with pain medication at the hospital, taken to the jail and then interrogated by two armed officers?" Jesse could have objected on several grounds, but let it slide. She did take note about how smooth Dasher was about changing innocent words of his client, like, 'talk' to 'interrogate.' She would have to remember that for when they were in front of the jury.

"Yes. I thought they were Kentucky police men because they didn't tell me who they were."

"So they were not in uniform?"

"No. They were in regular clothes, but they did have guns and stuff."

"Were you scared?

Jesse stood up. "Objection, leading." She refrained from adding in a speaking objection that she had been letting Dasher get away with leading the defendant, but had now had enough. Being in her hometown, she knew Judge Doverman frowned upon speaking objections.

"Mr. Dasher, response?" The Judge looked at the defense attorney.

"I'll rephrase, Your Honor."

Jesse knew exactly how he was going to rephrase the question. It was an old defense attorney trick – ask the leading question with the answer you want in the question and then after an objection is sustained re-ask the question as an open-ended question. The witness will always answer with the answer that was suggested in the first place.

"Kerri, how did two armed officers interrogating you make you feel?"

"I was scared."

Jesse knew the Judge would see through the answer, so she was not concerned.

"So tell the Judge what happened when the officers came and

interrogated you."

"Well, I hadn't been at the jail long. They had already made me put on an orange jump suit and took me to a cell. Then, as soon as I laid down, they came and got me and took me into a small room where the two officers were."

"Did you get to sleep at all?"

"No, I was exhausted, but they came and got me before I had a chance to sleep any."

"What did the officers tell you when you were taken into the room?"

Jesse stood again. "Objection, hearsay." Even though the answer to this question didn't matter, Jesse did not want to set the tone that she was going to allow a lot of hearsay to come in through the defendant's testimony. Many people use the word hearsay in everyday language, but hardly anyone knew what it actually meant, including some attorneys. Hearsay is a statement, other than one made by the declarant while testifying at the trial or hearing, offered in evidence to prove the truth of the matter asserted.

"Judge, both of the officers are here and will testify, so it is not hearsay."

Jesse quickly responded, "Your Honor, Florida Statute 90.801 clearly defines a statement that is not hearsay." Jesse was looking at her cheat sheet that had all of the Florida Evidence Code listed on it. "Paragraph two clearly states, 'A statement is not hearsay if the declarant testifies at the trial or hearing and is subject to cross-examination concerning the statement and the statement is: (a)

Inconsistent with the declarant's testimony and was given under oath subject to the penalty of perjury at a trial, hearing, or other proceeding or in a deposition; (b) Consistent with the declarant's testimony and is offered to rebut an express or implied charge against the declarant of improper influence, motive, or recent fabrication; or (c) One of identification of a person made after perceiving the person.' None of the subparagraphs, 'a,' 'b' or 'c' apply in this circumstance."

Ronald Dasher started to respond, but the Judge held up his hand and said, "I'll allow it, but will only give it the weight that it is worth."

The ruling irritated Jesse because that ruling was not a proper ruling. There was no exception to hearsay to 'give it the weight it is worth,' but nearly all of the judges she appeared in front of gave that response. What Jesse didn't know is that the judges talked about ruling on hearsay exceptions at the various judicial colleges that they attended. Judges statewide made this type of ruling, though it had absolutely zero legal bearing.

"Okay, Kerri, you can answer the question now." Dasher beamed at his client.

"I'm sorry, what was the question?" Hall truly did have a look of confusion on her face. Perhaps Jesse needed to change her strategy and start objecting more because it seemed as though interjecting objections was throwing Hall off of her script.

"Most certainly. What did the officers tell you when you were taken into the room?"

"Oh, right. Well, nothing really. They just started asking me questions."

"Kerri, do you know what I mean when I say, "Miranda Warning?""

"No, not really."

"Did the officers advise you that you did not have to talk to them and that you could have an attorney present?"

"I don't remember them doing that."

Hall's response made Jesse mad. She knew that this hearing was about to turn into flat out lies.

"Now Kerri, we have received discovery from the government, right?" Dasher asked.

Jesse noticed that he called the prosecution, 'the government.' It was yet another tactic that defense attorneys usually used in front of juries, but typically did not do in front of judges. Perhaps some local attorneys had given Dasher bum advice about the Judge's political background.

"Yes, that's the police reports, right?"

"Yes, that's right, Kerri." Dasher walked over to his table and thumbed through a file before pulling a paper from within. He briefly held it up in front of Jesse' face as he walked back to the lectern. "Kerri, I'm going to show you a piece of paper, okay?" Dasher looked at the Judge. "May I approach the witness?"

"You may," Judge Doverman responded.

"Do you recognize this?" Dasher was not creating a good record because he did not identify the exhibit number that he was referring to when he asked his client the question.

"Yes."

"How do you recognize it?"

"You showed it to me."

"Before I showed it to you, had you ever seen this before?"

"No, I don't think so."

"Now, look at the bottom here, okay? There is a signature line. Is that your signature?"

"No, it is not."

Dasher turned to the Judge and said, "Defense moves defense Exhibit 1 into evidence."

The Judge looked at Jesse and asked, "Any objection?"

"No, Your Honor, no objection." Technically, Jesse could have objected because Dasher did not lay the proper foundation, but Jesse was going to move a copy of the Miranda Waiver into evidence anyway, so she did not object.

"Kerri, do you remember the interrogation with the officers?"

"Not a whole lot, like I said, I was really tired and drugged up."

Dasher gave a nearly imperceptible start. "By drugged up, you mean that you had pain medication administered to you, right?"

"Yes. Yes, of course. That is what I meant."

"Is there anything that you do remember about the interrogation?"

"Yes."

"And what is that?"

"I asked for a lawyer."

"Really?" Dasher feigned surprise.

"Yes."

"How is it that you remember asking for a lawyer?"

207

"Well, two things really. First, as you know, my father is a successful businessman. My whole life, I've heard him say, 'My lawyer this, my lawyer that.' Whenever anything started to not go his way, he always said that he was going to call his lawyer. So, it just made sense that I was in jail, so I should call my dad's lawyer."

"Okay, and what is the second thing that makes you remember asking for a lawyer?"

"Well, this one is a little silly, but I watch a lot of T.V. and you always see the bad guy ask for a lawyer." She recognized her poor choice of words. "I mean, you know, the person that the police arrest; they always ask for a lawyer."

"Did the police officers stop interrogating you when you asked for a lawyer?"

"No."

"How can you be certain?"

"Well, in the stuff the prosecutor gave you, there is a video of the second time they came and talked to me and they talked about the first interview and I seemed at the time to remember what they were talking about. So, from watching the video, it kind of makes it to where I just know that they kept asking me questions."

Jesse could not believe Hall's answer. The defense just opened the door to her bringing in the video tape of the second interview. That was good because the detectives talked to Kerri about the first interview while they were conducting the second taped interview. Jesse knew the worst thing about this whole case was that neither detective recorded the initial interview. If the interview had taken place at the criminal division at the local sheriff's office, then the entire thing would have been audio and video recorded. They had a special interview room set up to where the camera started rolling as soon as the lights came on. But, seeing as how the detectives traveled hundreds of miles to conduct this interview, it was understandable that they did not have a digital recorder or even a tape recorder with them. At least that was what Jesse was going to argue to the Judge.

"Did the officers promise you anything?"

"Yes."

"What did they promise you?"

"They were saying something about charging me with a misdemeanor or maybe even nothing at all if I talked to them; that I could help myself out."

"So they didn't tell you that they were planning on charging you with murder?"

"No! Not at all."

"Why did you keep talking to the police?"

"They made it seem like if I talked to them, nothing would happen to me."

"Nothing further, Your Honor." Dasher sat down.

The Judge turned to Jesse, "Cross?"

Jesse stood and gathered her notepad and pen. "Yes, Your Honor, thank you." Jesse walked over to the lectern where Dasher had just been standing. She faced the defendant and smiled. She was going to start off with easy, rosy-path questions. "Ms. Hall, you were at the hospital before going to the jail, right?"

"Yes."

"You broke your right wrist?"

"Yes."

"The doctor bandaged up your whole arm, right?"

"Yes."

"That must have been hard for you, wasn't it?"

"Yes."

"You are right handed?"

"Yes."

Jesse was done laying the foundation for more questions that she would ask later, so she moved on. "Two detectives came to talk to you at the jail, right?"

"Yes."

"They introduced themselves to you."

"I don't remember that." Hall responded.

"They told you that they were going to ask you some questions."

"I don't remember."

"The detectives were not wearing a uniform with a full gun belt like the bailiff over there, were they?"

Hall looked over at the bailiff and shook her head no.

"You have to answer out loud, Ms. Hall. The court reporter is typing everything being said and she can't take down you nodding or shaking your head."

Hall quickly leaned forward and responded, "No" in to the microphone.

"Even though they did not have a uniform on, they did have

210

badges on their belts, didn't they?"

"Um, I'm not sure."

"You had no doubt that they were law enforcement officers, did you?"

"No. I knew they were cops."

"They never pulled their guns out of their holsters, did they?"

"No."

"They just sat down and talked to you, right?"

"Yes."

"They never raised their voices at you, did they?"

"No, I don't think so."

"Detective Wescott took a card out and read from it, didn't he?"

"I don't remember that."

Jesse just looked at her before going on. "Really?" She asked incredulously. "You're telling me that you do not remember Detective Wescott reading from a card to you."

"No, I don't remember that at all."

Just in case Hall was playing with semantics, Jesse phrased it another way, "Do you remember either detective reading to you from a card?"

Hall paused for a moment and looked furtively at her attorney. "Um, maybe. Maybe one of them did."

Jesse was now on to the plan between defendant and defense attorney. She would have bet anything that Dasher had advised his client to be less than forthcoming in this area. It was an easy out and a way to get out of a perjury charge if Hall claimed confusion as to the

211

names of the detectives. Jesse would have to be more careful in how she phrased her cross examination questions. "You have heard of the Miranda Warning before, haven't you?"

"I don't know."

"Well, you told the detectives that you knew your Miranda Rights, didn't you?"

Hall looked like she was caught between a rock and a hard place. "I might have said something about my rights." Hall looked at her attorney for approval.

Jesse decided to ease up a bit and ask some softball questions. "Ms. Hall, you watch crime shows on TV, right?"

Hall looked a little surprised by the question. "Um, sure."

"You've seen the police officers on television reading the 'rights' to the perpetrators."

"Yes. That is what I said earlier."

"Sometimes the bad guy asks for an attorney, right?"

"Yes."

"And the TV officers stop questioning?"

"Yes." She paused. "Well, sometimes yes."

"The detectives had you sign a form stating that they read you your rights."

"No, I don't think so."

"You told them that you wouldn't sign it."

Hall was surprised at the way the question was asked and decided to change tracks on the spot. "That's right."

"In actuality, you were playing a joke on the detectives because

212

you broke your right arm."

"I don't understand the question."

"Your right hand, wrist and arm was bandaged at the hospital, right?"

"Yes."

"Normally you use your right hand to write, don't you?"

Suddenly it dawned on Hall where Jesse was going with the questioning. She answered it in a slightly lower tone, "Yes."

"You ultimately used your left hand to sign the form."

Hall looked at her attorney again. He just stared back at her, not daring to get caught giving his client assistance during her testimony. "Um, I don't remember."

"Let me show you Defense Exhibit 1 again." Jesse walked over to the Deputy Clerk and picked up the exhibit. She looked at the Judge and asked, "May I approach the witness, Your Honor?"

"You may," the Judge responded.

"Ms. Hall. Take a good hard look at Defense Exhibit 1." Jesse held it in front of the defendant's face. "Is it your testimony that you did *not* sign this form with your left hand?"

"I don't remember signing it." Hall wasn't budging.

Jesse had proven her point, so she moved on, asking the next question as she walked over to the Deputy Clerk to return the exhibit. "You never specifically said that you wanted a lawyer, did you?"

"I asked for a lawyer, yes."

"Ms. Hall, were not your exact words, 'I think I should talk to a lawyer'?"

"I don't remember my exact words, but that is asking for a lawyer no matter how you look at it."

Jesse was pleased with that response and would address it in argument, but wanted to go a little further. "So if the detectives come in here and say that you said, 'I think I should talk to a lawyer,' they would not be lying?"

Hall thought about her answer. She didn't understand what the trick behind the question was. "I asked for a lawyer. I do not remember my exact words."

Jesse decided to leave it alone. There was plenty of fertile ground for closing argument. "Ms. Hall, the detectives never promised you anything for talking to them, did they?"

"Yes."

"Really?" Jesse acted surprised. "So you are saying the detectives promised that you would not be charged?

"Yes, basically."

"In actuality, the detectives never promised to make your charges go away, did they?"

"Yes, they did."

"Ms. Hall, the detectives repeatedly told you that they did not know what would happen to you, didn't they?"

"They said if I talked to them that I would help myself. That it was self-defense, so I wouldn't be charged."

Jesse was actually surprised that she got that much of a response out of Hall. "Actually, didn't they tell you that *if* you were acting in self-defense that you *may* not be charged?"

Hall exclaimed, "It's all the same thing!"

Jesse had enough for the record and for legal argument, so she saved her favorite question for last, "You were under the influence of methamphetamine when you were taken to the hospital, weren't you?"

Ronald Dasher quickly stood up while simultaneously slapping the table. "Objection, Your Honor. Prejudicial, beyond the scope and relevance. I never talked about anything like that during direct."

The Judge just looked at Jesse for her response.

Jesse responded, "Your Honor, during direct, Ms. Hall responded, and I quote, 'I was really tired and drugged up.'"

Dasher interrupted, "At which time I clarified with her that by drugged up she meant with pain medication."

Normally Jesse would have been peeved at a defense attorney interrupting her, but was actually glad that Dasher pointed it out that he was the one that clarified pain medication, thereby directing his client's response. "Exactly, Your Honor. I would submit to the Court that Ms. Hall opened the door with her initial response and it was not until defense counsel led her in the direction that he wanted to take her that she gave the response about pain medication that was prescribed for her at the hospital." Jesse took a deep breath, "Additionally, Your Honor, this goes to the very core of the defense motion. The law in Florida is very well established that voluntary intoxication is not a defense. If the defendant was under the influence of methamphetamine, of her own accord, she cannot then turn and use her illegal action as a defense against a statement that she gave to the detectives."

"Your Honor," Dasher interjected just as the Judge was about to speak. "Absolutely nothing has been said about use of methamphetamine, it is simply beyond the scope of direct examination."

The Judge looked at Dasher and said, "Your objection is overruled."

Dasher quickly came back, "Your Honor, I also object on the basis of self-incrimination. My client cannot be compelled to testify against herself." Dasher didn't want his client to admit to using methamphetamine.

The Judge glanced at the Indictment and said to Dasher, "I do not see that she has been charged with a drug crime in Florida, so how could her answer be self-incriminating?"

Jesse just stood there and enjoyed the show.

"Your Honor, my client was charged with possession of methamphetamine in Kentucky. For her to testify about using methamphetamine, would just incriminate her." Even Dasher recognized his circular argument.

"Ms. Bradshaw? Do you wish to be heard?"

"Yes, Your Honor. While it is a crime to possess methamphetamine, it is not a crime to consume, or to have consumed methamphetamine. The mere fact that the defendant had methamphetamine in her system does not go to prove or disprove whether she possessed the methamphetamine in her purse, where it was found. Quite frankly, the usage itself would be inadmissible any way you look at these facts."

"You're getting into facts that I do not know about." The Judge paused and went on, "Disregarding the comment about drugs in the purse, I find that the question about methamphetamine usage may be asked, but do not ask anything about what, if anything, was found in her purse or about any pending charges in Kentucky."

"Certainly, Your. Honor." Jesse turned back to the defendant. "Ms. Hall, before you were taken to the jail, you had been using methamphetamine, hadn't you?"

Hall quickly weighed her options. She didn't know the law, but she was pretty sure if she lied, that the prosecutor would pull out her blood work from the hospital, which showed methamphetamine in her system. She knew the prosecution had her blood work because a copy had been given to her attorney in discovery. Not knowing what else she could do, Hall responded, "Yes."

Jesse announced to the Judge, "Nothing further, Your Honor."

The Judge turned to Ronald Dasher and asked, "Do you have any further re-direct?"

Dasher stood where he was rather than walking back to the lectern, "Just briefly, Your Honor." He then turned to his client, "Kerri, if the officers hadn't promised you that you wouldn't be charged, you wouldn't have – "

"Objection!" Jesse was on her feet. "Leading! This is re-direct, not cross examination." She broke her own rule of a speaking objection in front of Judge Doverman. At least it wasn't a really long speaking objection.

The Judge didn't even give Dasher a chance to respond. "Mr.

Dasher, you know better than that," he said in a dolling voice.

"Your Honor, I - ," Dasher stopped midsentence and reconsidered what he was going to say. "Nevermind." He faced his client again, "Kerri, why did you talk to the police?"

Hall looked at the Judge. "Because, they made me think that I had to."

"Nothing further, Your Honor."

The Judge looked at Jesse. "Re-cross?"

Jesse stood, "No, Your Honor."

Judge Doverman looked at Hall and said, "You may step down."

The bailiff once again stood between Kerri Hall and the court reporter as Hall stepped out of the witness box and shuffled back to her seat.

"Next witness," the Judge said.

Dasher stood to address the Court. "No further witnesses at this time, Your Honor. It is the defense position that we have presented a sufficient showing that the statement made by my client was not voluntary. Therefore, the burden should now shift to the State."

"Ms. Bradshaw, your position?" The Judge asked.

"Your Honor, while the State does not concede that the defense has presented a credible showing that the statement made by the defendant was involuntary, in the interest of judicial economy, I will just go ahead and call my witnesses so you can get a full picture of what actually transpired."

Dasher snapped back, "Your Honor, I object to the characterizations in Ms. Bradshaw's argument. This isn't argument

218

and it is not proper."

The Judge looked at Dasher, "Duly noted, Mr. Dasher. I've been doing this quite a while and I know when to give weight to a statement or argument and when I should not. With no further defense witnesses, State get ready to call your first witness. I've received a message from my judicial assistant that I have an important telephone call to return. We will be in recess for ten minutes."

With that announcement, the Judge stood up and walked out his private entrance behind the bench.

Jesse stood and turned around. Mark McCullers was still sitting in the front row. "Hey, you stayed?" she asked.

"Of course. I wouldn't miss any part of this case. I wouldn't want to do anything that would disadvantage my client." He looked over to make sure Ronald Dasher was still in conversation with his client and then stepped up closer to the banister and leaned in to whisper to Jesse, "Plus, I kind of like the view from where I'm sitting."

Jesse immediately blushed and whispered back, "Shut up. I can't believe you are saying something like that in open court. Digital recording is still running and I know from personal experience that it can pick up voices, even as far away as you are."

"Eh, I'm not worried. Besides, no one would ever listen to it unless you draw their attention to it; which if you keep it up, you will definitely do so."

Jesse took a quick glance around the room. One bailiff was talking to the court reporter and the other was still sitting next to the defendant. The Deputy Clerk was typing something on her computer.

No one seemed to be paying them any attention. "Okay, fine. You win. Just please don't say stuff like that in public in the future. You know how paranoid I am about us getting discovered."

He smiled at her. "I know, but sometimes I can't resist."

"Okay, I need a couple of minutes to gather my thoughts before I put on my witnesses. You are too much of a distraction." She smiled at him.

"All right, I will leave you alone. I'll just sit here and enjoy the view." He grinned, "I mean show. I will enjoy the rest of the show."

14

The recess ended up being a full thirty minutes before Judge Doverman took the bench again. As he came in he dismissively waved his hands at everyone to indicate that they should remain seated. The time delay didn't really matter to Jesse; she was ready to proceed with the testimony of the officers.

Judge Doverman looked at Jesse and said, "Ms. Bradshaw, I believe we left off with you about to call your first witness, correct?"

Jesse stood, "Yes, Your Honor. The state calls Detective Doug Wescott."

The bailiff at the rear of the courtroom stepped out into the hallway and brought the detective in. Without being told, Doug went directly to the witness stand and sat down since he had already been sworn in.

Jesse stepped up to the lectern and laid out her notebook with her questions. "Good morning, will you please state your name for the record."

"My name is Douglas Wescott."

Jesse had to get all of the background questions out of the way before she could go into the substantive issues. "Where do you work?"

"I work at the Columbia County Sheriff's Office."

"What is your position?"

"I am a detective."

"How long have you been a detective?"

"I have been a detective for fifteen years."

"Are you assigned to any particular unit?"

"We are a small agency, so we do not really have explicit units, such as white collar, drug and homicide."

"I see. What training did you have to go through in order to become an deputy?"

"I actually went to college and majored in criminal justice. I am from this area, so I moved back to Columbia County after graduation and started working for the sheriff's office. While working there, I attended a basic recruit training program and then took the State Officer Certification Examination. I passed the exam and became a sworn deputy."

"How many years total have you been at the sheriff's office?"

"I have worked there twenty years. The first five, I was a road deputy."

"During your employment at the sheriff's office, have you had the occasion to undergo any further training?"

"Yes, all officers have to undergo further training. Mine has included over 1,000 hours in drug investigation, domestic violence and homicide investigation, amongst various other topics."

"What about any training in interview techniques?" Jesse and Doug had already gone over his testimony prior to him testifying and he was supposed to have included his training in interview techniques in his last answer.

"Yes, of course. I've had many hours of training in interview techniques as well." He reached down to his brief case and held it up. "I have certificates from most of my courses available if you want to see them."

"No, that is okay. Mr. Dasher may want to examine them, but I trust you." Jesse was sending a subliminal message to the Judge. Jesse went on, "Over the course of your career, how many interviews would you say you have conducted?"

"I can't really say for certain, but it is definitely more than ten thousand."

"How are you able to make that determination?"

"Well, I've been working for twenty years, so even if I just conducted one interview a day, that would be seventy-three hundred interviews. I definitely average more than one interview a day. Even as a road deputy, I encountered more than one citizen a day and every contact is like an interview."

Jesse didn't want to get bogged down into the details of his math because it was not really relevant to where she wanted to go with her questioning. "Do you have any particular technique that you follow when you conduct an interrogation?"

"Yes."

"Could you explain that technique to the Judge?"

Doug turned to face Judge Doverman since he was about to give a narrative response. "In the context of an actual interrogation, I always

223

start with going over the Miranda Warning. I first read the warning to the individual and then ask if they understand what I've just read. I also hand a written copy to them that has the Miranda Warning written out, so they can read it for themselves if they want. At the bottom of that copy is a signature line which acknowledges that they have been advised of the Miranda Warning."

Jesse switched tracks to be case specific. "Detective Wescott, do you know an individual by the name, Kerri Hall?"

"Yes, I do."

"How did you come to know Ms. Hall?"

"During the course of the investigation of the murder of Dean Witherington, Detective Newsome and I travelled to Elizabethtown, Kentucky. While there, Ms. Hall was apprehended and we interviewed her at the local jail."

"Do you see Ms. Hall in the courtroom today?"

"Yes, she is seated at counsel's table, next to Mr. Dasher."

"Could you further identify her by an article of clothing?" This part was unnecessary during this type of motion, but Jesse just wanted to point out that Kerri Hall was wearing the unmistakable jail-orange jumpsuit.

"Sure, she is wearing the orange jumpsuit."

Jesse turned to the Judge, "May the record reflect the witness has identified the defendant."

Judge Doverman dryly responded, "It shall so reflect."

"Is the procedure that you outlined to us earlier the same procedure you followed when you interviewed Kerri Hall in Kentucky?"

"Yes. I believe I spoke to her very briefly about her banged up arm." Doug faltered a moment, thinking that he could have said something wrong. "Uh, when I say that, I mean that I just asked how she was feeling. Seeing as how she had just been in a wreck and all."

"Prior to administering the Miranda Warning, did you question Ms. Hall about anything dealing with the murder of Dean Witherington?"

"No."

"Did Ms. Hall sign the acknowledgement form?"

"Yes, but not at first."

"What do you mean?" Jesse asked.

"Well, she made a joke out of not signing the form. Eventually I realized she refused to sign because her writing hand was bandaged up. I asked her to at least make an 'X' with her other hand and she complied by writing her name with her other hand."

Jesse asked, "Did Ms. Hall acknowledge that she understood her rights?"

Doug responded, "Other than her little joke that I just referenced, yes, she indicated that she understood her rights."

"Tell me about Ms. Hall's demeanor throughout the interview."

"Well, she was definitely more compliant than she was at the scene of the crash."

"What do you mean?" Jesse asked.

"Well, she was not cooperative at all at the scene of the crash. Once we were at the jail, I guess you could say she was pretty meek and mild."

Jesse was glad that Dasher didn't make a big deal out of Doug referencing Hall's behavior at the crash site, seeing as how Doug wasn't even there. She moved on before he could object. "Was she responsive to your questions?"

"Most certainly. In fact, she engaged in quite a bit of conversation."

"Was she physically alert?"

Dasher was on his feet, "Objection, leading."

Jesse didn't wait for a ruling, she volunteered, "I'll rephrase, Your Honor." She turned back to Doug. "Detective Wescott, could you go into more detail regarding Ms. Hall's demeanor – both physical and mental."

"Sure. The worst thing that could be said is that she was tired. But so was I. It had been a long day for all of us."

"Did that affect her ability to answer your questions?"

Dasher stood again, "Objection, speculation."

Judge Doverman looked at Jesse.

Jesse was going to fight this objection, "Your Honor, I am not asking the witness to speculate as to anything dealing with Ms. Hall. I am simply asking the witness, whether in his opinion Ms. Hall was able to answer his questions."

Judge Doverman ruled, "Phrasing the question as just stated is fine, but do not go into what Ms. Hall was thinking."

"Yes, Your Honor." Jesse turned back to Doug, "Was Ms. Hall able to answer your questions despite her appearance of being tired?"

"Yes, absolutely."

226

"When I say, was she able to answer your questions, I specifically mean, was she able to answer responsively to the question that was asked?"

"Most definitely. In fact, she engaged in a back and forth conversation. She was even witty at times."

"Did Ms. Hall appear to be under the influence of any controlled substance?"

Dasher stood yet again, "Objection, calls for speculation, Your Honor." His voice grew louder as he said, 'Your Honor.'

Jesse responded, "Judge, Detective Wescott is trained in the enforcement of drugs as well. He has been an officer for twenty years and around plenty of people that are under the influence. Additionally, he is a drug recognition expert, which requires even more training."

Judge Doverman responded, "While that may be true, you and I both know that information from other hearings, you have not established that predicate at this time. The objection is sustained, with leave to explore again once the proper background is laid."

Jesse immediately turned to Doug and asked, "Does your training include being a drug recognition expert?" She couldn't believe that she didn't notice that he did not volunteer that information earlier in the questioning. That objection came as a direct result of not paying enough attention to Doug's responses; instead, she was looking ahead to her next question. Quite a rooky mistake!

"Yes."

"What does it mean to be a drug recognition expert?"

"In order to be a drug recognition expert, or 'DRE,' you have to go through an eighty hour specialized training course. You are trained to evaluate suspects to determine if they are impaired, what drug category is causing the impairment and whether a medical condition is causing the impairment."

"How long have you been a DRE?"

"I've been certified for ten years."

"Are you currently certified as a DRE?"

"Yes."

"Were you also certified as a DRE at the time you conducted the interview in Kentucky with Kerri Hall?"

"Yes."

"Now I ask you again, Detective Wescott, did Kerri Hall appear to be under the influence of any controlled substance at the time of the first interview?" Jesse turned and stared at Ronald Dasher, daring him to stand up and object.

Dasher complied with Jesse' challenge, "Your Honor, I must object again. This witness is not competent to testify as to his opinion."

"Ms. Bradshaw?" Judge Doverman inquired.

"Your Honor, we are not in front of a jury. But, if the Court so desires, I tender this witness as an expert in the field of drug recognition, to include being able to assess whether a person is under the influence and to determine what is causing the impairment, as well as whether it is a medical condition causing the impairment." Jesse thought she could detect a smirk on the judge's face.

"The Court does not desire anything, Ms. Bradshaw." He turned to

Mr. Dasher, "Do you wish to voir dire regarding this officer's training as a drug recognition expert?"

"No, Your Honor." The wind was taken out of Ronald Dasher's sails.

"Then without objection, Detective Wescott will be allowed to render an opinion as a drug recognition expert, including the assessment of whether a person is under the influence, what is causing the impairment and whether the impairment is being caused by a medical condition." Judge Doverman never recognized witnesses as an "expert," not even when it was a bench trial or hearing; instead, he just allowed the witness to render an opinion, which was the whole purpose of having a witness qualified as an expert.

Jesse now phrased her question slightly differently, "Detective Wescott, in your opinion, was Kerri Hall under the influence of any controlled substance at the time of the first interview?"

"No."

Jesse went on, "In your opinion, was Kerri Hall impaired in any way at the time of the first interview?"

"No."

"In your opinion, was any sort of a medical condition causing any impairment?"

"No. But with that said, I could tell she was in a little pain, but not to the extent that she was non-responsive to my questioning."

Jesse didn't care for the commentary that Doug added on, but let it slide, instead asking, "Was there anything about Ms. Hall's demeanor or presentation that made you think her statement was not knowingly,

229

voluntarily and intelligently made?"

Dasher started to stand to object, but decided to save it for argument instead.

Doug responded to the question, "No."

Jesse moved on to the next area of the defense's motion. "Detective Wescott, did you or Detective Newsome make any promises to Ms. Hall during the initial interview?"

"No, not at all."

"Was there any discussion about a deal?"

"No, not about a deal." He went on, "Now, I did talk to her about what type of charges she could be facing if what she was telling us was true, but I never told her she would get a specific deal or that she would be charged with anything less than murder. The bottom line is that I told her the State would make the ultimate charging decision."

Not seeing any point in going further in that area of the defense's motion, Jesse went on to the final area of attack. "Detective Wescott, did Ms. Hall ever ask for an attorney?"

Doug paused before explaining, "No, she never explicitly said that she wanted an attorney."

"Did she talk about an attorney at all?"

"Yes."

"What were her exact words?"

"She said, 'I think I should talk to a lawyer.'"

Jesse knew that Ronald Dasher would hammer Doug on this point, so she wanted to soften the blow a little, "How do you remember exactly what she said?"

Doug had his answer pre-planned and was ready for the question. "I am always extremely sensitive when the suspect even utters the word 'attorney' or 'lawyer.' She did not specifically say that she wanted a lawyer, just that she *thought* that she should talk to a lawyer. I have had training and discussions with the State Attorney's Office before about what is an equivocal versus unequivocal request for a lawyer. Ms. Hall made an equivocal statement and I'm not under any obligation to clarify what she meant by *thinking* that she needed a lawyer."

Jesse was satisfied with the response, but wanted to clear up one more damaging area before cross examination began. "Detective Wescott, did you record this interview?"

"No."

"Why not?"

"If we had been in our own jurisdiction, recording would not have been a problem. However, we were at a different agency. I guess we just made an assumption that the interview room had a camera." The comment about making an assumption would open the door for some scathing cross-examination from Ronald Dasher.

Doug went on, "When we found out that the first interview was not recorded, we made arrangements to conduct the second interview in a room that had a video camera. We used the intoxilyzer room when we came back to interview the defendant the next day."

"Thank you, detective. I don't have any more questions for you." Jesse turned to Judge Doverman, "Your Honor, I tender this witness for cross examination."

15

Ronald Dasher made a show out of briskly walking up to the lectern and going right into questioning. "Mr. Wescott, so it's your testimony that every contact is an interrogation, right?"

Doug paused and thought before answering, "Not really – I said that every contact is like an interview."

"So that is how you are coming to your number of saying that you have interviewed at least seventy-three hundred people a year."

"In coming to that rough estimate, sir, I am accounting for all citizen contacts. Even if - "

Dasher cut him off and quickly said, "Oh so you are now lumping in citizen contacts?"

Jesse stood as fast as she could and said "Objection, Your Honor. Counsel is not allowing the witness to answer the question."

The Judge looked at Ronald Dasher for a response.

Dasher simply said, "Judge, he will get every opportunity to say what he wants. If not on cross, then on re-direct."

Judge Doverman admonished, "Let the witness answer the questions you ask fully and completely. If he is not responsive, then you may ask for intervention from the court."

Dasher was not pleased, but answered, "Yes, Your Honor." He turned back to the witness and went right back to his last question, still not recognizing that the witness was not done with his last response. "So, Mr. Wescott in coming to your *rough estimate* you are lumping in all citizen encounters, not just interviews, correct?"

"Yes sir."

"Now a citizen encounter could be as simple as you just seeing someone and saying hello, correct?"

"No sir."

"No?" Dasher feigned astonishment. "So, if you encounter a citizen on the street and say hello, that is not a citizen encounter?"

"No sir, not in the context of what I meant by citizen encounter. In the plain meaning of the words, sure, but I mean when I actually have conversation with the citizen other than small chit chat."

Dasher said with a smirk, "So your definition is a moving target. I see."

Doug started to try to answer to that comment, but Dasher went on to the next question too quickly.

"In coming to your estimation of seventy–three hundred interviews, you did what? Multiplied twenty years times three hundred and sixty-five days a year?"

"Yes sir, just as a way to come to a rough estimate."

"Now it is fair to say that you do not work every day out of the year, correct?"

"Yes sir."

"In fact, at most, you only work five days a week, right?"

"As a detective, yes sir. I work five days a week."

"So, there are fifty-two weeks in a year, multiplied by five actual working days, so your total per year is actually two hundred and sixty a year, not three hundred and sixty-five, right?"

"Sir, I interview multiple people in any given day. You are correct that I should have done my math differently, but I don't claim to be a mathematician. However, factoring in that I interview more than one person a day, I stand by my estimate that I previously gave."

Dasher knew better than to get into a pissing match over math. "But you would agree detective, that an interview is not the same as an interrogation?"

"Yes and no." Doug answered.

"Oh really? Yes *and* no?"

"Yes sir. In general, interviews do not become antagonistic; they are simply interviews of people who are not suspects in a crime, but may have information leading to an arrest for a crime that they witnessed or have some information about. An actual interrogation deals with a suspect. I approach the two differently."

"So the bottom line is that you have far fewer interrogations than you do interviews?"

"As far as raw numbers, yes sir. But the technique used in questioning citizens and suspects is similar."

Dasher finally realized he was belaboring a minute point, so he moved on. "Now you said that Ms. Hall did not suffer any sort of medical condition causing any impairment, correct?"

"Yes sir."

234

"In fact, she had been in a car wreck and her right arm was in a temporary cast and a sling, was it not?"

"Yes sir."

"That certainly was an impairment, wasn't it?"

"Well, yes, I suppose so. But what I meant was she wasn't suffering a mental impairment based on her medical condition."

"We all heard what you said, Mr. Wescott. That she wasn't suffering from any impairment."

"I also said that she had a banged up arm." Doug quipped back.

Ronald Dasher gave Doug a scathing look and said, "Deputy, I will ask the questions here. Now, moving on to your testimony about not recording the interview – you said that you assumed that the room had a camera, correct?"

"Yes sir."

"So that is at least one assumption that you admit to making in this case?"

"That is the only assumption that I made in this case."

"You would agree, Mr. Wescott, that the best evidence of that happened during the interview would be a video tape, wouldn't you?"

"I have testified as to what happened in that room."

"That is not the question. Would you not agree that the best evidence would be a video recording so that every utterance, movement and comment could be viewed by this court?"

"Yes sir, a video recording would show all of that, but I have testified as to everything that is relevant."

"Ahhh! You have testified as to everything that is relevant. And *you*, the investigating officer, *you* are the one that determines what is relevant, aren't you?" Dasher's voice got louder with each word he uttered.

"I have responded to the questions that have been asked. I would be more than happy to answer all of your questions, sir." Doug said, '*sir*' with more than a hint of sarcasm.

"Well, I certainly appreciate that Mr. Wescott." Dasher gave a dose of sarcasm right back to Doug. "You would agree that Kerri was tired during the interview, wouldn't you?"

"I think that is fair to say."

"Well, she was yawning, wasn't she?"

"Yes sir, she did yawn. But then again, I probably did too."

"You were not with Kerri the entire day, were you?"

"No, sir."

"So you do not know how long she had been up by the time you started interrogating her."

"No, sir."

Dasher snatched his notepad off of the lectern and announced to the Judge, "No further questions, Your Honor."

It was all a bit too much of gamesmanship for Jesse, but she knew that the attorney was just putting on a dramatic show for his client. Jesse stood, not even waiting for the Judge to ask her if she had any re-direct. She went right into her questioning. "Detective Wescott, did Ms. Hall respond to your questions appropriately?"

"Yes, she did."

Jesse clarified, "By that, I mean - were her responses appropriate for the questions being asked. Not whether she gave the right answer, but if you asked her the time of day, did she respond with the time of day, not with the color of the sky?"

"Well, I never asked her the time of day, but yes, her answers to my questions were in response to the subject matter that I asked her about."

"Did Ms. Hall ever ask for you to stop questioning her so that she could get some rest?"

"No, she did not." Doug shot a look across the room at Dasher.

"Did Ms. Hall ever indicate that she would like to stop questioning and resume after the pain medication was out of her system."

"No, she did not."

"In your experience as a DRE, was Ms. Hall under the influence of either illegal or legal drugs to the extent that her normal faculties were impaired?"

"No."

"Specifically, when I say normal faculties, I am referring to the ability to see, hear, walk, talk, judge distances, make judgments and in general, the ability to perform the many mental and physical acts of our daily lives." Jesse had tried so many DUI cases in her career that she knew the jury instruction for defining "normal faculties" by heart. She recited it almost verbatim, leaving out only a couple of irrelevant terms.

"Yes, absolutely. She definitely had her normal faculties about her."

Jesse stepped back over to her table and announced to the Court,

237

"Nothing further, Your Honor."

Dasher quickly stepped back over to the lectern, firing off his first question before he even got there. "Mr. Wescott, you did not conduct a DUI investigation here, did you?"

"No."

"In fact, you did not administer any FSE's to my client, did you?"

"No sir, I did not administer any Field Sobriety Exercises to your client."

"Wouldn't you agree that in conducting a DUI investigation, you administer FSE's, to determine whether someone's normal faculties are impaired?"

"Yes sir, I do."

"But you didn't do that here."

"No, I did not." Doug said with finality.

Dasher turned to the Judge, "Nothing further, Your Honor."

Jesse quickly contemplated whether she should ask anything else of Doug, but decided against belaboring her point. Judge Doverman knew that her position was that Kerri Hall was not under the influence of any medication or illegal drugs to the extent that she was unresponsive to the questioning or was not able to make a voluntary waiver of her *Miranda* rights.

Judge Doverman inquired, "State, anything further of this witness?"

"No, Your Honor. He may step down, but we ask that he remain under subpoena."

Judge Doverman looked at Doug and said, "Detective, you may

step down at this time. The lawyers are done questioning you for now, but the State has asked that you remain under subpoena. As I admonished earlier, do not discuss this case or your testimony with anyone other than the lawyers." The Judge looked at Jesse, "Ms. Bradshaw, does Detective Wescott need to remain outside the courtroom or may he go about with his business and just remain on stand-by?"

Jesse had already spoken to Doug about staying at the courthouse. In fact, he wanted to so he could hear the closing arguments of counsel. "I'd ask that he remain in the courthouse, Your Honor. I have his cell number to be able to reach him if he would like to go somewhere other than the hallway."

"Not a problem, Your Honor. I will be right outside the door." Doug told the Judge as he stepped down from the witness stand.

Judge Doverman turned back to Jesse, "State, call your next witness."

"The State calls Detective Marty Newsome."

The bailiff stepped out into the hallway and brought Marty in.

Both Jesse's questions and the cross examination of Marty covered the same areas as Doug's testimony until Dasher harped on the detectives telling Kerri to *help herself out*.

Dasher asked Marty yet again, "Mr. Newsome, isn't it true that you repeatedly told my client that the only way she could help herself out was to talk to you?"

Marty replied, "No sir. Detective Wescott was the lead investigator, so he was asking the majority of the questions. Yes, those words were uttered that she could help herself out if she talked to us, but we never made any promises to her."

"So you admit that during the interrogation of my client, one of you told her that she could help herself out if she talked to you?"

Marty looked like a deer in the headlights for a moment before he responded, "Yes, but it was -"

Dasher cut him off, "Nothing further, Your Honor."

The Judge turned to Jesse, "State?"

"Detective Newsome, would you like to finish your response?" Jesse wanted to emphasize that Dasher was disregarding the Judge's earlier admonishment to let the witnesses finish their responses.

"Yes, what I was saying is that we did tell her that she could help herself out by talking to us, but it was in the context that it would look better for her if she cooperated with us. We didn't have the final say so, that is always up to the State, but we told her that it would be better for her if she talked to us before Sessions talked to us; that she shouldn't throw her life away to protect someone like him."

Jesse didn't care for all of the extra narrative that Marty added in, but she thought it was best to leave things as they were and just address it all in argument rather than eliciting any more testimony. "Nothing further, Your Honor."

In an exercise of great restraint, Dasher did something that defense attorneys rarely do, he resisted the temptation to re-cross Marty even more. Perhaps he was picking up on the Judge's irritation of jury trial tactics at a bench hearing. Dasher simply said to the Judge, "Nothing further from the defense."

240

Judge Doverman turned to Marty and said, "You may step down." He then turned to Jesse and asked, "Do you wish for Detective Newsome to remain subject to his subpoena as well?" Marty just stood there waiting for instructions on what to do.

Jesse responded, "Yes, Your Honor. However, the State will be resting as soon as I submit these hospital records into evidence. If Mr. Dasher does not have any further witnesses, I would ask that the Rule be lifted and both Detective Newsome and Detective Wescott be allowed to re-enter the courtroom to watch our closing arguments."

Dasher reached out, took the hospital report Jesse was referring to, and thumbed through it. "Your Honor, I object to this coming in."

The Judge asked Dasher, "legal basis for your objection?"

Dasher responded without a hint of a delay, "Your Honor, we have no way of knowing what this report means. Just because it says XY and Z doesn't mean that we know what XY and Z mean without an expert and the State obviously isn't putting on an expert."

Jesse knew Judge Doverman did not like speaking objections, but she was ready to respond as he looked at her. "Judge, prior to the hearing, I filed a Notice of Intent to Rely on Business Records. The business records certification is attached to Kerri Hall's hospital records. Therefore, there is not a legal basis to keep the records out of evidence. It is the state's contention that the exact quantity of the various substances in Kerri Hall's system do not matter. What does matter is that she had methamphetamine, a controlled substance in her system. The defense will be arguing that Ms. Hall was *in*voluntarily intoxicated. While the State does not agree that she was intoxicated at

241

all, if this Court should rule with the defense on that point, then this report will show Your Honor that Ms. Hall *voluntarily* had illegal substances in her system." She emphasized the word, voluntarily.

Dasher started back in without the Judge giving him the go ahead, "Your Honor, the State cannot sit here and honestly say that my client was intoxicated due to illegal drugs! This report doesn't tell us anything!"

Jesse asked, "Your Honor, may I briefly respond?"

"You may." Judge Doverman responded.

"Your Honor, the State has presented sufficient evidence to show that Ms. Hall was not intoxicated. That is something that we will address in final arguments. But for the instant objection, which I can only assume the defense is objecting to relevance, the hospital records are relevant to show that Ms. Hall also had illegal substances in her system - substances that she ingested voluntarily."

Judge Doverman didn't give Dasher another opportunity to speak. "The objection is overruled; the medical records will be admitted into evidence. Anything else before the State rests?" He asked both counsel.

Jesse remained standing as she said, "No, Your Honor."

The Judge turned to Dasher at which point Dasher quickly spoke up, "We don't have any more witnesses, Judge."

The Judge asked Dasher, "Any objection to the Rule being lifted so the witnesses can watch the arguments?"

Dasher dismissively responded, "No objection."

"Very well, bailiff, please step out and tell Detective Wescott that

242

he may return to the courtroom." Marty, who had just been standing in the courtroom while all of the legal argument was taking place quietly went to the gallery and took a seat. Judge Doverman then addressed both counsel, "Are both of you ready to proceed?"

Jesse and Dasher both responded in unison, "Yes, Your Honor."

"Fine, we will take a five minute recess. When I return, defense, you will go first since this is your motion. State, you will be given an opportunity to respond. During your arguments, please keep your arguments brief and to the point. If you are not able to concisely state your arguments, you will be given an opportunity to follow up in writing." That was Judge Doverman's way of saying keep it short.

Jesse was concerned about Judge Doverman making such a comment in a capital case, but quickly evaluated his comment as to its prejudicial effect and whether it could rise to the level of Kerri Hall ultimately raising an Ineffective Assistance of Counsel, or IAOC claim, after she was convicted. "Yes, Your Honor." It wasn't worth initiating that battle with the Judge, seeing as how he did offer both attorneys a chance to follow up in writing, if needed.

Dasher was slightly taken aback, but kept his cool. "Yes, Your Honor."

With that Judge Doverman stood and left the bench.

16

Doug returned to the courtroom and sat next to Marty in the gallery while Jesse started sorting her case law. She always kept like cases together so that as she addressed the case, she could hand a copy to opposing counsel and to the judge, while retaining a copy for herself. There was just something about having that particular procedural flair that she liked doing as opposed to some attorneys that just handed a stack of case law to the opposing counsel and the judge at the beginning of their argument or as they came to their first case.

It was not long before Judge Doverman returned to the bench and instructed the defense to begin their argument.

Ronald Dasher stood, without leaving his table and began, "Your Honor, there are multiple reasons as to why Ms. Hall's statement to police should be suppressed. First and foremost, my client was under the influence of pain medication lawfully administered by the hospital at the time of the interrogation; she was involuntarily intoxicated to the extent that she was not able to knowingly, voluntarily and freely waive her rights.

Florida Statute 775.051 states that voluntary intoxication is not a defense. However, it is a defense when the 'consumption, injection or use of a controlled substance under chapter 893 was pursuant to a lawful prescription issued to the defendant by a practitioner as defined in s. 893.02. As you can see in the State's own evidence, Ms. Hall had hydrocodone in her system, which was prescribed by her doctor at the hospital. Not only that, but the combined effects of being sleep deprived along with the hydrocodone rendered Ms. Hall unable to knowingly waive her rights.

Ms. Hall testified that she could not remember a whole lot of what happened the night the police interrogated her because she was so doped up on pain medication. She had just been in a car wreck that resulted in her arm being broken. Not only that, but she also said that she was tired because she had been up for a long time. It is well established that police cannot use sleep deprivation as a tactic to get a confession. That is essentially what happened here. Now I anticipate the state will come and argue that the officers did not cause the sleep deprivation, but the bottom line is that Ms. Hall was operating on no sleep and was under the influence of lawfully prescribed pain medication to the extent that she could not give a voluntary confession.

Furthermore, Ms. Hall did not knowingly, freely and voluntarily waive her rights because the police used undue influence through implied promises." Dasher handed a stack of cases to Jesse and to the bailiff so the bailiff could in turn hand them to the Judge. "Your Honor, I'm handing you several cases. The first of which is _State v. Cohen_, which is a 2001 Circuit Court case, cited as 2001 WL 34001052. That Court properly addressed the rule that 'In assessing 'voluntariness,' the court is required to consider whether, in light of 'the totality of the circumstances' surrounding the confession, coercive police activity or direct or implied promises produced that confession.' *Cohen* then cites to *Traylor v. State* and *Johnson v. State*.

Cohen goes on to state, 'To exclude a confession or an inculpatory statement, it is not necessary that any direct promises or threats be made to the accused. It is sufficient if the circumstance or declarations of those present are calculated to delude the prisoner as to his true position and exert an improper influence over his mind. A confession or inculpatory statement is not freely and voluntarily given if it has been elicited by direct or implied promises, however slight.' The court was citing *Johnson* again.

Here, you have two officers repeatedly telling a young, inexperienced girl that had never had any dealings with law enforcement before and that was also so tired and under the influence of pain medication that she could not even think straight, that she could *help herself out* if she just talked to them. When the officers first arrived, they never even told my client that they were from Florida, they used trickery to imply that they were Kentucky officers, there to ask her about the Kentucky charges.

Once the officers slyly worked the death of Mr. Witherington into the interrogation, they confused my client about what charges she could actually be facing. They strongly implied that she would be facing a misdemeanor, or perhaps no charges at all since it was obviously a self-defense case. It was due to those promises that my client actually talked about what allegedly happened down here in Florida.

I'd also like to turn the Court's attention to *Day v. State*, 29 So. 3d 1178, a Fourth DCA cases from 2010." Jesse noticed Judge Doverman shuffling through the stack of cases that Dasher previously provided, trying to find the correct case. Dasher went on, "Your Honor, in the *Day* case, the defendant's confession was involuntary because the investigator made constant offers of help, followed by requests for information. The investigator did not clarify the limits of her authority and implied that she had significant authority. That court found that there was a causal nexus between the investigator's statements throughout the interview and the defendant's confession.

Those facts are almost identical to what we have here. We have two cops that come in and interrogate a young, scared, medicated, inexperienced woman – they constantly say things to her that made her think they had the authority to only pursue a misdemeanor or perhaps no charges at all because it was self-defense. The officers never clarified that they were the ones that would ultimately decide the charges she would be arrested on and that the State would decide the ultimate sentencing decision.

On the last page of the case, the court in *Day* aptly noted, 'It must be remembered that confessions, as such, are equally inadmissible when they are the fruits of hope as when they are the product of fear.' That cites to *Rusher v. State*. The court goes on, 'In the present case, based on the totality of the circumstances, the many offers of help and the statements implying authority to influence the process rendered appellant's confession inadmissible as improper *fruits of hope*.'

Judge, if you look at the totality of the circumstances in this case,

247

you will clearly see that all of the officers' actions combined with the mental state of my client render her statement to police involuntary. If we were here talking about physical evidence to be suppressed, then we would be talking about *fruit of the poisonous tree* – that law enforcement did something that violated the Fourth Amendment and therefore found physical evidence. That physical evidence is fruit of the poisonous tree. Well the police are not rewarded for their misconduct in that situation, just as they should not be rewarded for their misconduct in this situation. Ms. Hall's statement is inadmissible as improper *fruits of hope*.

Your Honor, one of the basic rights of the good people of our country is the right to have an attorney present with them during an interrogation, or even any questioning by a law enforcement officer. There are two scenarios in which law enforcement should immediately stop talking to a suspect. The first is when the suspect says that they don't want to talk to the officer. Now granted, if the suspect re-engages the officers on his own accord, the officers can resume questioning, but that is not what we are talking about here. I'm talking about the second basic tenant – that once a person asks for an attorney, the officers should immediately *stop* the interrogation. Once those magic words are uttered, you cannot unring the bell. As soon as Kerri said that she would like an attorney, the officers should have stopped, but they kept going, which is such a clear violation of the law.

Looking at the totality of the circumstances, Your Honor, my client could not have knowingly, voluntarily and freely waived her *Miranda* rights. She was coerced into signing the waiver form, she was tricked

248

by the officers as to who they really were, she was sleep deprived, she was under the influence of pain medication, she was lied to about the charges that she was facing and she was denied her request for an attorney. Any single one of these reasons is enough to suppress her statement to police, but certainly, taken as a whole, looking at the totality of the circumstances, her statement should be suppressed."

He went on, "Had the officers simply recorded the interview, we would not be here today. In this day and age, there are recorders small enough to fit in a pen. In fact there are recorders small enough to fit in eyeglasses. Those types of recorders were readily available to the officers, but instead, in a case of this magnitude, in which the State is asking to put my client to death, they chose to go into that interrogation room without any sort of a recording device. So here we are today, without the best evidence of what transpired.

Judge, I ask that you suppress the statements my client made to law enforcement. Under the totality of the circumstances, she could not have knowingly, voluntarily and intelligently waived her *Miranda* rights. The officers denied her request for an attorney and promised her things in which they knew they had no authority to promise. Because the first statement was poisoned by the fruits of hope, the second statement is tainted as fruits of the poisonous tree and should be suppressed as well. For all of these reasons, both individually and under the totality of the circumstance, I ask this Court to suppress Kerri Hall's statements to the police. Thank you, Your Honor." Dasher sat down.

Judge Doverman motioned to Jesse, "State?"

"Yes, Your Honor." Jesse stood at her table and began, "The defense is right in one regard – that this Court must consider whether the confession was given freely and voluntarily under the totality of the circumstances. The burden is on the State to prove by a preponderance of the evidence that the defendant knowingly, freely and intelligently provided her statement to police.

The Supreme Court has repeatedly held that to be admissible into evidence at trial, the State must show that a confession was voluntarily given. That holding was stated in *Brewer v. State*, 386 So.2d at page 235 of the reporter. Also stated on that same page of the reporter is that the burden is on the State to prove the voluntary confession by a preponderance of the evidence. The Court should look at the totality of the circumstances surrounding the confession to see whether direct or implied promises produced the confession, as stated in *Traylor v. State*, 596 So.2d at page 964 of the reporter and *Johnson v. State*, 696 So.2d at page 329 of the reporter." As Jesse cited each case, she handed a copy to opposing counsel and to the bailiff so the bailiff could hand the pre-highlighted copy of the case to the Judge.

"So what types of things do we need to look at here to see the totality of the circumstances? You have a woman that came in and spoke to the detectives. She answered the questions responsively, did not fall asleep during the interview and did not ask for the interview to end. Instead, she was coy about her arm being broken and that was the reason why she did not want to sign the *Miranda* form; not that she was not waiving her rights, but instead because she could not use her writing hand to actually sign.

250

As far as the detectives discussing what charges would be brought, they were always very clear with the defendant that they did not know what the State would ultimately do. They made it clear to her that the State would make the charging decision. Even if the detectives did imply to the defendant that she could 'help herself out' by talking to the detectives, that statement did not render her statement to the detectives involuntary. I would direct the Court's attention to *Cohen*, the Circuit Case that Mr. Dasher provided. On page seven of the reporter, the case states, 'Rather, the detectives only agreed to present Defendant's case to the State Attorney who would decide and by the Defendant's responses on the videotape he understood that the State Attorney was the ultimate authority who would decide what the Defendant would be charged with concerning Lisa White's death. *These statements by the detective did not render the confession involuntary.*'" Jesse emphasized the last sentence.

Jesse went on, "That is almost the exact same scenario that we have under the instant facts. The detective's job is to gather information, not to apprise a suspect of the potential punishment he or she is facing. As stated in *Stevens v. State*, 419 So.2d, 1058, a Supreme Court Case, on page 1063 of the reporter, 'A police interrogator must neither abuse a suspect, nor seek to obtain a statement by coercion or inducement, nor otherwise deprive him of Fifth or Sixth Amendment rights. As a safeguard against such improprieties, the *Miranda* warnings have been prescribed. But a police interrogator's job is to gain as much information about the alleged crime as possible without violating constitutional rights, and it

251

is not his duty to apprise a suspect of the possible punishment for the crime under the investigation. The ultimate punishment to be meted out upon one convicted of a crime depends on the nature of the formal charges filed, which is often a function of prosecutorial discretion, the outcome of the trial, and the exercise of discretion by the sentencing judge. At the investigatory stage of the criminal justice process, it is quite proper for an investigator to decline to speculate on the possible ultimate result.'

Here, the officers did not promise the defendant what would happen to her. As is almost always the case, if a suspect cooperates with law enforcement, the State usually goes lighter on the punishment. In fact, cooperation is a legal basis to deviate from the Criminal Punishment Code Scoresheet. The State would submit to you that the defendant's statement was not involuntary due to the alleged promises of the detectives.

Now, as to the voluntariness of the statement due the defendant being intoxicated with lawfully prescribed medication. As Your Honor can see in State's Exhibit 1, Ms. Hall had methamphetamine in her system when they took blood from her at the hospital. Florida Statute 775.051 states that 'Voluntary intoxication resulting from the consumption, injection, or other use of alcohol or other controlled substance as described in chapter 893 is not a defense to any offense proscribed by law. Evidence of a defendant's voluntary intoxication is not admissible to show that the defendant lacked the specific intent to commit an offense and is not admissible to show that the defendant was insane at the time of the offense, except when the consumption, injection, or use of a controlled substance under chapter 893 was pursuant to a lawful prescription issued to the defendant by a practitioner as defined in s. 893.02.'

Mr. Dasher made a big deal that the State did not present expert testimony as to what the levels of methamphetamine in the defendant's system meant. Your Honor, the State submits that the actual level doesn't matter. What matters is whether or not she was intoxicated. How can you tell whether a person is intoxicated? Are there scientific tests that can be performed to check levels in the blood? Absolutely, but those levels only give a presumption of being impaired. If Your Honor considers the definition of 'normal faculties' out of the DUI jury instructions, then Your Honor will clearly see that Ms. Hall was not impaired to the extent of being intoxicated.

The relevant portion of the normal faculties definition is the ability to see, hear, walk, talk, judge distances, make judgments and in general, the ability to perform the many mental and physical acts of our daily lives. Did Ms. Hall say she was not able to see, hear, walk, talk or respond appropriately to questioning? No, she didn't. What is interesting to note is that she selectively could not remember some things, but she clearly could remember asking for an attorney, but I will get to that aspect of things momentarily.

Both detectives testified that Ms. Hall was coherent and responsive to the questioning. If she were actually intoxicated by the pain medication or even by the methamphetamine, then she would not have been able to respond coherently and responsively to the questioning.

The defense pointed out that Ms. Hall did not sign the waiver form.

While the State's position is that Ms. Hall did sign the form, even if this Court were to take Ms. Hall at her word, it doesn't matter whether it was signed or not. Detective Wescott testified that he read the *Miranda* warning to the defendant and asked her if she understood what he had just read. He then gave her a copy so that she could read it herself and then asked her to sign it at the bottom. Ms. Hall made it into a joke that she wouldn't sign – not because she did not want to waive her rights, but because she couldn't sign with her arm in a sling."

Jesse handed the next case to Dasher and the bailiff. "In *Sinley v. State*, 699 So.2d, 662, a 1997 Florida Supreme Court case, the Court found that the evidence supported a determination that the capital murder defendant's confession was knowingly, intelligently and voluntarily made, even though the defendant did not sign the bottom of the Miranda warnings acknowledgement form. The officers in that case testified that they read the defendant his rights from the Miranda form and he acknowledged that he understood them and signed the top of the form. The reason why the other place for signature went unsigned is because the defendant started asking questions and distracted the officer. Ultimately, that defendant made a spontaneous confession.

Just as here, the defendant indicated that she understood her rights after Detective Wescott explained them to her. She also signed the acknowledgement form, though that is not even required by law.

Finally, Your Honor, as to the defense's most serious allegation that Ms. Hall requested an attorney, the law is clear that an ambiguous request for an attorney is not sufficient to trigger the Fifth or Sixth Amendment. I had brought my own cases to address this issue, but to keep the paperwork a little lighter for Your Honor, I will just cite to *State v. Cohen*, one of the cases Mr. Dasher provided. On page three of the printout, which also happens to be page three of the reporter, the court states, 'After having validly waiv[ed] his *Miranda* rights, when a defendant makes an equivocal or ambiguous utterance to terminate an interrogation, police in Florida need not ask clarifying questions.' The court then cites to *State v. Glatzmayer* and *State v. Owen*. The court goes on, 'Subsequently in *Almeida v. State,* the Florida Supreme Court explained that when an officer is not faced with an equivocal utterance, but with a clear question concerning the suspect's rights after the suspect had earlier waived his rights, the officer must stop the interview and make a good-faith effort to give a simple and straightforward answer.' The court found that *Almeida v. State* was 'not applicable to the subject facts because the Defendant did not ask a question concerning his rights, but rather made an equivocal or ambiguous utterance to which *State v. Owen* would apply.'

In *Cohen*, the defendant's comments regarding an attorney included 'we'll just have to let my lawyer handle this.' As well as, 'I'm not going to say nothing else until my attorney's present because . . .' at which time the detective said, 'It is my understanding that you want an attorney right now, is that what you want?' and the defendant responded, 'No. I just, I just don't understand all of this.' There was further discussion about a lawyer, but ultimately the defendant never clearly requested the presence of an attorney.

Ms. Hall wants to have her cake and eat it too. In one instance, she tells this Court that she was so tired and under the influence of pain pills that she can't remember what all was said, yet in the next breath she tells this Court that she asked for a lawyer; that she clearly remembers asking for a lawyer. The State submits to you that her testimony is not credible. Both officers testified that Ms. Hall said, 'I think I should talk to a lawyer.' Clearly, Your Honor, that is not an unequivocal request for the presence of counsel.

As stated in *Glatzmayer*, which explains *Owen*, the officers are *not* under an obligation to ask clarifying questions. Other than the defendant saying, 'I think I should talk to a lawyer,' she made no other reference to an attorney. She continued talking to the detectives without any problem or hesitation.

Your Honor, taking all of the circumstances as a whole, the defendant's statement to the detectives was knowingly, voluntarily and intelligently made and as such, the State would ask that you deny the Defense Motion to Suppress Statements Made to Law Enforcement. Thank you." Jesse sat down.

Dasher didn't immediately make a move to stand up to do a rebuttal nor did the Judge give him an extra moment to do so. Judge Doverman announced, "Very well, I will take this matter under advisement. You will have a ruling from me before we reconvene on the remaining motions next week.

Dasher stood and asked, "Would you like us to each submit a proposed order, Your Honor?"

Judge Doverman just looked at the defense attorney for a moment before responding, "No, that will not be necessary. I will write it *all* myself." He emphasized the word 'all.' Jesse was sure Dasher was aware that a prior judge in the Third Circuit was reversed on a capital case because the attorney prepared an order and the judge signed it without any editing. She suspected Dasher was trying to create error for an appeal. While it is common practice in both criminal and civil cases for attorneys to prepare the order for the judge, the presiding judge has to make at least some changes to where he or she can claim authorship of the ruling. Otherwise, it is just a rubber stamp for one side or the other.

With that, Judge Doverman stood and started to walk out. The bailiff came out of his daydream and said, "All rise." On normal pre-trial days, the bailiffs did not call the entire courtroom to order each and every time the Judge entered the courtroom. Jesse suspected that the bailiffs were somehow doing a hazing stunt for the new bailiff, Carey Sparkinski. Jesse almost felt sorry for him – she didn't know his back story yet. Oftentimes deputies ended up at the courthouse by request, but just looking at Sparkinski's diminutive size made Jesse think that he didn't have any street credibility.

Jesse stayed around to chat with the detectives for a few minutes after the Judge left the courtroom. She assured them that everything had gone well, that there should not be a problem. The only thing that was of concern is that the first interview was not recorded. Judge Doverman had a history of commenting on police actions or inactions and had specifically said a time or two that all interviews should be recorded. But, based on the testimony, even if the Court took every word the detectives said as false and every word the defendant said as true, the *Motion to Suppress* should still be denied.

Once the courtroom cleared out, Mark walked up to Jesse and congratulated her on a job well done. "Are we still on for tonight?"

Jesse looked around the courtroom even though she already knew it was empty. "Yes, you're coming to my place, right?"

"Yes ma'am. Will you have the Jacuzzi ready?

"Of course." Jesse smiled, "I think after today, I may even have to have a glass of wine. I know you won't join me in a drink, but I think I will splurge."

"Well, you deserve it. In all seriousness, you did a good job today."

"Thanks." She almost felt awkward for a moment, so she returned to where she always felt comfortable – talking about work. "Look, I've got a few things to finish up upstairs. I will see you later tonight, okay?"

"Okay."

17

Jesse spent a few more hours working before she finally went home for the day. When she walked though her front door, Xander anxiously greeted her. Some dogs were meant to be couch potatoes, but not Xander. He was a working line German Shepherd Dog and he wasn't one for just lying around. Jesse laid her purse and computer down on the loveseat as she headed for the backdoor to take Xander for a walk. He knew what was coming and started spinning in circles, as was his habit. That was the one thing that drove Jesse nuts about him because it was hard to hook the leash to his collar while he was spinning.

After Jesse finally got Xander to calm down a little and walked him out back, she went in and started to put her belongings away. It wasn't that she was a neat freak, but Mark would be coming over later and she never left her bags lying about. She took her gun out of her purse and put it in its nighttime resting place, in the drawer of her antique hall tree that stood by the front door. She then took her purse and computer to the office, where they would stay untouched for the evening.

It was already 8:30 so Jesse decided to go ahead and start drawing the bath water. Mark would be there any minute and there was nothing more like a mood killer than waiting for the Jacuzzi to fill up. As the water was running, she poured herself a glass of wine and lit a couple of tea light candles in the bathroom. Normally, she was a stickler for security and would never leave her door unlocked, but she lived in a quiet neighborhood. Nothing ever happened on her cul-de-sac and if it did, both of her elderly widowed neighbors would know about it. Scratching Xander on the head, she unlocked the front door and went back to the bathroom, where she turned out all of the lights, save for the tea light candles and climbed into the tub. She didn't bother with turning on the Jacuzzi part just yet, as she just wanted a few moments of peace and quiet.

"Well hello there."

Jesse startled awake. She was disoriented for a moment until she realized that she had dozed off while waiting for Mark to join her. She looked up at him, standing there naked and grinning like a Cheshire cat.

"You scared the crap out of me." She started to scoot around to the other side of the tub to make room for Mark at his usual spot.

"Sorry. How else was I supposed to wake you? Just jump right in?" He lowered himself into the tub and faced her.

"So much for my personal protection dog. What did he do when you came in? I didn't hear a thing."

"Eh, let's just say he and I have become buddies." What Mark left out is that he had brought a bully stick for a treat – a treat that Xander absolutely loved.

Jesse let it drop though it was highly suspect that Xander hadn't followed Mark into the bathroom. "Well, it's nice to see you."

"And you, but I've had the upper hand. I've been watching you for a large part of the day. You really did do a good job today."

"Thanks." She pondered for a moment, "You know, Ronald Dasher really wasn't all that impressive to me. For such a high priced attorney, I was expecting a whole lot more. I guess he even had me fooled prior to today."

"Yeah, I've noticed that about a lot of the private attorneys. It seems more and more that if you are just a good bullshit artist or can tell the client what they want to hear, that you can sign the case up. But it is the results that count."

She agreed with him. "True. Does it ever frustrate you that you earn a pittance compared to what some of these guys make, yet you can run circles around them in court?"

Mark thought about that for a minute as he rubbed Jesse's foot. "In a way, yes, but overall, no."

"What do you mean?"

"Well, I hate to see the client's families get hoodwinked into paying high dollar for the same service that they could have gotten had they just gone with the public defender. I mean, take Kerri Hall for example. Even though she comes from money, none of it is in her name, so she would have qualified for the PD's office. But no, her dad went out and paid a ton of money for Ronald Dasher. Now, not to take anything away from him because from what I hear, he is great in front of a jury, but after what I saw today, I really wasn't all that impressed either."

"Just think, you could have had her for a client instead of Sessions."

"Ugh, I don't know which is worse. . .the prima donna or my guy. Actually, he isn't all that bad."

"Oh?" Jesse asked.

"Nah, once he was in jail for a while and got the meth out of his system, he turned into a half decent fellow."

Jesse chuckled, "Well, you know you can't use voluntary intoxication as a defense, right?" She splashed a little water his way.

"What? You think I wasn't listening to your motion today?" He made a silly face at her, "Duh! I know I can't use that as a defense. I'm just saying he isn't a half bad guy when he isn't all messed up on drugs."

"I see."

"I went and saw him after your hearing today."

"Oh yeah?" Jesse was a little concerned with the direction of the conversation. While she and Mark technically were not violating any of the Florida Rules of Professional Conduct, they were certainly skirting them. Jesse had even looked it up to be certain. Rule 4-1.7(d) only prohibited lawyers related by blood or marriage from representing parties directly adverse to one another. Neither the rule nor the commentary mentioned lawyers involved in a relationship, or even the type of status she and Mark had, which was presently still undefined.

"Yeah. I told him how kick ass you were today."

"Oh, come on now."

"No, seriously, I did. He needs to know what he is up against. Besides, he is the one that asked about you."

"About me in particular?" That had Jesse a little concerned.

"No, not really. About the hearing. I gave him a copy of Dasher's motion. I've been monitoring all of their motions too, you know."

That was nothing new to Jesse. "I know."

"He actually is pretty helpful. He is a smart guy, really. He has behaved pretty well and they let him have library privileges. They won't make him a trustee, of course, due to the charges he is facing, but at least he is able to look in the law books to try to help himself out a little."

"Nothing like a good jailhouse lawyer, huh?"

"As you know, I normally can't stand a client that is acting like a back seat driver. But Sessions is different. He actually comes up with some good angles to follow." Mark started to move closer to her. "Besides, whenever he does bring you up, I tell him you are no one to be messed with – either in the courtroom or out."

Jesse feigned shock, "What is that supposed to mean?"

"What? Oh, I just tell him that you are kickass in the courtroom and are also kickass outside the courtroom. I mean look at the type of training you do with Xander. That isn't for the faint of heart."

Mark was referring to Jesse's secret indulgence in training Xander in Schutzhund. It was rare for anyone to actually be familiar with the sport, so she always gave a short explanation that it is a three phrase sport, comprising of tracking, obedience and protection. The part that

Mark was referring to as being hard core was the protection phase. "Well, it isn't any of his business what I do and I prefer that you leave me out of your conversations with him."

"Hey, I didn't mean anything by it; I was trying to compliment you. You really are kickass in the courtroom and outside of the courtroom."

Jesse wanted to hold a grudge, but she couldn't as Mark inched up right against her, wrapping his legs around her as he pulled her deep against his chest. All she could muster was a "Hmph" as he pulled her in for a kiss that was delivered like he meant it.

There wasn't going to be anymore talk of work tonight. That was for sure.

18

Even though LeAnne, Barry and Randy were all in Jesse's office discussing the case, Jesse was distracted. Jesse did not get much sleep the night before but she was very rested. Or perhaps she was just very satisfied. She did not like keeping such a big secret and her relationship with Mark was just that – a big secret. No one at the office knew. Perhaps some suspected that there was some sort of chemistry between them, but no one knew the extent of how far things had gone. Not to mention she was disappointed in herself for getting involved in another "secret" relationship. Though the reasoning behind the secretiveness with Mark was different than the reasoning behind the secretiveness with Doug, one thing remained the same – both were secret relationships.

Barry chuckled and said, "Hey, Jesse, did you see this part of Dasher's case law?" He looked up from the *Cohen* case that Ronald Dasher provided as part of his argument the previous day and then read, "The Court in this case admonished the police officers about adopting some sort of specific procedure for handling audio cassettes." He looked back up. "I bet you anything Judge Doverman will make

265

some sort of comment about the sheriff's office adopting a policy of always recording suspect interviews."

Barry's comments took Jesse away from her musings and back into the moment. "It's funny you should say that, Barry." Jesse responded. "He has already orally admonished them about that in the past. We had a motion to suppress on a drug trafficking case and the officers didn't record the interview even though they had digital recorders readily available. The Judge definitely was not happy with that."

"Did he suppress the evidence?"

Jesse smiled and shook her head at the young prosecutor, "No, of course not. As you will learn, if you haven't already, it is pretty rare that anything gets suppressed around here. We are the first line of suppression. In my opinion and what I teach the prosecutors that come through here is that we wear the white hat. If there was police misconduct, the case stops with a *No Information*. We don't rubber stamp misconduct and file on a case that should be suppressed in hopes that the defendant may enter a plea if we give a sweet deal."

"Yeah, I know. You've told me that before." He said with a sheepish grin.

LeAnne spoke up for the first time. "All right then, where are we at? What else needs to be done or researched?"

"Well, overall, I am in pretty good shape. We have the *Bruton* motion next week. I want to round table with you guys whether or not to file a *Motion in Limine* to exclude the victim's medical records to the extent that he had methamphetamine in his system."

"I don't think it hurts us at all." Randy said.

"How so?" LeAnne asked.

"Well, the elements Jesse has to prove don't have anything to do with whether or not the victim had drugs in his system. There isn't a valid defense to say that the victim was high, therefore it isn't murder. When you are dead, you are dead. Doesn't matter if you have drugs in your system or not."

LeAnne piped in, "True, but Kerri is going to argue self-defense. Her attorney could argue that Witherington was on a meth high and violent at the time. . . who knows, the list goes on."

"Yeah, but it doesn't matter. For one thing, the amount of meth in his system wasn't so high that it would have had an effect on him to change his personality. They haven't disclosed any medical experts that could testify about that, have they?" Randy asked Jesse.

"No, they haven't, but they could possibly use the ME, he is a doctor after all. If the jury finds out he had drugs in his system, Witherington definitely won't be as sympathetic, but the bottom line is that he is still dead. Besides, it also kind of plays in with our theory that Hall and Sessions killed Witherington while on a drug binge. It is also consistent with Hall and Witherington doing meth together the day the maid saw Hall at the house."

"So do you want the jury to know or not?" Randy asked.

Jesse thought to herself for a moment before responding, "I need to think about that. I think that I definitely do *not* want to do a *Motion in Limine* to keep it out. But I am really okay with it coming in. I very rarely go into a trial without knowing exactly what I will argue, but I think so long as I have the alternative theories planned ahead of time, it should be fine. So either way, whether it comes in or it never comes up, I am really okay with it."

LeAnne chuckled, "Well aren't you just mellow today. I have a feeling that once you think about it some more, you will decide one way or the other."

Perhaps there was some merit to LeAnne's observation. Jesse was feeling pretty mellow after the night she had just had with Mark. Jesse just rolled her eyes at LeAnne and jokingly said, "Whatever."

Barry asked, "What about filing the *Notice of Intent to Seek the Death Penalty?*"

"I haven't filed it yet." Jesse responded.

"For either of them?" Randy acted surprised.

"No, I know I have enough aggravating factors, but the defense really hasn't given me enough discovery to know what their mitigating factors are."

Barry was hesitant to ask, but did anyway, "Umm…isn't it getting pretty late in the game for them to produce that type of information?"

Jesse knew he was right, but she didn't want to diss Mark. She could care less about her colleague's opinion of Dasher. "Well, it could be that they don't have much for us."

Barry decided to go all in. "Forgive me for asking, but shouldn't that type of information be provided in discovery before the trial? Don't you go straight into the penalty phase of the trial immediately after the guilt phase of the trial?"

"Yes, you're right. When we select the jury, we will explain that the trial is a two phase trial; the first phase is solely to determine guilt.

Assuming we are going after the death penalty, then as soon as the defendant is found guilty as charged, then we will move into the penalty phase." Jesse explained to him.

"Okay, I may as well say it – we didn't learn this type of thing in law school. What exactly happens at the penalty phase?"

Jesse didn't mind explaining the process to the new prosecutor. Her philosophy was that a solid foundation creates a better attorney. "No problem at all. That is what I'm here for!" She smiled at him to put him a little more at ease.

"Ultimately, after hearing all of the evidence, the jury makes a recommendation to the judge – either a life sentence or the death penalty. For the penalty phase itself, both the prosecution and the defense puts on a case. As the State, we present aggravating factors listed in Florida Statute 921.141. What is neat about the penalty phase is that pretty much anything that is relevant comes in despite the rules of evidence. The only real limitation is that no evidence can be presented that was secured in violation of the Constitution of the United States."

Jesse went on, "The jury's job is to weigh the enumerated aggravating circumstances against both statutory and non-statutory mitigating circumstances. If the aggravating circumstances outweigh the mitigating circumstances, they should recommend death. After receiving the advisory sentence from the jury, the judge still has to make written findings, which supports the sentence. What is unique to these cases is that they automatically go to the Florida Supreme Court for a review of the judgment of conviction and sentence of death."

"Okay, I can understand if you have ten mitigating circumstances and only one aggravating circumstance, but I really don't see how anyone can say death or life if the aggravating and mitigating circumstances are close."

"Well, that is where our job comes in. I believe that if it is really that close we, as the prosecutors, need to exercise our discretion in seeking the death penalty. It costs more for the tax payers to house someone in prison and go through all of the appeals on a death case than on a life sentence. The average time spent on death row is about thirteen years. Not to mention, it is the right thing to do."

"So what are the aggravating factors?" Barry asked.

Jesse knew what they were, but was not able to recite them verbatim, so she opened up her statute book to 921.141(5) and read. "Okay, the aggravating factors include:

(a) The capital felony was committed by a person previously convicted of a felony and under sentence of imprisonment or placed on community control or on felony probation. (b) The defendant was previously convicted of another capital felony or of a felony involving the use or threat of violence to the person. (c) The defendant knowingly created a great risk of death to many persons. (d) The capital felony was committed while the defendant was engaged, or was an accomplice, in the commission of, or an attempt to commit, or

270

flight after committing or attempting to commit, any: robbery, sexual battery; aggravated child abuse; abuse of an elderly person or disabled adult resulting in great bodily harm, permanent disability, or permanent disfigurement; arson; burglary; kidnapping; aircraft piracy; or unlawful throwing, placing, or discharging of a destructive device or bomb. (e) The capital felony was committed for the purpose of avoiding or preventing a lawful arrest or effecting an escape from custody. (f) The capital felony was committed for pecuniary gain. (g) The capital felony was committed to disrupt or hinder the lawful exercise of any governmental function or the enforcement of law. (h) The capital felony was especially heinous, atrocious, or cruel. (i) The capital felony was a homicide and was committed in a cold, calculated, and premeditated manner without any pretense of moral or legal justification. (j) The victim of the capital felony was a law enforcement officer engaged in the performance of his or her official duties. (k) The victim of the capital felony was an elected or appointed public official engaged in the performance of his or her official duties if the motive for the capital felony was related, in whole or in part, to the victim's official capacity. (l) The victim of the capital felony was a person less than 12 years of age. (m) The victim of the capital felony was particularly vulnerable due to advanced age or disability, or because the defendant stood in a position of familial or custodial authority over the victim. (n) The capital felony was committed by a criminal street gang member, as defined in s. 874.03."

LeAnne joined back into the conversation. "So for Sessions, we have the first one – that he was on probation when he did it; the second one - that he had a prior robbery; possibly the fourth one – that the capital felony was committed while they were committing a robbery; the sixth one – that the capital felony was committed for pecuniary gain since they stole the credit cards and vehicle; probably the eighth one, assuming the jury believes that the victim was conscious enough to see the execution shot coming, so it was especially heinous, atrocious or cruel. But I'm really not sure that we can prove that it was premeditated."

"You're right on all counts, LeAnne." Jesse thought for a moment. "I don't think it is worth creating an appellate issue about claiming premeditation. I know they went there with a gun, but I don't know that they were planning on killing him all along. It could have always been the plan just to take money. Who knows?"

"Yeah, but premeditation only takes a second's thought." Randy argued.

Jesse conceded the point. "You're right, but it still isn't worth the additional appellate issue. Especially considering all of the other aggravating factors we already have.

Barry asked, "So do you think you will just seek life on Hall?"

Jesse had been thinking about this very issue a lot. "I really don't know. My inclination is to say that I am not going to seek death on her. She is young and doesn't have a violent criminal history. My gut says that she will come off as sweet and innocent in front of the jury – not to the extent that they find her not guilty, but to the extent that they will think Sessions pressured or influenced her to go along with him. I'm sure that is Dasher's play – that Hall got messed up with drugs because of Sessions and Sessions was the one that was the ringleader behind all of this. I suspect Mark might try to do the same thing, but that would be pretty hard to pull off and maintain credibility."

"Why do you think Sessions will claim Hall was the ringleader?" Barry asked.

Jesse had to be careful not to reveal the real basis for her suspicions. "Well. . . I don't know. It is just a strong hunch based off of some of what Mark McCullers has said in passing. I think Sessions is a lot brighter than we initially gave him credit for. He was the type of kid that grew up with deadbeat parents and didn't make it out of the dead-end life he was born into. But, he is actually a smart guy – he

273

just never applied himself."

Barry asked, "So you think that will come up during the penalty phase?"

"Absolutely. Like I said before, the defense is not limited to just statutory mitigating factors. They can present everything, including the kitchen sink. If there is a sob story to be had in the person's life, the defense is going to present it during the penalty phase. That is one thing you can count on."

Randy interjected "Okay, I'm totally changing subjects here, but where are we on the Jeep thing?"

"What do you mean?" Jesse asked.

"Are we bringing it to Florida or not?"

"The short answer is no. Mr. Robinson drew the line on the expenditures for this case. He said that if the defense wants to inspect that vehicle for some reason, then they can go to Kentucky to do it. I don't have to use it for evidence in any way. I mean, I can use pictures, but the Jeep doesn't really have any evidentiary value to me. Now, if we had the Excursion, that would be another story, but that thing has long since been chopped up for parts."

"Well, damn. I was hoping to go up there and escort the vehicle down."

Jesse laughed at him. "Why on earth do you want to go to Kentucky?"

"It's my wife. There are some caverns that she wants to take the kids to go see. I figured if I could get a room for one night on the state's dime, it would decrease my expenses for the trip."

"I see. Well, sorry to burst your bubble, but that isn't going to happen." Jesse smirked, "That's not to say your trip isn't going to happen, because I'm sure your wife will make sure of that, but you just aren't going to get to defray some of the costs onto the state!"

"Yeah, yeah. I know." Randy sighed.

19

The rest of the week flew by; time always seemed to pass quickly as a trial was approaching. The last major set of motions to do prior to the trial being set was the latest defense *Motion to Suppress*, which both defendants filed immediately after Jesse filed her *Notice of Co-Defendant Bruton Statements* and the State's *Motion to Sever Co-Defendants*. All of the attorneys were walking into the hearing knowing the State was seeking the death penalty on both defendants, as the elected State Attorney gave Jesse the go-ahead to file the *Notice of Intent to Seek Death Penalty*. What neither defense attorney knew was that the State was likely going to withdraw the notice as to Hall. It was a strategic move to try to get her to plea and testify against Sessions.

Hall and Sessions were indicted on the same Indictment so that they could be tried together. Jesse's reasoning at the time was that since this was the same offense, which would include all of the same evidence, the co-defendants should be charged together. It also prevented her witnesses from being deposed two separate times by different defense counsel. That was never a good thing because if the witness said something slightly differently, it would give the defense

276

more room to impeach the witness at trial. If the defendants had been charged separately, each defense counsel would have had an opportunity to depose all of the state's witnesses separately. It would also give the defense counsel an opportunity to share the transcripts of the depositions with each other.

Jesse, Mark and Ronald Dasher already had time reserved with Judge Doverman for the various motions. Even though all of the motions had not actually been filed at the time they reserved both the courtroom space and time on the Judge's calendar, the Judge was pretty understanding and gave the extra time since this was a death penalty case. It didn't hurt that they had scheduled the motions for 3:30 p.m. and Judge Doverman was known to keep his afternoons clear so that he could cut out early from time to time. Jesse gathered the last of her folders before heading down to the courtroom.

LeAnne popped her head in the door, "Hey, you need anything else?"

Jesse surveyed her cart that contained her laptop and all of the case files for the case. "No, I should be okay. I think I have everything."

"Want me to come and be your back-up?"

"You can come watch if you want, but this is pretty straight forward stuff. The bottom line is that the case needs to be severed. Logistically, there is no way we can try two capital cases together at the same time. I mean, we could try to have two juries but there is simply no room to have them both in the courtroom at the same time. And heaven forbid if Judge Doverman orders a combined trial – my solution to the Bruton statements would be to have Sessions' jury taken out while Hall's statement to police comes in and Hall's jury taken out while Sessions' statement comes in.

Then we would also have to have separate juries for closing argument. It would be a logistical nightmare and open the door for someone to slip up and say something during closing that shouldn't be said in front of that particular jury. I know I wouldn't make that mistake, but if the trial doesn't go well for Dasher, I wouldn't put it past him to make some sort of *"mistake"* in front of the jury that would cause a mistrial."

LeAnne laughed, "Um, yeah. I can see how confusing all of this gets. I know what you're talking about and I'm confused already!"

"It isn't that bad. But you're right. I will have to really break it down for the Judge so that it makes sense. I think realizing the amount of security and the difficulty of making the bailiffs understand what needs to happen in order to keep it as one trial will really make the Judge lean my way and sever the defendants so we have two separate trials."

"This won't create an appellate issue?"

"No, I don't think so. I mean, even if the defense objects to severing the case, which they will, this is more of a procedural issue. The DCA gives the trial court a lot of leeway with that sort of thing and would only reverse if they found that it was an abuse of discretion. There is no way they would reverse the case on that issue."

"Okay, well I will be up here if you need me. Just call."

"Thanks, I appreciate it." Jesse grabbed her purse so she would have her cell phone and stacked it on top of the "war cart" as she liked to refer to it. She surveyed the cart one last time. Satisfied that she had everything, she left her office for the short trek down to the courtroom.

****

Most criminal hearings and trials were heard in courtroom two, three or four. In fact, all of the hearings and pre-trials in this case had been in one of those courtrooms thus far, but since both defense counsel had to be heard during the current motions and their clients had to be present, courtroom one was being used. The reasoning was simple – there were three tables available. Therefore, each attorney and client could have their own table as well as Jesse having her own table. Each of the other courtrooms only had two counsel tables per room.

Jesse looked up as she pushed her war cart through the double doors and was surprised to see both defense attorneys already in the room. As she would later confirm with Mark, the two defense attorneys had arranged to meet before the motions being heard so they could strategize against her.

Jesse didn't reveal any surprise or intimidation on her face as she said collectively, "Good afternoon, gentlemen."

Both attorneys looked her way and responded, "Good afternoon."

Jesse arrived at her table and started unloading the files that she would need. As she did so, she asked the men, "Is there anything we need to talk about beforehand or any issues that we can agree on?"

Ronald Dasher walked over to her, as his table was the farthest away, "Well, I think we all agree that neither my client's statement nor Mr. Sessions' statement can be redacted in such a way that it would not be prejudicial to the other defendant. But from there, I think both myself and Mr. McCullers differ from you as to the correct course of action. We believe the statements should be suppressed as laid out in each of our *Motions to Suppress* and you think we should just sever the defendants and have two separate trials."

Jesse retorted, "Well, there is another option. We could have one trial with two separate juries. When Hall's statements about Sessions are coming into evidence, the Sessions jury would be taken out. And then when Sessions' statements about Hall are coming in, Hall's jury would be taken out. We would have to have separate opening statements and separate closing statements. What do you think about doing that?"

Jesse knew that procedure would practically double the length of time it would take to try the case. What she didn't know was whether Dasher's retainer was a flat fee, which would mean a longer trial would hurt his bottom line or whether he had already worked through the initial retainer and was now billing above and beyond the initial $100,000.00.

Dasher didn't show his hand at all. "We'll just have to see what the Judge says about that."

Mark just stood back and smiled at the exchange between Dasher and Jesse.

"Well that's why we're all here, isn't it?" Jesse quipped back.

280

Before Dasher had a chance to respond, the side door opened and a bailiff walked in, escorting Robert Sessions. Jesse never really looked at the inmate during the other pre-trial court dates. It was strange because she saw him but never really *saw* him. Today, however, she actually looked at Sessions and noticed how he appeared; something was different about him but she couldn't quite figure out what it was.

Carey Sparkinski, a relatively new bailiff, escorted the defendant to Mark's table and pulled out the chair for the him since Sessions' hands were shackled to his waist. Sessions' ankles were also shackled together. Every step he took made a distinctive rattling sound. Sparkinski called the other bailiff, Joe, over to shackle Sessions' leg irons to the foot bar that was built into the table. It had taken Jesse several years of working at the courthouse before she figured out what those bars were for, as they were rarely used. She supposed since they were getting close to the trial the bailiffs were being extra cautious in case Sessions might try something.

Early on in Jesse's career, she watched a person escape; perhaps escape wasn't the right legal term – he just ran. In retrospect, it was almost funny. It was at a courthouse in one of the smaller counties. There was nothing special about the day, as it was just a normal pre-trial day. The judge was taking a plea from a defendant and everything was going as it normally did. The defendant that was entering the plea was out on bond, so he wasn't even in custody at the time he was entering the plea. But, the guy got cold feet because he turned around and ran out of the courtroom during the middle of the plea colloquy. The guy must have done track in his younger years because he effortlessly jumped the small swinging gates that separated the gallery from the area near the judge's bench.

Everyone was shocked as to what had just happened. After what seemed like an eternity, the bailiffs started chasing after the guy. Both of the bailiffs had to be well into their sixties, so it wasn't exactly much of a chase. By the time the bailiffs ran out of the back of the courtroom, they looked out the solid glass entryway to the courthouse and saw that the defendant was already a long way down the street. They didn't pursue.

The "escape" itself wasn't that impressive, as that particular courthouse didn't have any security measures. Nor was it comforting to know that anyone could walk in with a weapon at any time; especially if you were the person that was asking the judge to sentence someone to prison. Fortunately, the Columbia County Courthouse was much more modern. Unlike the smaller courthouse, the entryway had a metal detector and there were cameras everywhere.

Shortly after the bailiffs escorted Sessions in, an additional bailiff escorted Kerri Hall to her table. Surprisingly, they followed the same procedure and shackled Kerri to her respective table just as they had done with Sessions. Dasher wasn't happy with the bailiffs shackling his client to the table, but he knew he didn't have a leg to stand on to argue with them. If a jury had been present, they would never know his client was incarcerated because she would be in street clothes with an electronic thigh brace under her clothing. If she tried anything, it would shock her in a debilitating manner so she could not move. But since this was a bench hearing, the bailiffs could do as they pleased with the inmates so long as it fell under the hat of "security" as had been proven at prior hearings.

With everyone in place, Joe radioed to an unknown bailiff that Judge Doverman could be brought into the courtroom. The Judge must have been hovering at the secure entryway because the door opened almost immediately. As the Judge walked in, Elaine Davis, one of the supervising bailiffs announced that everyone should rise. Judge Doverman quickly told everyone to take their seats as he sat down himself.

"Okay, it looks like we are here on several motions." The court reporter was taking down everything the Judge said. "The State filed a *Motion to Sever Co-Defendants*, Mr. McCullers filed a *Motion in Limine* and both counsel for Mr. Sessions and counsel for Ms. Hall filed a *Motion to Suppress.* Speaking of motions to suppress, Ms. Bradshaw and Mr. Dasher, I denied the defense *Motion to Suppress* that I just heard. My judicial assistant is sending each of you a copy of my written ruling as we speak. While I did not see the need to put in it writing, I do want to admonish the State as to one area of great concern."

Jesse's back stiffened. She had no idea what she had done wrong and was not used to being called out by a judge.

Judge Doverman went on, "While it is not completely detrimental to the State's case and does not warrant suppression of the defendant's statements, the fact that recording devices are so readily available but were not used at the initial interview is inexcusable. The best way to know exactly what happened in any given situation is to have a recording. They make digital recorders so small these days that law enforcement officers can easily conceal the fact that they are recording an interview. The Court strongly suggests that the Sheriff's Office adopt some specific procedures dealing with recording suspect interviews so that in the future we will not have this problem. Ultimately, it will be up to the jury to decide the credibility of the witnesses." By witnesses, he meant the detectives because Dasher would surely make a big deal about the interview not being recorded.

Jesse loosened up a little. While she didn't like being admonished by the Court, she had not done anything wrong. In fact, she was a strong proponent of recording interviews and had relayed as such to the Sheriff himself. She could do nothing but take Judge Doverman's commentary in stride. "Yes, Your Honor. I will most certainly relay the Court's concern to the Sheriff's Office."

"With that out of the way, I think we can speed things along with the motions that are pending." Judge Doverman took his glasses off and rubbed his eyes. "Mr. McCullers, as far as your client's flight from Florida being evidence of consciousness of guilt, do you want to have any argument, or rely on your well written motion?"

Mark knew Judge Doverman well enough to recognize the way he said 'well written motion' was a clue to not ask for more time to make legal argument. He stood to address the court. "No, Your Honor, I stand by my argument as laid out in the motion."

"Very well. State, do you wish to be heard other than what was stated in your response?"

Jesse stood to address the court. "No, Your Honor."

284

The Judge addressed Mark and Jesse together, "Very well, then I will issue a written ruling as to whether or not the jury can hear evidence pertaining to flight being consciousness of guilt or cannot hear it because they will find out the defendant was on probation and absconded."

Judge Doverman shuffled a few papers on the bench and went on, "Gentleman, as to your respective *Motions to Suppress* – each of you are seeking to exclude the other co-defendant's statement from the trial against your own client, correct?"

Both Mark and Dasher responded simultaneously, "Yes, Your Honor."

"Would not both of you agree that suppression issues deal with the Fourth Amendment?"

Evidently the question was rhetorical because he went on without giving either attorney a chance to respond. "That suppression is called for when the government has performed some sort of wrong against a citizen, such as an unlawful search or seizure?"

Neither attorney responded, so Judge Doverman went on, "What we have here are statements that were made after being advised of the Miranda Warning. I've already dealt with Mr. Dasher's request to suppress Ms. Hall's statement, but what you are specifically asking is that – well, let me rephrase this. Mr. McCullers, you are asking that I exclude Ms. Halls' statements that were made that incriminate your client because you cannot force her to testify because that would violate her Fifth Amendment right to remain silent, your client's Sixth Amendment right to confront all witnesses and your client's

Fourteenth Amendment guarantee of due process of law, right?"

Mark responded, "Yes, Your Honor."

"And Mr. Dasher, you are asking this Court to exclude Mr. Sessions' statements that he made that incriminate your client because you cannot force Mr. Sessions to testify, as that would violate his Fifth Amendment right to remain silent, your client's Sixth Amendment right to confront all witnesses and your client's Fourteenth Amendment guarantee of due process of law, right?"

Ronald Dasher hesitantly responded, "Yes, Your Honor."

"Basically we have statements that Kerri Hall made that inculpate Robert Sessions and statements that Robert Sessions made that inculpate Kerri Hall and if the statements come into evidence, you can't cross examine either defendant about their statement to police, right?" He looked back and forth between counselors.

"Essentially, that is the crux of the issue, Your Honor." Dasher sounded more sure of himself this time.

"And am I correct that both defense counsel object to the State's *Motion to Sever Defendants*?"

Both men again answered in unison, "Yes, Your Honor."

"Well then, looking at all of your motions combined, including the State's *Motion to Sever Defendants*, I think we have our solution. Part of Florida Rule of Criminal Procedure 3.152 addresses when a defendant moves for severance of defendants based on a statement the codefendant made in reference to him or her but is not admissible. The Court is supposed to make a determination as to whether or not the statement is admissible."

Judge Doverman put his glasses back on and picked up a paper from the bench, "In looking at the State's *Notice of Bruton Statements*, I find that the statements made by Kerri Hall are not admissible against Robert Sessions. I also find that the statements made by Robert Sessions are not admissible against Kerri Hall."

Jesse was a little confused as to where the Judge was going with this because it was the State that moved to sever the defendants, not the defendants and he was quoting the part of the rule applicable to defendants moving to sever.

"Now the rule gives the State three options in a situation like this, one of which is to sever the defendants."

Ronald Dasher stood and interrupted the Judge, "Your Honor, if I may – the provision of the rule you are talking about is only applicable when it is the defendant that moves for a severance from the other defendant. Here, it was the State that Moved to Sever." From experience, both Jesse and Mark knew it was a bad idea to interrupt Judge Doverman; or any judge for that matter.

Surprisingly, Judge Doverman did not explode as he is known to sometimes do. Instead, he again removed his glasses, this time glaring directly at Ronald Dasher. "Mr. Dasher, there is a time and a place when you are to speak. When I am speaking, it is neither your time nor your place. Do you understand me?" The tone of his voice was harsh enough to make a grown man cry.

"Yes, Your Honor." Ronald Dasher quickly sat back down.

"Now, as I was saying. Rule 3.152 addresses the remedy when the defense moves for a severance, but it also provides the remedy when

287

the State asks for a severance." He looked at Ronald Dasher as if to say, *You see, Dummy, I was getting there.*

Judge Doverman put his glasses back on and picked up another piece of paper to read. "3.152(b)(1) states, 'On motion of the state or a defendant, the court shall order a severance of defendants and separate trials: (A) before trial, on a showing that the order is necessary to protect a defendant's right to speedy trial, or is appropriate to promote a fair determination of the guilt or innocence of one or more defendants.'"

Jesse knew right then and there that she was going to get the severance without even having to go through all of her legal and technical arguments.

"I believe I can make my ruling based on the written motions that each of you filed, along with the *Notice of Bruton Statements*. Before I rule, do any of you wish to make legal argument or have any testimony that you would like to present?" The question was loaded – Judge Doverman already had his mind made up and did not want to listen to legal argument from any of the attorneys.

Ronald Dasher weighed his options. Of course he wanted to argue with where the Judge was going but after he had already been redressed once, he thought better of it.

Jesse took the lead. She stood and said, "Nothing from the State, Your Honor."

Mark was running through his mind whether or not he should do anything else at this point. He certainly didn't want to piss the Judge off, but he also wanted to preserve the record for an appeal.

Ultimately, he decided to object to the ruling after it was made. There wasn't anything he could add at this point that would affect an appeal. "Nothing from Mr. Sessions, Your Honor."

Begrudgingly, Dasher said, "Nothing from Ms. Hall, Your Honor."

"Very well. I am denying both of the *Motions to Suppress* and I am granting the State's *Motion to Sever*. Rule 3.152 allows the trial court to grant severance when the jury could be confused or improperly influenced by evidence that applies to only one of several defendants. A type of evidence that can cause confusion is the confession of a defendant which, by implication, affects a codefendant, but which the jury is supposed to consider as to the confessing defendant and not as to the others. A severance is always required in this circumstance." He looked up from what he was reading and went on, "That language is almost verbatim from <u>Bryant v. State</u>, a Florida Supreme court case which cites to <u>Bruton v. United States</u>, the United States Supreme Court case.

He looked over to Jesse, "Ms. Bradshaw, since your motion has been granted, you will need to elect which defendant will be tried first. Since we are all here, I would like to take care of the scheduling now. Are you in a position to do so at this time?"

Jesse had actually put a lot of thought as to who should be tried first. While there were pros and cons to each, she ultimately decided to try Sessions first. That would give Hall one final chance to help herself and testify against Sessions. "Yes, Your Honor. The State elects to try Robert Sessions first. I have already spoken to court administration about space availability during the next trial term. I do not anticipate that the trial itself will take more than a week, but jury selection may take a few extra days because they will have to be death qualified. We have a courtroom reserved for a two week time span."

"And when would you try Ms. Hall?"

"The following trial term, Your Honor. And again, in the abundance of caution and in case Your Honor granted my motion, I already took the liberty of talking to court administration to reserve a courtroom for two weeks." She knew she just scored brownie points with the Judge for being prepared.

Judge Doverman looked at Mark. "Mr. McCullers? Will you be ready to try this case during the next trial term?"

Mark stood, "Yes, Your Honor. We are ready for trial."

"How about you, Mr. Dasher, will you be ready for trial the following trial term?"

"Well, Your Honor, I need to check my calendar to be positive, but I actually think that I have a civil trial that would conflict with this."

That was not the right thing to say. "You mean to tell me that a civil trial would take precedence over a death penalty case, Mr. Dasher?" Judge Doverman did not like anyone ever telling him that another judge's courtroom was more important. He was like a federal judge in that respect.

"Uh, no Your Honor. That isn't what I meant at all. I . . . uh, well, I'm sure I'm free."

A look of satisfaction crossed the Judge's face. "Good. It is settled then. State v. Robert Sessions will be heard next month during the next trial term. I will block two weeks off for this case. The following month, I will hear State v. Kerri Hall and will likewise block two weeks off. Are there any other matters to come before the court?"

Mark stood and said, "Very briefly, Your Honor. For record purposes, Mr. Sessions objects to the severance."

Realizing that he almost didn't preserve his objection, Dasher stood and repeated Mark's objection.

"Duly noted. Now is there anything else to come before the Court?"

Jesse joined the contemporaneous male chorus and replied, "No, Your Honor."

With that, Judge Doverman picked up the papers that he had brought in with him and walked out.

The same bailiff that had been standing near Kerri Hall the entire time unhooked her ankle chain from the table and escorted her through the door to the secure hallway.

Carey, the bailiff that had escorted Robert Sessions in followed suit after he had been given the go ahead that the hallway was clear and that Kerri Hall had been secured in her holding cell.

Each of the attorneys gathered their folders and papers in silence. Jesse finally spoke to the men, "If there are any last minute matters, please let me know. Mr. Dasher, when the venire comes out for your client's trial, you will be able to get a copy from the clerk's office. I'm not sure if they charge private attorneys for a copy or not." She didn't have to tell Mark because the clerk's office automatically sent a copy of the venire to the public defender's office.

"Yes, that will be fine. Thank you." Ronald Dasher said curtly.

He could not help but feel as though he was continuously getting home schooled, which was a phrase commonly used to describe a local judge and local attorney ganging up against an out of town attorney. Had he been thinking rationally, he would have realized that Mark McCullers had received the same rulings.

Mark looked at Jesse and cut his eyes towards the door, indicating that he wanted to talk to Jesse before she left. Jesse gathered the last two folders off of the table and added them to the array of other files and folders on her war cart.

The two walked out the double doors almost at the same time. No one was near them in the hallway. "So, should I come over tonight?" Mark asked.

With the trial just around the corner, Jesse was feeling more and more like they were doing something wrong by seeing each other even though it was on their own time and it did not violate the ethics rules. *Technically* it did not violate the ethics rules.

"I – uh." Jesse faltered, which almost never happened. "I really don't know. You know how I feel about this. We've talked about it so many times, I almost feel blue in the face. And it is all so real now, with the trial set and all, you know?"

Mark was disappointed. He enjoyed the time he got to spend with Jesse and he was extremely attracted to her. He had other options in the wings but Jesse didn't need to know everything.

"Come on, one last Jacuzzi, for old times sake?" He had a mischievous glint in his eye.

Jesse weighed her options. The truth be told, she was developing stronger feelings for Mark and could even see a future with him. She wasn't completely over Doug, but the passage of time and distraction by Mark certainly helped. For now she didn't have any problem with putting their budding relationship on hold until after the case was over. But at the same time, she didn't want to stop seeing him. What would one more night hurt?

Jesse smiled and even blushed a little as she said, "All right, but this is the last time, at least until the trial is over. Okay?"

Mark had won her over yet again. "Yes, ma'am."

"Come in the back door. I'll leave it open for you."

"Really? You're finally going to let me come in your back door?"

It took a moment for Jesse to realize what she had just said. She laughed as she lightly punched him in the arm. "Stop it. You know what I meant."

Mark just grinned like a kid caught with his hand in the cookie jar as he walked off. "See ya."

20

Jesse had only been in her office for about fifteen minutes before LeAnne came by. "How did it go?" LeAnne asked.

"Fine."

"Just fine?"

Jesse knew she wouldn't be able to leave it at that with LeAnne. "No, more than fine. The Judge ruled with me on everything. The defendants are severed and Sessions is going first. Next trial term in fact."

"Shoot."

"What?"

"I'm selecting a jury next trial term on Marx Abrams."

Jesse was actually disappointed because she wanted to be around to help with the Abrams trial, if needed. "Well, ditto."

Marx Abrams was one of the biggest drug dealers in the region. He had multiple twenty-five year minimum mandatory trafficking charges pending against him. The case was pretty important, as the State Attorney's Office was going to send a message to the drug community when Abrams was sentenced to multiple consecutive minimum mandatory sentences.

"Man, this sucks. I really wanted to be there for your trial."

Whenever there was a death penalty case, many attorneys usually watched, both from the defense bar and from the State Attorney's Office.

Jesse responded, "And I wanted to be there for yours too. Marx Abrams really needs to go down on this. He always has a way of getting off. I just don't get it." Jesse actually suspected that Abrams was tampering with juries but as of yet, the allegations were not substantiated and she didn't want to needlessly worry LeAnne.

Darby buzzed in over the intercom, "Jesse?" She sounded panicked.

"Yes?"

"I just got a call from Sergeant Jenkins. We need to go on lock down. I've already locked the front office door, but no one is allowed to use the stairway either." While there was access to a stairway within the halls of the State Attorney's Office, it was seldom used. Once you entered the stairway and the door shut behind you, you could not get back onto the floor from which you entered. The only way to exit was on the main floor.

"What's going on?" This had never happened since Jesse had been the supervisor of the office.

"Robert Sessions escaped!"

Jesse was blindsided. "What do you mean, he escaped?"

"That's all I know right now. Sgt. Jenkins said that he will contact you when he can. I think the new bailiff got hurt."

"You mean it happened in the courthouse?" Carey Sparkinski was a new bailiff in the courthouse, but he was not part of the transport group of officers.

"Yes."

Jesse and LeAnne just stared at each other. "Okay, tell you what. Send out an e-mail to all staff that until further notice, they are not to leave the office. There is an emergency situation in the courthouse and I will speak to them as soon as possible. Actually, just say that I will hold a staff meeting as soon as I know something, but they are to stay off of the phone lines. I don't want a situation to occur where all of our business lines are tied up because of people calling out to gossip about what is going on."

"Yes ma'am." Darby replied.

"And Darby, if you hear anything, let me know. As calls come in, just send them to voicemail. I do *not* want the phone lines tied up." Jesse knew she could trust Darby even though she was very excitable in stressful situations.

"Okay. I'm sending the e-mail now."

Jesse pressed the intercom button to make sure she was disconnected from Darby.

"What can I do?" LeAnne asked.

"Nothing right now. I need to find out what is going on. I will let you know something when I do." Jesse was trying to give LeAnne a gentle hint to leave her alone.

"Okay, I can make calls to some deputies."

"No, that is not necessary." Jesse wondered if LeAnne had actually listened to what she had just told Darby. No calls meant no calls. No gossip meant no gossip. It really was not that difficult to grasp. "Please pull my door shut on your way out." Evidently a stronger hint was necessary.

LeAnne got the point and left without saying another word.

****

As soon as LeAnne closed the door on her way out, Jesse pulled her cell phone out of her purse and sent Mark McCullers a text to see if he had heard that his client escaped and to see if Mark was all right. While doing that, she also dialed Sgt. Jenkins, using the land line. She looked at the lights on the phone. None of them were lit up, which meant her employees were actually listening to her instructions about staying off of the phone.

"Jenkins." The gruff voice answered.

"Sgt. Jenkins. This is Jesse Bradshaw. I just heard that Robert Sessions escaped. What is the status of things?"

"I have the whole building on lockdown. I am 99% sure he got out of the building, but I have someone reviewing the video just to make sure."

"But how - "

"Look, all I know for sure right now is that Carey Sparkinski was choked and knocked out and Sessions took his clothes, gun belt and key card. It appears that the key card was used to access the hallway from the holding cells and from there, the stairwell. That is why I am

297

reasonably certain that Sessions made it out of the building."

"Is Sparkinski okay?"

"I think he will be okay. He'll have a pretty good concussion."

"Do you have the crime scene unit coming?" Jesse didn't want to suggest to Sgt. Jenkins how to do his job but he normally didn't conduct investigations - he was only in charge of courthouse security. To Jesse's knowledge, nothing like this had ever happened at the Columbia County courthouse; certainly not an escape involving a defendant charged with first degree murder.

"Ms. Bradshaw, I know how to do my job." The formality of using her last name confirmed Sgt. Jenkins was not happy with Jesse meddling.

"I know that, but please understand that I have a very vested interest in this. I'm looking to put a needle in this guy's arm. He killed a man in cold blood and I believe he would do it again in a heartbeat if it meant his own survival."

"I know. We're doing everything we can right now." He paused for a moment and Jesse heard him talking to someone else. Sgt. Jenkins returned to the line. "Okay, it is confirmed. He is out of the building. The computer tech verified that Sparkinski's swipe key was used to get into the stairwell and the video shows it happening. The last video footage we can see is Sessions exiting the building through the employee entrance."

The employee entrance had been a hot topic a few years prior. For a while, all employees had to enter through the metal detector at the front entrance, just like the visitors to the courthouse. Prior to that

298

time, employees were allowed to come and go through a side entrance with their key card. The only caveat was that they were not supposed to allow anyone else into the courthouse with them. Of course, not everybody followed the rules and the privilege of using the side entrance was taken away. But, as time passed, things got lax again and the employees were allowed to come and go through the side door. The employee side door happened to be adjacent to the stairwell that Sessions used to escape.

"Any intel on where he may have gone?"

"Just a minute."

Jesse could hear him talking to someone else again. This time, his side conversation took a little longer.

"Well, the Sheriff is going to love this." Sgt. Jenkins said to Jesse.

"What?" Jesse asked.

"Sessions stole Sparkinski's patrol car."

It made perfect sense. The bailiffs were each allotted a patrol car to drive home each day. Since Sessions stole Sparkinski's keys, that would be the easiest way to drive away.

"Do you know anything about his history?" Jesse asked.

"Not really, why?"

"He used to be involved in a car syndicate. He will likely ditch the patrol car and steal another car." Jesse risked insulting Jenkins again by making further suggestions. "He may head to Wal-Mart or somewhere with a lot of cars and take a vehicle that isn't so conspicuous."

"That's a good point. I didn't know he had the know-how to wire a car. Thanks for that tid bit." Apparently Jesse hadn't pissed him off again.

"How long will we be on lock down?"

"Not much longer. I need to relay all of this to the Sheriff and then one of us will let your office know."

"Okay, thanks."

"Jesse?"

"Yes?"

"Do you think he is going to run or stick around?"

Jesse pondered the question for the moment. She really didn't see any reason why he would stay in town. He would be a hunted man; his face would be all over the television, newspapers and Internet. "I really don't see why he would stick around. That is, unless he has to lay low to make arrangements to get out of town. But as far as I know, he doesn't receive visitors at the jail. I've had Randy listen to the recorded telephone calls from time to time and there are hardly any to listen to."

"Yeah, I need to get all of his jail calls pulled and get someone to listen to them all."

"Randy should still be here. He has access to the jail phone calls. I'll get him on it right away." It wasn't like Randy could do anything else at the moment. Like it or not, he was part of the lock down. Not to mention Sgt. Jenkins was short staffed.

"Thanks. I appreciate that; one less thing for me to do. I'll let you know shortly when you can let your people go."

"Okay, thanks." They hung up. Jesse immediately started

responding back to Mark's text message that came in while she was talking to Sgt. Jenkins. It was obvious from his message that he didn't know what was going on. That wasn't surprising since the bailiffs tended to treat the public defenders as the enemy. Almost all of the bailiffs had been a road deputy at one time or another and therefore subject to many depositions at the hands of defense attorneys.

Before Jesse could finish the text message, her cell phone rang. "Hello?"

"Hey. What is going on?" There was no need for Mark to identify himself. "Our office is on lockdown but we don't know why."

"Robert Sessions escaped."

There was dead silence on the other end of the phone. Finally, Mark asked, "What?"

"You heard me. He knocked Sparkinski out, stole his clothes, key card and keys to his patrol car. He made it out of the building and off of the premises."

"Unbelievable."

"Do you have any idea where he might go?"

"No." There was no hesitation in Mark's response. Lawyers are bound to keep communications confidential except in limited circumstances. One of the exceptions was when someone else was in danger of imminent harm.

Jesse believed him. "Did he ever give any indication that he might do something like this?"

"No. I mean, he has been surprisingly optimistic about his odds of going to trial, but I just attributed that to him being off of drugs and

301

having a better outlook on life. Maybe he has been planning this all along. I really don't know."

"They will probably come interview you."

"That's fine. I can't tell them anything. Just because I represent the guy doesn't mean I know what his plans are." He added as an afterthought, "Or were."

"Do you know if he still has any connections in the area?"

"I really don't know how to respond to that. I mean, I have mitigation witnesses in mind for the penalty phase of the trial, family members to talk about how he was abused as a child and all. But in all of my communications with them, I never got the feeling that they were especially close. Or that they even talk to him anymore."

"I'm just trying to figure out if he has someone on the outside that is going to be helping him. I assume he is going to skip town as soon as possible and just try to disappear."

Mark shook his head, "If I were him, that is what I would do, but you and I both know he isn't exactly the brightest bulb in the box."

"Do you think Kerri Hall was the brains behind them fleeing from Columbia County before?"

Even though the conversation was treading on off-limits territory between the two, they continued their conversation. Mark answered honestly, "It makes sense that she was the brains. She was the one that knew Witherington. She was the one that knew about the hunting camp. She was the one that knew about the cabin in Kentucky. But look at Sessions - he is a car thief. He doesn't have a violent history. It seems like he was just along for the ride. He could have easily hidden the body in the pond and just stayed here to finish out his time on probation. "

As much as Jesse had always thought that Sessions was behind the plot to kill the victim, she did give Mark's statement some consideration. "Well, maybe he will follow suit with what they did before and just take off. I think he sees the writing on the wall – that if he stays, he is going to get the death penalty."

"I don't know that he sees it that way. Like I said, he was really optimistic about the trial. He has maintained his. . ." Mark had to be careful in how he phrased his words because even though his client had escaped, Robert Sessions was still his client and he could not break the attorney client privilege. "Well, let's just say Robert Sessions maintains he is not guilty of everything the State says he is guilty of."

"Which is why we have the jury system to figure it all out."

Just then, Darby buzzed Jesse's intercom. "Jesse, Sgt. Jenkins is here to see you."

"Okay, send him back."

"Call me back and let me know what is going on, okay?" Mark asked before Jesse could tell him she needed to go.

"I will when I can. Bye."

Sgt. Jenkins must have already been on the way back to Jesse's office before Darby was done talking to Jesse because he was looming in her doorway as she put down her cell phone.

"Where are we with things?" she asked.

"You've got to see this." Sgt. Jenkins held up a DVD.

"What is it?"

"I had the computer guys pull the video from the time Sessions was taken from the courtroom to the time he was put in the holding cell. They then followed him from camera to camera as he went down the stairs and exited the building."

"Okay, let's see it." Jesse took the DVD and inserted it into her laptop. She turned the monitor so they could both see.

What the monitor revealed was nothing short of a repeat of a very similar escape by one of the most notorious defendants ever tried and sentenced to death in the Third Judicial Circuit. Theodore Bundy.

Ted Bundy didn't escape from custody while residing in any of the Third Circuit Jails. He actually escaped while in Colorado. The first time he escaped was actually from the Pitkin County Courthouse in Aspen, Colorado. The escape was simple. While at the courthouse for a hearing, he visited a law library, where he merely opened a window that was hidden away behind a bookcase and jumped from the second story window to his freedom on the ground. Bundy knew that he needed to change his appearance, so he shed his outer layer of clothing, tied a bandana to his head, put a patch on his nose and walked right by all of the police cars reporting to the courthouse.

They caught him within six days. The second escape was from his jail cell. He somehow acquired hack saw blades and cut through the ceiling fixture. The opening was small, so he had to lose at least fifteen pounds to fit through. Other inmates heard Bundy in the crawl space, but either the guard didn't believe them or didn't care.

Bundy stole two shirts and walked right out the door and headed to

Florida where he committed a litany of new crimes. Commonly known as the Chi Omega murders, Bundy killed two women and injured two others at a sorority house in Tallahassee, Florida. But that was not enough. After leaving the sorority house, he broke into a nearby apartment and attacked another woman, severely injuring her.

Bundy left Tallahassee, went to Jacksonville and then backtracked to Lake City, Florida, where he kidnapped Kimberly Diane Leach, a twelve year old junior high student. Her body was finally found seven weeks later near the Suwannee River State Park, across the river from Pirate Land, a small canoe rental and gas station.

The trial wasn't actually held in Columbia County. Because of all of the pre-trial publicity, the trial was moved to Orlando, where Bundy was found guilty and sentenced to death. As with all death sentences, it took some time before Bundy was executed, but nearly all of the prosecutors in the Third Circuit still had pride that it was their small office that put away one of the most notorious serial killers in the United States.

Apparently Robert Sessions had read about Ted Bundy because his escape was based on the same principles. Watching the images on the screen, nothing was eventful as Sparkinski transported Sessions from the courtroom down the hallway to the holding cell. The camera view changed several different times as they walked towards the ultimate destination. Sparkinski secured Sessions in the holding cell, where Sessions was all alone.

Sgt. Jenkins narrated a little to tell Jesse that Kerri Hall had been in the neighboring cell, but was taken to the van to be transported back to the jail while Sessions was kept in the other holding cell. Isolated.

Following Sgt. Jenkins' instructions, Jesse advanced the DVD until she saw Sessions get up from the bench and go to the toilet. While the screen shot did not show the bailiff's control desk, Sgt. Jenkins told her that he had reviewed it simultaneously as the current video and it was obvious that Sparkinski was not watching Sessions on the video monitor, nor was he actually watching the cell, which was within eyesight of the control desk.

What followed was quite clever. Sessions' hands were still shackled to the waist chain, but he was able to get enough leeway to reach into his shirt and start pulling toilet paper out, which he quickly deposited into the toilet. Sessions clothes went from being snug to hanging off of his body. Sessions then shifted his bound hands back and forth to make the waist chain shimmy down with the movement of his hands. Once the waist chain was past his butt, Sessions simply sat on the toilet and pulled his feet through the circular waist chain. Sessions was deliberate and efficient in every move he made. It was obvious he had rehearsed his actions.

Instead of getting up off of the toilet, be pulled his hands back to the front of his waist, and gathered the chain into his hands and bent over. He stayed there until Sparkinski came to the door and ordered Sessions to get up. You could tell from the video that they argued back and forth. Finally, Sparkinski gave up and opened the cell door. He did not follow protocol. Officers were never supposed to go into a cell to get an inmate unless there were other officers present. It could have been a deadly mistake.

Sparkinski walked the few steps to Sessions and reached out to touch Sessions. But before Sparkinski knew what hit him, Sessions grabbed Sparkinski's arm and maneuvered himself behind Sparkinski, pinning Sparkinski's arm in the process. At the same time, Sessions took the waist chain with his other hand and looped it around Sparkinski's neck. Sessions height gave him an advantage.

Sparkinski was young and inexperienced. He didn't know whether to use his free hand to try to release the pressure against his neck or if he should try to reach around and grab Sessions somehow. Even the slightest movement sent bolts of pain through his right arm that was securely pinned behind his back.

It did not take long for Sparkinski to pass out. You could see his body go limp in the video. Sessions continued to hold on for good measure. Finally, Sessions let the body sag to the floor, where he quickly searched the bailiff for a key to the handcuffs. The search did not take long. With his hands now free, Sessions ripped his own clothes off. While he stood there in only his underwear, Jesse could see that he was emaciated. Sessions had been planning this for a long time.

Sessions took the bailiff's clothes off and put them on. He did the same with the gun belt. Sessions was now armed. Sessions bought himself a little extra time by dressing the bailiff in the orange uniform and laying him down on the bench, with his back to the camera. If one of the other bailiffs happened to look at the monitor that displayed the holding cell, nothing would appear awry. To assure that Sparkinski would not wake up, Sessions pistol whipped him. Hard. Sparkinski didn't move.

Having placed Sparkinski exactly as he wanted, Sessions turned to the camera and saluted. He knew this video would be watched over and over. The camera view changed to a different camera angle as Sessions used Sparkinski's key card to leave the holding cell area. There was a brief walk in the secure hallway, which led to the stairwell. There weren't any cameras in the stairwell, but it didn't matter because all of the cameras were synced together and displayed the time in the lower right corner. Sessions appeared moments later on screen, only now he was on the landing of the ground floor.

The sign said emergency exit only, but all of the employees used it as a way of ingress and egress. Sessions did the same. He walked out of the courthouse as if he belonged there. He walked casually away from the courthouse until he was out of the camera's viewpoint.

Jesse asked, "Did he know which patrol car was Sparkinski's?"

"I don't know if he knew or if he got lucky. Sparkinski is new and wants to make a good impression, so he is always one of the first ones to get here. As a result, he parks in one of the closest parking spaces. The bottom line is that Sessions made a clean escape."

"Will Sparkinski be okay?"

"I don't know. They were able to rouse him, but he is still pretty incoherent. They took him to the hospital."

"Any hits on the BOLO for the patrol car?"

"Not yet. I imagine he will ditch it and exchange it for another car like you suggested."

"What about LoJack or some sort of GPS positioning device on the

308

patrol car? Can you find it that way?"

"If it were one of the newer cars, then yes. But Sparkinski is new and he has one of the oldest cars in the fleet. It barely has functioning air conditioning."

"Okay, well are we off of lockdown yet?"

"Yes, but I wanted you to see the video first. The Sheriff has also seen a copy. He agreed that we can let people leave the courthouse, but we are deactivating all of the key cards. No one gets into this building unless they first go through security."

"What about the employee exit?"

"Put a memo out to your employees that no one is to use that door until further notice. They won't be able to get in because I'm deactivating their cards, but they should not use it as an exit either. And by all means, they should not let anyone in that door so someone can avoid the metal detectors."

Jesse had always thought it should be like that anyway. She did not argue with Sgt. Jenkins. "I'll send the memo out right now. I will also let them know that they can go home."

"That is fine."

"Do you mind if I keep this?" Jesse gestured to the DVD that she was removing from her laptop.

"Sure. I had the computer guy make several copies."

"Thank you for coming and keeping me informed." Jesse was sincere.

"You're welcome."

With that, Sgt. Jenkins left as quickly as he had come. Jesse immediately started composing the memo to send to her staff. She attached the memo to the e-mail and in the body of the message requested that everyone meet in the conference room in five minutes.

The impromptu staff meeting did not last long. Jesse did not show the DVD, but she did tell them that Sessions escaped, that Carey Sparkinski was injured but they did not know the extent of the injuries at this time. She wanted everyone to go home and advised them to take anything they might need with them, as they would not have access to the courthouse except during regular business hours.

Jesse wanted to take her own advice and leave work. It had been a long day. Jesse was tired. All she wanted to do was go home, pour a glass of wine and relax with Xander until Mark came over. Unfortunately for her, that is not what the evening held in store.

21

Jesse stayed late at work so it was dark outside when she arrived home. Xander met her at the door, happy as always, but perhaps a little more wired than usual. Jesse dropped her purse, laptop and briefcase onto the loveseat on her way to the backdoor. With such a hectic day, she had not come home at lunch to let Xander out and he was very anxious to go outside.

Once outside, Xander was on high alert, with his ears forward and nose out, sniffing the night air. He didn't care to saunter around as he usually did. Instead, he purposefully paced the perimeter of the backyard until he was satisfied that no one was there.

Jesse didn't think anything of it. She figured one of the neighborhood cats must have jumped the fence earlier in the day and tormented Xander through the glass door, as had happened before. After having not discovered an intruder in his yard, Xander relieved himself and wanted to go back inside. He was hungry. Actually, he was always hungry. Sometimes Jesse thought the dog would eat her out of house and home.

Jesse prepared Xander's food and he eagerly devoured it. While Xander ate, Jesse put her state issued gun in the hall tree by the front door and took her purse and briefcase to the office. She wanted to do something to make her evening with Mark special, so she opted for candles. She set out five large votives throughout the bedroom. Since they were big, she went ahead and lit them. They would not burn out. She didn't know what time Mark was going to get there, so she just set the small tea light candles in the bathroom to light them later.

She started the bath water and headed towards the kitchen. Jesse took out her wine chiller and a bottle of the best Chardonnay she had on hand. Jesse's tastes were simple and paying $50.00 for a bottle of wine was a splurge for her. Since tonight would be the last time she would be having Mark over for a while, she figured she might as well make the most of it.

She opened the wine and poured herself a glass. The first sip went down smoothly. She placed the wine bottle in the chiller and hooked her arm around it so that she could carry it and the two glasses to the bathroom in one trip. The bath water was about to reach the perfect level. She laid the wine chiller and glasses down and turned the water off. She walked out of the master suite and found Xander chewing a bone on his bed in the living room. He was going to have to stay out in the living room because Jesse didn't want to risk him jumping up and burning himself on a candle or hot candle wax in the bedroom.

She scratched his head. "Okay, boy. You be good, okay?" He just wagged his tail and looked up at her. She went and checked the doors to make sure they were locked. She had planned on leaving the back door unlocked, but with the events of the day, thought it wiser to keep her cell phone with her and just go open the door when Mark

312

arrived.

Jesse shut the bedroom door and set up her iPod dock to play easy listening music and then went and sank into the tub. She usually waited for Mark to join her before turning on the Jacuzzi jets, but it had been a long day and she just wanted to relax for a while. Jesse was dozing peacefully within minutes.

Between the music playing, the water jets making noise and Jesse being asleep, Jesse was clueless as to what was transpiring in the living room. Robert Sessions had not fled the state. He had not even fled the county. Instead, he had traded out the patrol car for a 2000 Honda Civic, his clothes for a pair of jeans and a plaid shirt and acquired a few other supplies by stealing them. He wanted to see Jesse Bradshaw in person.

Finding Jesse Bradshaw's home had been easy for Sessions earlier that day. He simply went to the library and looked up her name on the property appraiser's website. Since he was only vaguely familiar with the neighborhood, he clicked on the aerial map and saw the street names. He could see the roof of Jesse's home but had not paid attention to the chimney. At that time, he had no idea that it would be instrumental in gaining entrance to the residence.

After he escaped, found a new car and clothes, Sessions scoped out Jesse's house to find a way in. He tried all of the obvious things first – the windows and doors. They were all locked. But while he was in the backyard, he noticed a small door at ground level. At first he thought the door might access a crawl space, but then realized that it was actually a door that would allow the homeowner to place firewood into a storage cabinet inside the home without carrying the wood through the house. He assumed there was another door inside the home that could be opened up to access the storage space. He assumed correctly.

It was not unusual for homes in North Florida to have a fireplace. But it wasn't common either. Sessions had lucked out. He tried the small wood door and much to his delight, it opened. He looked inside and was pleased to see that his body would be able to fit; not to mention it was empty. It would be cramped, but he would fit. He crawled halfway into the space so that he could push on the interior door. It opened with minimal resistance. He was about to take a cursory look inside the house when he heard a low, deep growl. He had forgotten that his attorney told him that the prosecutor trained dogs. He quickly shut the small door and backed all the way out.

He had to go find a way to neutralize the dog; otherwise, he would not be able to carry out his plan. So, Sessions broke into a nearby veterinarian's office and stole a large bottle Diazepam. Once upon a time, before Sessions got messed up with drugs, he wanted to be a vet tech. He had shadowed a cousin at a veterinarian's office for a whole week. Even in those days, he must have had an interest in drugs, because he remembered that Diazepam was used to sedate animals. He figured if he gave enough of it, he could at least knock the dog out, if not kill him.

Sessions was back at Jesse's house for at least an hour before she arrived home. He couldn't neutralize the dog before the prosecutor arrived home or she would know something was amiss. So, he hid behind the bushes of a house across the street that had a for sale sign in its yard. After the prosecutor got home, the lights were on for less than half an hour before the house went dark. It was show time.

Sessions entered the backyard through the gate. So far, so good, he thought. He had seen floodlights at each corner of the house, but apparently they were not motion sensitive. That was one less problem to deal with.

Sessions quickly went to the firewood storage door. He left his small bag of supplies outside the exterior small door and quickly stuck his head and chest into the empty storage space. He had already put several Diazepam pills into individual Pill Pockets, a pliable treat that pet owners use to wrap around pills so that the animal will swallow the pill. He threw several laced Pill Pockets into the living room and left the door slightly cracked so that he could watch what transpired within. The lighting was very dim, with only a slight green glow in the room, presumably coming from the appliances in the nearby kitchen.

Xander suddenly stopped chewing his bone. The intruder was back. The big black dog stealthily approached the firebox. Xander knew he had to protect his master. The powerful dog emitted a low growl as he took one deliberate step after another, inching closer and closer to the cracked door.

On high alert, the muscle bound dog smelled sweat on the man; it smelled like fear. Xander knew there was a threat but he also smelled a treat on the floor. Was it possible that his beloved master had dropped treats for him and he had not found them? He put aside his desire to sniff the delicious smelling treats and inched closer to the intruder. He heard the man mutter something and shut the door.

Xander just stood there for what seemed like an eternity. He didn't move a muscle. He didn't even open his mouth to breathe. He was intent on making sure the threat had passed. Not smelling or hearing anything, Xander finally decided he could partake in the goodies sprinkled on the floor. He ate them up without even chewing, as was normal for him.

Xander checked out the rest of the living room to make sure he had not missed any other treats - not to mention he also wanted to make sure nothing else was out of order within the house. Everything seemed fine, but he was extremely tired. So tired, he could not even make it back to his dog bed. The eighty-five pound dog collapsed on the floor.

The dog scared Sessions as he approached the hiding place. So Sessions closed the door and backed out of the wood storage area. He would have to give the dog a chance to eat the Diazepam. After about fifteen minutes, Sessions checked to see if the dog was still a threat.

Sessions crawled back to where he had been earlier. He cracked the interior door and did not see anything. He tapped on the door so that it would make a little noise. The dog still did not appear. He got a little braver and pushed the door open a few inches wider, still no sign of the dog. The treats laced with Diazepam were gone. That was a good sign.

Sessions made a quiet tsk'ing noise by striking his tongue against the back of his teeth. The dog was nowhere to be seen. Perhaps the pills had worked. Sessions backed out and grabbed his goody bag from outside. He went for it and entered the living room through the small wood storage area. He still didn't see the dog.

It took no time for Sessions to make entry and stand up in the living room. He stood still so that his eyes would adjust to the dim lighting. There was music coming from behind a closed door. He figured that must be the master bedroom. He also heard the sound of water jets. Perhaps he would be lucky and catch the prosecutor unaware in the tub. He walked around to acquaint himself with his surroundings and to make sure there was no one else in the home. The living room was neither too large nor too small. Everything was tidy and in order, which matched the personality of the prosecutor that he had come to know and hear about.

On the other side of the loveseat, lying motionless, was the dog. He kicked the dog and received no response. He was safe. Sessions continued his tour and saw a second bathroom that separated two bedrooms. One of the bedrooms was used as an office. Satisfied that he was alone, he headed towards the master bedroom but not before kicking the dog one more time for good measure. He couldn't be too cautious.

Sessions reached into his bag and pulled out a gun. The safety was off and a bullet was chambered. He slowly and quietly opened the master bedroom door. There was no sign of the prosecutor. He walked down the short hallway to his right, which led to the master bedroom. Sessions could see everything clearly, as there were candles throughout the room. The prosecutor was not there. She must be in

317

the bathroom.

Sessions quietly made his way to the bathroom. The door was cracked slightly; he pushed it far enough open to gain admittance. The sleeping prosecutor was within five feet of him. His pulse quickened. This was the moment he had been planning for oh so long.

Jesse was in the stage of sleeping to where she was dreaming, yet still semi-conscious of her surroundings. She must have sensed something was wrong because she opened her eyes. It only took a few seconds to focus. The first thing she saw was a gun pointing at her. Then she saw who was holding the gun. Robert Sessions, the escaped murderer. Could this really be happening?

Sessions found his voice and said, "Hello, Ms. Bradshaw. I've been waiting for this moment for a very long time."

Jesse was speechless, but only for a moment. Her training kicked in and she knew she had to take control. "Mr. Sessions, I would have thought that you would flee the area."

"No, I only have one thing that I need to do before I leave and that is to talk to you."

Jesse's heart was pounding. What could she do? Her first thought was to call Xander; he was trained to bite a person on command, but only when the person was wearing a training sleeve. He had never actually bitten a person directly. But where was he? There was no way he would've let someone in her house. She was terrified Sessions had already hurt him.

Her cell phone was lying on the vanity but it was across the room. Her work gun was in the hall tree, but it was by the front door. Her razor was lying next to her, but with the protective covering, it was useless as a weapon. Her .38 caliber handgun was in her nightstand, but it was too far away. The tea light candles in the bathroom were useless and the votives in the bedroom were out of reach. The bottom line was that she had nothing to use to defend herself except her hands and her words.

"Well, this isn't exactly a good moment for me to talk to you. Do you mind if I put some clothes on?" She did her best to not let her voice quiver.

Sessions leered at the exposed, curvy body below him. He had to admit, the prosecutor definitely had it going on. But he had to focus. He was there for a reason. The prosecutor had to know the truth about what happened and then he was going to get the hell out of Columbia County. He would never look back.

"Stand up," Sessions commanded. While still holding the gun, Sessions felt the pockets of Jesse's robe that was hanging on the towel rack. There was nothing in the pockets.

Jesse stood up. Sessions took his time to admire the naked woman in front of him before he threw the robe at her. Jesse caught it midair and quickly put it on, not even attempting to dry off.

Jesse stepped out of the tub and forced herself to not look at her cell phone lying on the vanity. She did not think Sessions had seen the phone. She wanted to keep it that way.

"Go sit on the bed." Sessions backed up a step and gestured behind him.

Jesse considered her options. The cell phone would be within reach as she walked towards the bedroom. If she tried to grab it, he may see her. If she didn't, she may not get another chance. Jesse decided to go for it. She purposefully looked over Sessions' left shoulder, which tricked him into looking behind himself to see what she was looking at. During that split second, Jesse slid the cell phone into her robe pocket without missing a step.

Jesse then did as she was told and went to sit on the end of the bed. She thought about her next move. She couldn't put her hands in the robe without being noticed. She couldn't do the voice activated dialing without the phone making a noise. If she received a call, a text message or even an e-mail, her phone would alert the crazed man before her. Perhaps she made a mistake in grabbing the phone.

Jesse thought about her other options again, but even the hope of getting to the .38 in the nightstand was not plausible. She decided to keep Sessions talking. Mark was due to be there any minute. That scared her, but also gave her hope.

"Mr. Sessions, what is it you wanted to talk to me about?" She decided to distract him. She knew from the limited discovery that the defense had given her that Robert Sessions was a paranoid schizophrenic. It was the key part of the defense strategy for the penalty phase. Perhaps she could use the man's delusions to her advantage.

"I did not kill that man."

Jesse did not react outwardly, though she could barely concentrate over the sound of her pounding heart; it felt as though the organ were in her head instead of her chest. "Okay. Well, Mr. Sessions, I think you would agree we are here under unusual circumstances. But I feel compelled to tell you that I am not allowed to speak to you directly. You are represented by counsel and I cannot talk to you without your counsel present." Jesse didn't know what to say. She just knew she had to say something, so as silly as it sounded, the first thing that came to mind was advising Sessions about her ethical obligation.

Sessions just laughed at her. He pointed the gun directly at her forehead and then waved it back and forth. "I'm waiving all of that, lady. Get it? You are going to talk to me or the gun is going to talk to you." Sessions thought for a moment, "You know what? It doesn't even matter if you talk. You just need to listen. You are going to listen to me. I have told my lawyer over and over and over. I did not kill that man. That bitch, Kerri Hall, it was all her plan. She's the one. She set me up. I see it all now. I didn't know it at the time, but I see it all now."

Jesse just sat there and listened. She did her best not to show any emotion.

Sessions continued, "That bitch had it planned all along to kill Witherington. She used me. She uses everybody. Everybody that knows her knows that she will use you until she is done with you and then dump you just to move on to the next person."

Jessed decided to break her silence, "Okay, how did she use you?"

"She set me up. She is the one that shot that guy. After she did it, I didn't know what to do. I'm the one that was on probation. I'm the one that would have gotten fingered for killing him. So I did what she told me to - I cleaned up the mess, patched the hole in the wall and hid the body. She promised that no one would be the wiser that he was missing. We could just leave and there was no way that we would get caught. And you know what? If that man hadn't been out there hunting and come across the body, we may have pulled it off."

"Why do you think she set you up? How did she do that?" What had Sessions done to her dog? She had to concentrate even harder to focus on keeping Sessions from shooting her. If she thought about Xander, she may lose it completely.

"I've read the discovery. I know what she told those detectives from here when they interviewed her in Kentucky. I know she is the one that said I pulled the trigger. But she is lying. She is the one that pulled the trigger. She shot him twice - in cold blood! She shot him in the chest and then stood right over him, with him begging for his life and shot him point-blank in the head."

Sessions had Jesse's attention. It was possible that Sessions had figured out a story that was consistent with the trajectories of the bullets. But it didn't make sense that he would go to such great lengths to escape, risk getting caught by going to her house to tell her these things when all he had to do was flee the county to escape the murder charges. Maybe he was telling the truth?

Jesse decided to play into Sessions' ego. "Mr. Sessions, if what you are saying is true, it can be proven by forensics. You have a trial scheduled. That is what a jury is for – to hear both sides of the story, not just the State's side. You will be given an opportunity to testify if you want to testify."

"Oh, that's bullshit! Yeah, my attorney told me that it is my

choice to testify, but if I do, I'm just signing my own death warrant."
He started pacing and waving the gun as he spoke. His voice got
louder and louder with each word that crossed his lips. "The only way
you would believe me is if I came and told you the truth. Do you think
I would have stuck around otherwise? I could have been scot-free by
now, but no – I stuck around so I could tell you how it really
happened." He turned and faced her again, pointing the gun straight at
her. "Don't you see? You wouldn't have believed me any other
way!"

"So what is your plan? Kill me after you just told me you were not
guilty of murdering Witherington?"

Sessions ignored her. "Have those detectives reopen the case and
investigate. Kerri kited me a letter. I have it. I gave it to a buddy at
the jail because I knew my cell would be tossed after I escaped."

Jesse knew that the term "kite" meant that a letter was sent from
one inmate to another through one of the trustees; usually, one of the
people doing the laundry or delivering the food.

"What did she say in the letter?" Jesse asked.

"She admits everything. She said that she set me up. She knew
that I would take the rap and that she would be able to claim self-
defense. She said that she was sorry but it was just the way it had to
be. Ultimately things didn't work out the way she wanted. She had a
big plan to get Witherington's money for us. Her father was cutting
her off. Nobody knows that, even to this day, since he ended up
bankrolling her defense anyway. But before all of this happened, he
was going to cut her off completely."

323

Jesse did not know that Thomas Hall had cut his daughter off. But if she survived this, she would certainly have the detectives check it out.

Sessions went on, "Dean Witherington was going to be Kerri's salvation. All she needed to do was have him disappear. That bitch pulled a long con. She gained access to all of his accounts and passwords. He had offshore accounts that no one knew about and she had all of that stuff. We just needed a little bit of time. If I hadn't been so stupid and partied with her, we would have been able to flee the country."

"How could you have done that?" Jesse asked. "You were a fugitive. You should've known that as soon as you absconded, there would be a warrant out for your arrest."

Sessions was on stage now. The spotlight was on him and him alone. It was time to show just how smart he truly was. "She had a person lined up to create passports for us. We had new identities and everything. It cost her thirty large to get two passports made. She put half up front and was going to pay the other half when we got the ID's."

"Then why did you use the credit cards? If you had all of this money and everything all figured out, why do something so stupid? Why do something that could so easily identify your location?"

"*I didn't* use the credit cards, *she did*. That's what makes it so obvious that she was trying to set me up. She wanted to get caught." He just sat there staring past Jesse. He then looked at her and imploringly said, "She wanted *me* to get caught. Don't you see that?"

"I don't understand why she would want to get caught."

"Well, in her letter to me, she didn't want to get caught, she wanted me to get caught. Her plan got screwed up when that Elizabethtown cop tracked us all day and caught her. If only I had been quicker, I would have gotten away. I should have been smarter and cut my losses and run." He started pacing again. "I don't know why I went back to that cabin." He muttered the last bit to himself, as though he were talking to one of the voices in his head.

Jesse sat there, watching and thinking. She needed to use the phone to her advantage. She shivered as though she was cold, then she discreetly stuck her hands into her robe pockets and pulled her shoulders together, shivering. What she was really trying to do was distract Sessions but he didn't seem to be paying attention to her anyway. By touch alone, she put her phone on silent. She was careful to turn the phone upside down first so the glow from the face of the phone would not shine through the robe pocket.

Jesse was afraid to call 911 because they would arrive with lights flashing and maybe even sirens that would agitate Sessions and then there would be a hostage situation. Instead, she used the speed dial to dial Mark. She pressed the earpiece part of the phone down against her thigh while keeping the microphone part sticking out. She did not want Mark to unknowingly walk into this situation.

Jesse could feel a slight vibration on her leg each time Mark said, *"Hello? Hello? Jesse, are you all right? I can't hear you, what's wrong?"*

All the while, Sessions was still talking – sometimes to himself and sometimes focusing his attention on the exposed prosecutor. The vibrations stopped. Jesse prayed Mark was actually listening and had not hung up, thinking it was a bad connection. Not feeling any more vibrations, Jesse took her hand off of the phone and prayed.

22

Mark was one block from Jesse's house when his phone rang. He answered by pressing the call answer button on his steering wheel.

"Hello?"

He did not hear an immediate response but thought he could hear music. Perhaps she had butt dialed him.

"Hello?

Still nothing. Mark thought there was something wrong with his Bluetooth connection so he picked his phone up off of the console and deactivated the car's Bluetooth. He placed the phone against his ear.

"Jesse, are you all right? I can't hear you, what's wrong?"

That is when he heard the man's voice. The speech was garbled, but he was able to pick out a few words. He heard Kerri Hall's name mentioned and the police. It only took a moment for Mark to realize the voice he was hearing belonged to Robert Sessions, his escaped client.

Mark had to think quickly. He was within a hundred yards of Jesse's driveway. Instead of pulling in and alerting Sessions, he killed his lights and parked along the road, three houses away from Jesse's.

He knew he should call the police, but he was afraid they would bungle things up and he, Jesse, or both of them would wind up dead. Mark decided to try and handle things on his own; after all he had a pretty good rapport with his client. Or so he thought.

Under the cover of darkness, Mark jogged up to Jesse's front door. Without making a noise, he tried the handle. It was locked. Mark immediately ran around to the back of the house. Could Jesse have been so stupid as to leave the back door open for him, knowing that an alleged murderer had escaped?

He reached out and tried the glass door. It was locked too. Mark tried to look into the dark house, but could not see anything. The clock lights from the kitchen stove and microwave were not illuminating the room enough. Mark went in search of the hidden key.

Jesse had a little bit of a sick sense of humor. Since she owned a large dog, it was not unusual for large piles of dog poop to be scattered in the yard. Mark had to find the fake pile amongst the real ones. Fortunately for Mark, he found the right pile on the first try. Mark wasn't a dog person so he didn't realize that dogs typically relieve themselves in the same area, time after time. The lone pile near the bushes was by itself for a reason.

Mark wasted no time in letting himself into the back of the house. He was silent in his movements. He looked around the room as well as he could as his eyes adjusted. Where was Xander? Mark knew that Jesse kept her office issued gun in the hall tree by the front door, so he headed there to arm himself. He could only assume that Sessions had found a way to arm himself.

As he stepped around the loveseat, he saw Xander, lying still on the floor. He had grown fond of the dog, but there was no time to check on him. Jesse was in danger. Mark stepped over to the halltree and opened the single drawer that was below the beveled antique mirror. The gun was there.

Mark took the gun and silently made his way over to the bedroom door. The music was still playing, so even if he did make a noise, it was masked. Mark stood in the open doorway and listened. Sessions was telling Jesse that Kerri Hall still had a plan to get out of all of the trouble that she was currently in.

The angle of the hallway blocked a direct view of Jesse, but he could see the side of her face in the dresser mirror's reflection. His view of Sessions was unobstructed as Sessions was standing a few feet from the end of the bed. He had to figure out how to get into the room. But there really wasn't a way to do it without being seen.

Sessions was antsy and pacing the room. He walked towards the dresser. Jesse's eyes followed him. That was when she noticed the shadow in the doorway reflecting back at her in the mirror. Mark was in her house!

Jesse realized she had to communicate with Mark before he acted alone. So she started engaging Sessions. "Your attorney knows how to handle these types of situations. It has to be a coordinated effort."

Sessions stopped pacing and faced her. "What are you talking about?"

Jesse had to somehow make her secret communication to Mark relate to Sessions more. "Well, I just meant that your attorney and

Kerri Hall's attorney had to work together, against the state. Each of

the attorneys was trying to exonerate their own client. It's when

your attorney does a *coordinated effort* that he stands the best chance

of winning."

Jesse hoped that Mark understood her hidden message – they

needed to work together to stop Sessions. The closest "weapon" Jesse

could get to was the melted candle wax. But she had to convey her

idea about the hot candle wax to Mark. Her mind was reeling to come

up with something. After just a moment, it finally hit her. Her iPod

had been playing the whole time Sessions had been holding her

hostage. She could make up something about a song.

Jesse said to Sessions, "Look, would you mind if I turn my iPod

off? I know this playlist like the back of my hand and the next song is

'Counting on You' by Mikey *Wax*. I'd really rather not hear that song

right now."

Jesse looked directly at Mark's reflection as she said the words,

'Counting on you' and 'Wax.' She hoped that would be enough to

make Mark understand that she was telling him that she would throw

the hot molten wax onto Sessions at the same time that Mark barged

into the room.

Sessions exploded, "I don't give a fuck about the music! Turn it

down, turn it off, I don't care."

Jesse got up and prayed with all of her might that Mark understood

her message. Sessions kept the gun trained on Jesse. She would only

have an instant to disguise the motion of reaching for the candle with

one hand while reaching for the iPod with her other hand. Jesse stepped up to her dresser and used her body to block Sessions' view of her left hand. She used her right hand to reach for the iPod and at the same time used her left hand to grab the candle. She fumbled with the iPod, causing it to fall. The commotion drew Sessions attention.

Jesse grabbed the candle and quickly turned around and threw the hot wax into Sessions' face before he even knew what was happening. At the same time, Mark charged into the room, with a gun drawn on Sessions.

Mark screamed, "Drop the gun! Drop the gun!"

But as soon as the hot wax hit Sessions' skin, he involuntarily raised both hands to his face and started screaming, "You fucking bitch!" Unfortunately, Jesse's aim could have been better. While the wax did hit Sessions in the face, it did not make contact with his eyes. He was hurt, but not immobilized. Unfortunately, he still had the gun in his hand, though it was no longer pointed at its target.

Mark was still yelling at Sessions to drop the gun as Jesse took the risk of running to her nightstand to grab the .38. After arming herself, she aimed her gun at Sessions also.

By the time Sessions could pull his hands down from his face, he knew he was outnumbered, but he wasn't going to give up. He figured if he was going to die anyway, he might as well do something to deserve it. He would take the man with the gun and the prosecutor with him.

After he got his bearings, realization hit Sessions' face like a Mac Truck. The man with a gun was his attorney. "What the fuck?" he exclaimed.

Without interpretation, both Jesse and Mark knew what Sessions meant. How was it that his very own attorney was at the prosecutor's house at night?

"What the fuck are you doing here? You're my attorney!"

"I should ask you the same, Robert. Why did you come here?"

"I told you, man. I'm innocent. Kerri Hall set me up. You wouldn't listen to me, so I figured I would tell the prosecutor. You wouldn't ever let me talk to her, so I took matters into my own hands."

Sessions was pointing his gun at Mark. Jesse made a slight movement, which caught Sessions' eye and he quickly turned the gun on her. Sessions was backed into a corner and knew he had to make his way to the bedroom door if he was going to stand a chance of getting out of this situation alive. Nothing was going like he had planned. Why was his attorney there?

Mark wanted to draw the attention back onto himself. "Look, there is a way out of this without anyone getting hurt."

"Let me guess – I turn myself in, right?"

There was no way around the answer. "Yes."

"You are my attorney, you were supposed to be fighting for me."

"I was fighting for you and I still will fight for you, but not like this."

"All the while you've been banging the prosecutor, haven't you?" Sessions was furious. All of his conspiracy theories were being vindicated.

"Look, I have done nothing wrong here. My relations with Ms. Bradshaw are separate and distinct from me representing you." Mark's words sounded like a pathetic attempt to make excuses. It was no wonder Sessions didn't believe him.

"That's bullshit and you know it! Are you honestly going to stand there and tell me that you two have never had pillow talk about my case?"

Mark tried to take another tactic. "So what if we did? Do you really think it would hurt your case? If anything, it would help you."

Sessions exploded, "Don't treat me like I'm an idiot! I know better than that!"

Mark didn't want Sessions to blow up and possibly fire the gun. "Look, just calm down and we can talk about this. We can figure a way out of it."

"Really? You really want me to believe I'm walking out of this?" Sessions was incredulous.

It was time to change tactics again. "Look, as far as anyone knows, you escaped. No one knows that you are here. I didn't call anyone before coming in here."

"Why should I believe you? All you have done is lie to me."

"Here," Sessions reached for his back pocket while still keeping the gun pointed at Sessions. "Look at my phone. The last action you will see is - " Mark caught himself before he said that Jesse had called him. There was no reason to make the situation worse. "Just look at my last sent call. It is an 850 area code. I called a buddy in Tallahassee, not the cops."

"Yeah, you just want me to look at your phone so I'm distracted. You really do think I'm an idiot, don't you?"

"No, I don't. I just want to prove to you that I am not lying."

Sessions was starting lose what control he had left. "You can go fuck yourself!" He pointed the gun at Mark. "Tell me one good reason why I shouldn't put a bullet in you right now!"

The situation was escalating. Jesse started mentally preparing herself to pull the trigger but before she knew what was happening, Xander appeared out of nowhere and with every ounce of strength he had left in his body, he silently launched himself at Robert Sessions.

Sessions reacted surprisingly quick, firing his gun at the weakened dog. Without missing a beat, Mark yelled and ran forward. Time stood still for Jesse. She reacted, without thinking. Jesse did not see Mark running forward or hear him yelling at her to get down. She did not hear Sessions yelling after being attacked by Xander. All she knew is that she was not going to let her dog die. Jesse fired her gun the one and only time she had ever fired a gun at a human being.

Sessions fell to the ground, taking Xander along with him. They hit the ground with a dull thud. Jesse couldn't move for what seemed like an eternity. In reality, it was less than a second. The adrenaline that had rushed through her body a millisecond before peaked and she was now shaking uncontrollably.

Jesse screamed, "Xander!" The sound came out of her mouth at a pitch so high that it was nearly non-human. It is very rare in life that you hear a true blood-curdling scream.

He couldn't be dead. *Please, God, don't let him be dead*, Jesse thought. She ran to him, hitting the ground hard with her knees. The dog was not moving. He had warm blood on him. But whose was it?

Xander's or Sessions'?

Sirens were approaching, but Jesse did not hear them; all she cared about was saving her dog. Mark tried to pull Jesse away from the two lifeless bodies; all he cared about was saving Jesse. What if Sessions wasn't dead? He did not want to risk Sessions shooting Jesse. Jesse jerked her shoulders out of Mark's grasp. She grabbed a hold of Xander and drew him up into her arms, cradling him like a baby. At that moment, nothing else mattered.

23

Doug blew past the S.W.A.T. team after they used the battering ram to break in Jesse's front door. He broke procedure, but he didn't care – Jesse was in harm's way. Doug had been in this house so many times that he knew exactly where he was going, even without hearing the noises coming from the master bedroom.

Doug momentarily stopped dead in his tracks after entering the bedroom. As a law enforcement officer, you never know what is going to happen in a take-down situation. He didn't know what he would be talking in to – until he saw Jesse crumpled on the floor. Blood was everywhere.

"Jesse!" he yelled as he ran to her, disregarding his own safety as he pushed a man out of the way. He grabbed a hold of Jesse from behind. Emotions beyond anything he could ever comprehend flooded him.

Mark's back had been to the door, so he did not even realize the officers were in the house despite the crashing sound as the front door gave way. His adrenaline was still flowing and with the music from the iPod still playing, he hadn't even realized the officers had made entry into the house.

"Oh, God! Jesse, are you hurt?"

The sound of Doug's voice brought Jesse into the moment. "Doug, we've got to get him to the emergency vet."

Doug was confused. "Wh – " Then he saw Xander, covered in blood on the floor. He immediately took charge. "Are you hurt?"

"No, but Xander – " Jesse finally broke down and started to cry. "I don't know if he was hit. Sessions fired the gun at him and . . . I don't know. It all happened so fast. I think Xander managed to bite Sessions and then I fired my gun and then," she stopped as realization hit her. "Oh, God! What if I'm the one that shot him!"

Doug pulled Jesse into him, holding her tightly despite her pulling away to hold on to her dog. "Calm down, it's going to be okay. Let me take him to my car. We'll go to the pet emergency right now."

Jesse broke away from his embrace and tried to lift Xander's lifeless body. He was too heavy for her.

"Here, let me." Doug reached down and effortlessly picked up the dog.

By this time, the rest of the S.W.A.T. team had cleared the house and was standing in the bedroom's hallway.

"Move out of the way!" Doug yelled at them as he carried Xander out of the bedroom with Jesse on his heels.

"Ms. Bradshaw, you can't leave. This is a crime scene."

Jesse glared at the Roy, the S.W.A.T. leader, and sneered, "Watch me."

Not a single man dared step in the path of the head prosecutor. They had all had dealings with her at one point or another and knew

337

she was a force to be reckoned with.

Mark attempted to follow suit behind Jesse, but Roy stepped in his path. "You're not going anywhere, buddy."

"Look, I'll give you a statement, but I need to be there for her right now."

"Not a chance. Now sit down."

****

Jesse and Doug rode in silence to UF's Emergency Vet Clinic. Normally, the drive would have taken about forty-five minutes, but with the lights and sirens on, the drive was cut in half. Jesse sat in the back seat of the Crown Vic, holding onto Xander. Jesse had enough sense about her to hold a mirror to the dog's nose to see if he was breathing. Amazingly, he was, though the breaths were extremely slow and shallow.

It was touch and go for the first few hours, but Xander pulled through it, without any damage. The blood on him turned out to belong to Sessions. Xander had not been hit by any flying bullets.

Doug stayed in the waiting room, holding Jesse the entire time. They didn't have to say anything to one another. It was if all of those months had not passed and they were still together.

They were supposed to be together, at least that is all Doug could think as he sat there holding her. What if he had lost her? What if he had never told her how much he loved her? The thought of losing her completely was more than he could stand. Seeing Jesse covered in

338

blood, not knowing if she was hurt, made everything picture clear to him. He was wrong. What he did was wrong. Jesse was the woman he was meant to be with. It would be hard figuring out how to deal with the possibility of another man coming into his son's life, as Alice would inevitably move on, but he would have to find a way to deal with it.

****

Even though Sessions did not live to testify in front of a jury, he did leave a letter detailing his involvement in the Witherington murder. He maintained his innocence, laying blame completely on Kerri Hall. Sessions wrote in the letter that Kerri's letter that she kited to him was in the possession of an inmate nicknamed, "Turtle." A search of all known aliases did not reveal a person named Turtle residing at the jail. Doug personally interviewed all of the inmates but he never discovered a letter purported to be written by Kerri Hall.

Was Sessions telling the truth? Was Kerri Hall truly the mastermind? Could Kerri have located the person in possession of her letter and bought them off? Or was Sessions truly the person that pulled the trigger, killing Dean Witherington?

Ultimately, no one would ever know. Exactly four weeks after Sessions escaped, Kerri Hall entered a plea to life in prison. Jesse had been taught early on in her career that the victim has a story, the defendant has a story and the truth was somewhere in the middle. Nothing could be further from the truth.

Made in the USA
Lexington, KY
12 December 2014